Microeconomic Modeling and Policy Analysis

Studies in Residential Energy Demand

This is a volume in
ECONOMIC THEORY, ECONOMETRICS, AND MATHEMATICAL
  ECONOMICS

A Series of Monographs and Textbooks

Consulting Editor: KARL SHELL

A complete list of titles in this series appears at the end of this volume.

Microeconomic Modeling and Policy Analysis

Studies in Residential Energy Demand

THOMAS G. COWING
Department of Economics
State University of New York at Binghamton
Binghamton, New York

DANIEL L. MCFADDEN
Department of Economics
Massachusetts Institute of Technology
Cambridge, Massachusetts

1984

ACADEMIC PRESS, INC.
(Harcourt Brace Jovanovich, Publishers)
Orlando   San Diego   New York   London
Toronto   Montreal   Sydney   Tokyo

ACADEMIC PRESS, INC.
Orlando, Florida 32887

United Kingdom Edition published by
ACADEMIC PRESS, INC. (LONDON) LTD.
24/28 Oval Road, London NW1 7DX

Library of Congress Cataloging in Publication Data

Cowing, Thomas G.
   Microeconomic modeling and policy analysis.

   (Economic theory, econometrics and mathematical
economics)
   Bibliography: p.
   Includes index.
   1. Housing--Energy consumption--Mathematical models.
I. McFadden, Daniel. II. Title. III. Series.
HD9502.A2C69 1984   333.79   84-6296
ISBN 0-12-194060-8 (alk. paper)

PRINTED IN THE UNITED STATES OF AMERICA

84 85 86 87   9 8 7 6 5 4 3 2 1

Contents

v

Preface

One of the more important developments in econometric modeling which has taken place during the past decade has been the increasing use of microeconomic simulation, or microsimulation, models in policy analysis. Such models involve detailed behavioral equations specified at highly disaggregate levels, for example, the firm, household, or individual consumer level, and have been used for policy analysis in such diverse fields as housing, transportation, labor markets, and energy. Several of the most recent developments in this area have been prompted by the need for improved analysis of alternative energy policies during the last 10 years or so, particularly with respect to residential energy demand.

The purpose of this study is threefold: first, to present a comprehensive discussion of the various approaches, limitations, and model structures required to accurately simulate residential energy consumption in general; second, to present a detailed empirical analysis of the aggregate and distributional impacts from several representative energy policies as they relate to residential energy usage; and third, to quantitatively evaluate the comparative performance of two state-of-the-art microsimulation models of residential energy demand. The two models analyzed in this study are the Oak Ridge National Laboratory Residential Energy Consumption

(ORNL) model and the Electric Power Research Institute Residential
End-Use Energy Planning System (REEPS) model. Both models simulate
energy-related economic activity at the household level within frame-
works which differentiate appliance choice, utilization, and energy consumption by a variety of dimensions, among them: type of housing, type
of fuel, and end use. The predictive performance of each model is individually analyzed in Chapters V and VI, respectively, while Chapter VII
contains a comparative evaluation of the two models' forecasts.

Since there is at present only a limited literature on the design and use
of microsimulation models of residential energy demand, none of which is
easily accessible, there is a real need for a comprehensive discussion of
the conceptual and empirical issues involved in using microsimulation
models of energy demand in policy analysis as well as a detailed comparative evaluation of actual model performance. As a result, three types of
readers may find this book beneficial: (i) readers with a general interest in
policy analysis, not necessarily energy related, who would like to keep
abreast of recent developments; (ii) econometric modelers who may be
more interested in the technical aspects of microsimulation model design
and structure; and (iii) energy policy analysts interested in both policy
analysis and the use of microsimulation models of energy demand to aid in
such analysis.

Acknowledgments

A number of institutions and individuals were crucial to the succesful completion of the research effort presented in this study. In terms of finance, we are indebted to the National Science Foundation and the Electric Power Research Institute who provided support at several stages. In particular, we would like to thank Jim Blackman and Larry Rosenberg at the National Science Foundation and Steve Braithwait at the Electric Power Research Institute for their encouragement and support over the past several years. A number of other individuals also played significant roles. We especially wish to thank several former graduate students at the Massachusetts Institute of Technology, among them Jim Berkovec, Jeff Dubin, and John Rust, whose roles as research assistants were particularly invaluable. Without their efforts, this study might have never been completed. John Rust also read the entire manuscript and provided helpful suggestions for improving the final content and organization. Other individuals who provided suggestions and advice at vaious stages of the project include Andy Goett of Cambridge Systematics, Inc. and Eric Hirst and Terry Vineyard of the Oak Ridge National Laboratory. Alice Sanderson at the MIT Energy Laboratory provided word-processing support for the preparation of the final manuscript under rather trying circumstances, and we are especially grateful for her assistance. Finally, Professor Cowing would like to acknowledge the financial support of the National Science Foundation and the Massachusetts Institute of Technology which made it possible to spend a year on leave in the Department of Economics and the Energy Laboratory at MIT.

We are particularly indebted to organizations and individuals who provided materials and support for portions of this book. Chapter II draws heavily on the introductory material in an evaluation of the Oak Ridge National Laboratory Model written by Daniel McFadden (1982) for the Energy Model Analysis Program of the MIT Energy Laboratory, sponsored by the Electric Power Research Institute, and in addition, on research conducted by McFadden at Cambridge Systematics for the Electric Power Research Institute. Section III.2 is edited from McFadden (1982). Section III.3 is edited from A. Goett and D. McFadden, *Residential End-Use Energy Planning System*, final report prepared by Cambridge Systematics Inc. for the Electric Power Research Institute. We thank A. Goett, Cambridge Systematics, and the Electric Power Research Institute for permission to publish edited versions of these materials. Chapters IV– VII were prepared on the basis of research conducted at the MIT Energy Laboratory by T. Cowing and D. McFadden under the sponsorship of Office of the Secretary, U.S. Department of Energy, as part of the program *Studies in Energy and the American Economy*. We thank David Wood who was director of this program and instrumental in arranging support, particularly in the difficult days after cancellation of U.S. Department of Energy scientific research programs in 1981.

We thank the MIT Center for Energy Policy Research, which has supported the preparation of this manuscript.

CHAPTER **I**

Introduction

The use of econometric models for analyzing the potential impacts of alternative economic policies, as contrasted with other techniques of policy analysis, has gained widespread acceptance at all levels of government in recent years. Beginning with the earlier and more familiar macroeconomic models of aggregate economic activity, microeconomic models of sectoral and industry activity have more recently begun to be used as serious analytical tools for exploring policy options and implications in such areas as housing, transportation, labor markets, and energy. Given this increasing use and the accompanying interest in the performance of such models for analyzing a variety of both policy and exogenous shock impacts, it is important to understand the strengths and limitations of such models in general, as well as the relative performance of specific microeconomic models.

The purpose of this book is to present a detailed analysis of both the aggregate and distributional impacts from alternative energy policies as they relate to residential energy demand and the adequacy of existing microsimulation models of residential energy consumption for such analyses. Two such models are examined at length: the Oak Ridge National Laboratory

1

Residential Energy Consumption (ORNL) model[1] and the Electric Power Research Institute Residential End-Use Energy Planning System (REEPS) model.[2] Both models represent state-of-the-art attempts to simulate energy-related economic activity at the household level and include such detail as type of housing (old, new, single-family, multiple-family, mobile home), type of fuel (electricity, natural gas, fuel oil), and a number of end-use consumption categories (space heating, water heating, air conditioning, cooking, etc.). Thus, a variety of dimensions, including time, are modeled so that a wide range of both alternative policies and policy impacts can be analyzed.

In particular, three alternative energy policies and their likely impacts on residential energy consumption are examined in this study—a base case scenario, using 1981 price projections and existing energy policy; an accelerated natural gas deregulation scenario; and a mandated thermal efficiency standard for new housing. The first two scenarios represent alternative energy pricing policies in that the economic impacts in each case result from changes in the prices of residential fuels, while the third policy scenario represents a nonprice policy in which minimum standards on new housing thermal efficiency are assumed. Thus, a wide range of possible energy policies are depicted by the three representative scenarios analyzed in detail in this study, including several which have been given active consideration recently by Federal energy policymakers.

Although an analysis of the aggregate or total impacts of energy policy is included, the primary focus of our analysis is upon the distributive effects—especially income and regional impacts—of alternative residential energy policies. The distributive impacts of economic policy are an important but typically neglected dimension of policy analysis in general, but they are especially important in the case of energy policy analysis given the widespread and pervasive nature of energy-related economic activity. For example, mandatory thermal efficiency standards for new housing generally result in initial increases in investment expenditures for additional insulation and future reductions in energy expenditures, but the impacts are likely to vary substantially among various groups. First, buyers of new housing, who bear the initial burden of the increased investment costs, are likely to represent income groups and geographic locations differing from both renters and owners of existing housing. Second, although they bear the initial burden, new home buyers also benefit from future reduced fuel expenditures so that the associated benefits will also have similar distributional impacts. Third, there may be differences in capital costs and/or availability across income groups in particular, with higher income households facing lower interest rates with which to finance the additional investment expenditures than lower income households. Finally, many of these impacts depend in a fundamental way upon weather so that significant differences across regions are also likely to exist. Other distributive dimensions which are also important in the case of residential energy policy include differential effects across type of household, race, age and size of household, type of housing, owners versus renters, and rural versus urban location. Some of these additional dimensions can be analyzed using the two models examined in this study, although the two models differ fundamentally in their ability to accurately simulate the impacts of many of these effects.

A second major focus of the analyses presented in this study is model performance, including the internal consistency and predictive performance of each of the models. Since these two models differ significantly in terms of their underlying structure and general approach to modeling residential energy demand, this comparative evaluation of the two models should shed considerable light upon the issues of microsimulation model performance in general and the problems and potential for modeling residential energy demand in particular.

This book is organized basically in terms of two parts. The first, including Chapters II and III, contains a discussion of energy use modeling and the use of microsimulation both in general and in terms of the two models — REEPS and ORNL — examined in this study. The second part, Chapters IV – VII, presents a discussion and analysis of the alternative policy scenarios and the results from running each of three policy scenarios using each of two models. In particular, Chapter VII presents a detailed evaluation of the comparative performance of the two models in a variety of both aggregate and disaggregate dimensions. A number of implications for both model construction and energy policy are discussed in Chapters VIII and IX by way of conclusion.

[1] The ORNL Residential Energy Consumption model was developed by Eric Hirst and a number of his associates at the Oak Ridge National Laboratory. The model is coded in FORTRAN and is available from the Oak Ridge National Laboratory, Oak Ridge, TN 37830. For further documentation of the model, see Eric Hirst and Janet Carney, "The ORNL Engineering-Economic Model of Residential Energy Use," ORNL/CON-24 (July, 1978), Oak Ridge National Laboratory; and "RESENU — A Model of Residential Energy Use," CET-002/RESENU (undated), Engineering Physics Information Centers, Oak Ridge National Laboratory.

[2] The EPRI Residential End-Use Energy Planning System model was designed by Andrew Goett and Daniel McFadden and developed by Cambridge Systematics, Inc. for the Electric Power Research Institute. The model is coded in FORTRAN and is available from the Electric Power Research Institute, 3412 Hillview Avenue, Palo Alto, CA 94304. For detailed documentation of the model, see "Residential End-Use Energy Planning System (REEPS)," EA-2512, Project 1211-2, Final Report (July 1982), Electric Power Research Institute, and "Household Appliance Choice: Revision of REEPS Behavioral Models," EA-3409, Project 1918-1, Final Report (February 1984), Electric Power Research Institute.

CHAPTER **II**

Approaches to Energy Use Modeling

II.1. ISSUES IN SIMULATION MODEL DESIGN

A. Modeling Strategy

The purpose of developing a policy simulation model is to provide a device which can produce plausible quantitative forecasts of the impacts of alternative energy policies. This establishes certain features the simulation system should have: It should accept as inputs the policy alternatives of interest, ideally in a form in which they are naturally described by policy makers. It should provide as outputs the full range of information required to assess impacts through time and across individuals.

Any forecasting system, whether simple or complex, can be viewed as a black box in which background factors and policies are linked and modu-

4

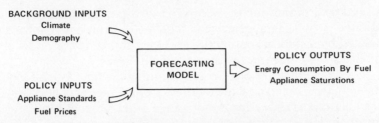

Fig. II.1   A simulation model.

lated to produce forecasts; see Fig. II.1.   The internal workings of the black box may be constructed from historical data on technology and behavior by using econometric – statistical techniques or some method of engineering design and simulation.   One criterion for assessing the plausibility of a forecasting model is *realism in process:* Are the detailed technical and behavioral linkages inside the black box realistic descriptions of how energy-using equipment is acquired and operated, and how this behavior is influenced by external factors?   A second criterion for assessing plausibility is *realism in performance:* Is the model successful in "backcasting" response to historical events or in forecasting recent behavior?

In general, satisfaction of one of these criteria is neither necessary nor sufficient for satisfaction of the other.   A complex model the elements of which each appear to be plausible descriptions of the linkage process may contain fallacies of composition or ecological instabilities which result in implausible performance.   It is extremely difficult to design large dynamic models without unintentionally building in unstable feedbacks which lead to implausible long-run behavior.   On the other hand, a model with a good record for realism in performance may exploit inertia in the real system and be correct for the wrong reasons.   Consequently, it may seriously err when attempting to forecast response to policy which changes behavioral linkages.

Realism in performance is the bottom line for a forecasting model.   Since the whole objective of modeling is to abstract the key linkages of reality, it is not the case that a more realistic model is always better.   When the task of the analyst is primarily to prepare baseline forecasts or consider policies which are mild variations on historical experience, there are many advantages to simplistic econometric – time-series analysis models which exploit system continuity.   On the other hand, when policy alternatives depart radically from historical experience, it is reasonable to expect that a realistic process model will extrapolate more plausibly than a simpler forecasting system.   These comments have two implications.   First, it may be useful for the analyst to have a portfolio of simulation models ranging from simple models, designed primarily for short-term baseline forecasting, to complex process models, designed primarily for long-term forecasts of the impacts of significant policy innovations. Second, in any specific simulation model, it is desirable to build in a structure in which short-run baseline behavior is modulated by historical continuities and long-run behavior under alternative policies is bounded by realistic process linkages.

A second feature of the black box containing the forecasting model is its flexibility in terms of being able to address a wide range of policy alternatives or provide outputs answering a wide range of policy questions. A related characteristic is the robustness of the system in terms of being able to respond to policy questions not anticipated at the time of design. Generally, the more flexible or robust a model, the more complex it must be made to capture the required degree of realism in process, and the greater the associated burden in time and cost placed on the analyst both to calibrate and validate the model and to prepare and interpret the policy runs. Current microeconomic policy simulation models, and in particular the two systems analyzed in this book, are rather ambitious in accepting model complexity to gain flexibility. It would be desirable in addition to develop limited and specialized versions of existing models, or new simplified models, for more specialized policy arenas.

A final feature of the black box is its internal organization. A simulation system can be viewed as having a structure much like the internal organization of a firm, as illustrated schematically in Fig. II.2. The core of a simulation model is the *line* function of accepting model inputs, processing them through the equations that link inputs to outputs, and producing policy outputs. A good simulation system will be organized functionally under a supervisor with the capacity to tailor the production process to specific tasks.

A variety of staff functions in the simulation will service the line function. An accounting and auditing function will organize input and output files, run consistency and validation checks, and maintain records of simulation model performance and cost. A processing technology function will provide and update linkage equations and system parameters, integrating information such as household survey data as it becomes available. This function is in turn served by a research and development function which evaluates model validation results and results from alternative systems and determines where additional model improvements will be most productive. In most current simulation models, only the line production function resides as software in a computer. The remaining functions are less formal and are often not developed as part of the model design process. However, good practice in systems design would place more stress on integrating the supervisory and monitoring functions into the architecture of the system.

In most current energy simulation models, the line-processing function is designed as a single-purpose top–down recursive process. The same sequence of steps is performed, in the same order, no matter what the policy

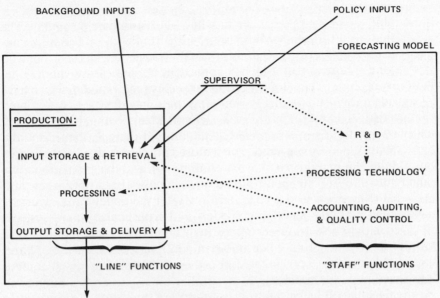

Fig. II.2   Simulation system organization.

under consideration or the policy outputs desired.   This is the simplest of a variety of ways of organizing a processing system.   Alternatively, we could house several independent models within one simulation system, perhaps with common input and output structures, with the supervisor assigning work to the most appropriate model.   With vertical modularity and/or parallel processing, we may simplify some stages of the simulation or build in redundancy to be used for consistency checking and validation.   Good systems architecture will choose modular and functional model designs that are amenable to operation in various mixed modes.   One ideal is to develop the models in terms of some high level simulation language permitting easy modification, rather than as hard-wired modules.   However, the current generation of simulation languages does not appear to be powerful or efficient enough to handle systems as complex as the current generation of energy simulation models.

B. Inputs and Outputs

A key question in simulation design is the extent to which the system should be vertically integrated to accept inputs and provide outputs in the natural language of policy analysts.   A fully vertically integrated system will be highly user-oriented; however, building in user convenience usually requires building in rigidities which may limit what the system can do. The best solution to this problem is to provide the user with an operating language which defaults to a very simple form for inexperienced users, but with flexibility for experienced users who can then choose to override the defaults. So far this has not been an issue for energy policy models which have mostly been written without consideration for user operation.

One important question with respect to vertical integration is the extent to which the model attempts to forecast equilibrium in the markets it is studying, or in the economy as a whole, as compared to an analysis of shifts on only one side of the market, i.e., partial equilibrium analysis. There are two major advantages to an equilibrium approach. First, only the policy variables are exogenous to the system; the market prices and quantities are determined by the model, eliminating the need to provide auxiliary forecasts of these variables or to worry about their consistency with equilibrium. Second, within-model equilibration permits a complete accounting of direct and indirect impacts and can capture effects which a more casual analysis may overlook. The drawbacks of an equilibrium model are scale and complexity, particularly when multiple markets are involved. This results in practical problems of calibration and of computation of the equilibrium forecasts.

The current generation of microeconomic energy models for residential energy demand do not incorporate supply and are sufficiently large so that it would be difficult to expand them into practical equilibrium systems. On the other hand, the equilibrium energy models which have been operated successfully, notably Hudson and Jorgenson (1974), have operated on far too aggregate a level to address directly the relevant micro policy questions with respect to residential energy consumption. In principle, by using modular design and simplified models of complex modules, we should be able to design systems in which complex supply and demand modules are operated separately and then used to fit consistent simplified demand and supply surfaces. These can then be equilibrated and approximate equilibrium prices fed back to produce final detailed demand and supply impacts. This scheme is illustrated in Fig. II.3. Although this approach has not been used systematically, some current uses of complex demand modules along with price impacts calculated from aggregate demand and supply elasticities are in the spirit of this proposed methodology.

A second aspect of simulation model inputs and outputs is that large quantities of data are often involved, requiring some degree of database management. If the simulation system runs within the environment of a good database manager, then the latter system can be used to provide some of the user-oriented capacities desired, such as provision for modifying and

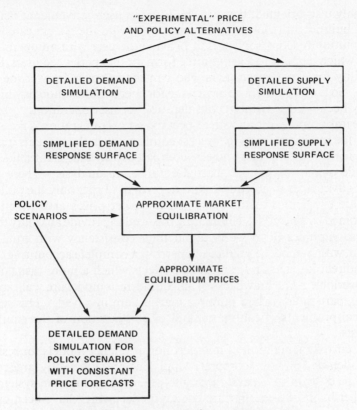

Fig. II.3 System for establishing equilibrium prices.

checking inputs and summarizing and tabulating outputs. In general, it is a good idea to choose a database manager that has the capacity to do some arithmetic and statistical calculations to aid in constructing inputs and summarizing outputs. There are also advantages in using a standard data manager language.

C. Structure

The usefulness of modular functional structure in the design of the simulator processing system has already been stressed. Ideally, a processor can be organized as a "job shop" in which flexibility and robustness in handling a variety of policy problems are achieved by employing a selection of appropriate modules. The capacity to handcraft critical steps and to use standard or simplified outputs for noncritical steps is a clear advantage. It is desirable to have computer software which facilitates such adaptations; it usually will not be necessary or desirable to automate the entire management of adaptation.

One way of achieving flexibility and economy in the same system is to have interchangeable modules which process the same intermediate inputs and outputs at various levels of precision and complexity. For example, one may have a very precise module which forecasts appliance purchases by explicit aggregation over a large simulated population and simpler alternative which forecasts the same behavior directly for regional aggregates. A second example is a simple reduced form module which forecasts energy consumption as a function of price, in place of more complex modules for modeling appliance purchases, determination of appliance efficiency, and appliance usage.

It is possible to develop interchangeable modules independently, perhaps by drawing blocks of equations from various existing systems. However, an approach which has a better chance of preserving the integrity of the system is to develop the simpler modules as *models* of their more complex alternatives. For example, a simple model for aggregate appliance purchases could be estimated as a reduced form regression of the disaggregate model on its inputs, called a *response surface*. In this way, one could construct a consistent hierarchy of models in which the most precise and complex modules would be utilized only when they are critical to a particular policy analysis.

Some of these ideas have been applied piecemeal in many simulation systems. For example, the *Elasticity Estimator* module in the Oak Ridge National Laboratory model can be interpreted as providing a response surface for a more complex system (in a *staff* rather than a *line* capacity). However, they have not been applied systematically, at least for energy policy simulators, and there are some research questions involved in their implementation: Is it practical in sequential modular calculations to go from a simplified coarse module to a complex fine one without compromising the consistency of the complex calculation, and what is the best way to make this transition? In fitting simple response surfaces to complex modules, how should data at the level of detail of the response surface be weighed, and how should this information be used in assessing and upgrading the complex module?

D. Calibration

The calibration of contemporary energy simulation model parameters in the presence of a variety of innovative policies has placed an immense burden on model builders. Behavioral response parameters are required in areas where data have never been collected or where the appropriate experiments have never been performed. Technical parameters are required in areas where the experiments or working models required for careful analysis are unavailable. The approaches taken have usually been to restrict model structure and limit model objectives or to guess model parameters relying on downstream consistency checks to limit the damage caused by poor judgment. Quality control with the second alternative is very difficult. In general, widespread and sometimes cavalier judgments about model parameters are a fundamental weakness in current energy forecasting models. The need for improvement suggests that poorly supported judgments should be flagged, subjected to sensitivity analysis to measure their impact, and when possible checked against auxiliary data and tested for internal consistency with engineering and behavioral laws.

The statistical and specification errors certainly present in complex data-poor systems should be faced resolutely, and not ducked by use of spuriously precise judgmental or engineering parameters. Error transmission should be modeled and reported as part of simulation outputs. The demand of policy makers for point estimates is legendary. (Lyndon Johnson once said in response to bounds on a GNP forecast, "Ranges are for cattle.") Nevertheless, modelers only damage their own cause by implying false precision. It is much more prudent, and sobering, to estimate error bounds which incorporate forecasting experience, classical calibration error, and judgments on the reliability of model specification.

E. Validation

The need for policy tools has led in general to the uncritical use of simulation models without adequate testing and validation. In particular, energy policy simulators are complex systems which are relatively innovative but untested. If these models are to be a useful input to important policy decisions, then it is important that they be designed and managed correctly and that they be widely accepted as reliable.

A common method for validation is within-calibration-period forecasting compared to actual outcomes. This is a useful exercise, but requires two cautions. First, since model development and calibration is an ongoing process, it is important to freeze the system and conduct arms-length validation on outputs which have not previously been used in calibration. Second, in a parameter-rich system, it is very easy to over-fit in the calibration period and thereby lose accuracy in the forecast period.

A valuable validation method is to backcast prior to the calibration period. If the model cannot simply be reversed and run backward in time, then it must be provided with starting values and exogenous variables for the backcast period. Validation is sufficiently important to make the availability of such variables a consideration in model design.

Sensitivity analysis of model parameters and equation specifications is also a useful way to learn about model characteristics and consistency. However, note that while sensitivity analysis may *invalidate* a model by showing that it is implausibly sensitive (or insensitive) to some factors, it cannot by itself validate a model.

The most valuable information on model validity comes from the cumulative experience in using the model for policy forecasting. The primary difficulty with this approach, however, is that the policy user has little day-to-day interest in model validation or in systematic data collection for validation purposes. Impressionistic reports on model performance are typically resorted to instead and are clearly often biased. A serious evaluative effort requires a systematic arms-length monitoring of policy applications and consequences.

Questions which must be answered in setting up a validation study are which model outputs are to be tested for accuracy and under what range of environments and information conditions are standards for acceptable precision to be imposed. Models differ in focus, coverage, time frame, complexity, input requirements, output detail, and range of policy sensitivity. It should be obvious, however, that validity along one direction does not imply validity along a second. The objectives of a validation study are then primarily to determine the boundaries of satisfactory operation of models and indicate which model is best for which purpose, rather than to rank in terms of accuracy models which are otherwise incomparable.

Consider, for example, two models of the energy market, one of which simulates energy demand taking energy prices as inputs, and the second of which simulates both demand and supply and outputs both prices and quantities. How can the accuracy of these two models be compared? The answer depends on the way the models will be used. If the application requires forecasts of actual market quantities, then the demand simulation must be combined with another system which forecasts energy prices. The accuracy of the quantity forecasts is then determined by the joint accuracy of the demand simulator and the exogenous price forecasts and may well be limited by the latter. It is this measure of accuracy that should be compared to the accuracy of the equilibrium simulator. In cases where a complete formal description of the process of exogenous price forecasting is unavailable, it may be necessary to treat it as a black box and to infer the statistical properties of its forecasting errors from historical observation. When the application requires only forecasts of demand patterns conditioned on market prices, however, the demand simulator can be tested directly for accuracy, but the equilibrium simulator outputs require further analysis. One method of obtaining conditional forecasts from an equilibrium system is to vary exogenous variables or policy instruments to achieve the required price levels. Except in very simple models, this may require in practice that a response surface be fitted to model inputs and outputs and the conditional forecasts obtained by interpolation on the response surface.

F. Data Limits

An energy simulation model is typically required to forecast baseline energy consumption by fuel and year given exogenous forecasts on demography, income, and prices; and to forecast the variations in consumption induced by various policies such as fuel price changes, time-of-day electricity pricing, appliance standards, or insulation tax credits. Behavioral models of response require either historical or experimental data from which parameter values can be inferred. In addition, a simulation model requires base year starting values.

At the level of geographical aggregates such as states, time series data are generally available on energy expenditures and physical consumption levels, incomes, prices, and demographic variables. These permit calibration of some baseline forecasting models, but lack the detail on interactions necessary to calibrate even baseline models with full end-use disaggregation. For many policy alternatives, indirect evidence on response can be deduced by translation into price equivalents; however, the behavioral-engineering judgments required for the translation are often difficult to justify. For example, the discount rate implicit in water-heater fuel choice may also apply to choice among levels of water-heater insulation. However, this inference requires inadequately supported assumptions on the market price of insulation, perceptions of efficiency gains, and uniformity of behavior.

Cross-section surveys of individual households which have recently become available permit the calibration of more detailed behavioral models of appliance choice and consumption. However, these surveys are generally not sufficient to determine appliance efficiency or to provide a behavioral foundation for the current life-cycle cost-minimizing models of appliance efficiency choice.

G. Simulation Methodology

The necessary steps in simulating the effects of energy policies, given a calibrated model of behavioral response are, first, to prepare inputs of exogenous and predetermined variables, second, to translate the policies of interest into scenarios stated in terms which can be understood by the model, and third, to operate the model and collect the outputs relevant to policy evaluation.

Consider the first step, preparation of inputs of exogenous and predetermined variables. A characteristic of energy simulation models is that they have a dynamic structure, with current behavior dependent on past history. Thus, it is necessary to supply a predetermined initial state for the base year of the simulation process. This is typically done by supplying actual base year data on stocks and flows. For comparison of alternative scenarios, it is not necessarily important that base year starting conditions conform exactly to observations. However, realism is enhanced if base conditions are reasonably accurate. Furthermore, observed base year data are more likely to be internally consistent in terms of the satisfaction of basic accounting identities.

Several cautions on the specification of base-year conditions are necessary, however. First, reliable base-year data may not be available for all model variables. Often only marginals, such as electricity consumption aggregated over end uses, are observed. Further, data collected from disparate sources may involve differences in variable definitions, coverage, and sampling procedures which will lead to violation of accounting checks. Two broad guidelines should govern the process of filling out and reconciling base-year numbers.

1. Most of the questions of variable definition and measurement procedure also arise in preparation of the database for calibration. It is essential for consistency that the *same* procedures be used in preparation of calibration and simulation data.

2. Implicit in the behavioral and technological equations of the model are relationships between detailed and aggregated quantities. In the absence of direct observations on detailed quantities, one should adopt allocations which are compatible with model relationships.

A second caution regards the dynamic structure of the simulation model and the effect of starting conditions. First, we consider the case of models which are dynamically stable. With stationary driving variables, this kind of model will have an equilibrium with a characteristic pattern of stocks and flows. When started from a nonequilibrium point, the model may exhibit sharp and unrealistic transients in the first few years of simulation output. If this occurs for properly measured base-year data, it is evidence against the validity of the model. However, one may believe a model to have realistic long-run behavior even if short-run transients are implausible. In this case, it may be desirable for policy analysis purposes to start up the model several years before the time interval in which alternative policies are to be compared to allow transients to disappear. This has the effect of taking the original base year to be an equilibrium configuration rather than the observed configuration.

On the other hand, suppose the simulation model is dynamically unstable. In large systems, it is not uncommon for this to occur as a consequence of estimation even if the real system is stable. When driven by stationary but noisy exogenous variables, a model such as this will tend to explode, eventually violating accounting or technological constraints. (In sufficiently nonlinear systems, local instability combined with bounds imposed by technology may produce cyclic behavior which is not obviously implausible.) In this case, long-run policy simulation is unlikely to be reliable. The first implication of this result is that the dynamic stability of the calibrated model should be tested, analytically if possible, or otherwise by extended simulation runs with stationary driving variables. Second, if the system is indeed found to be unstable, the short-run simulation behavior of the system is likely to be more realistic than its long-run behavior. Consequently, the base year is best chosen close to the time interval for policy comparisons, with base-year variables set to observed levels.

Most energy simulation models have a partial equilibrium structure, requiring exogenous inputs over the period of the simulation. Thus, an energy simulation model may require exogenous projections of population, income, or households by dwelling type. Beyond this, if only one side of energy markets is being simulated, exogenous price or quantity inputs may be required. The first issue is the quality of these projections and their impact on policy conclusions. It is useful to distinguish between *background* inputs such as population which are unlikely to be influenced by energy policy and *foreground* inputs such as energy prices which in truth are jointly determined with the dependent variables in the simulation model.

It is possible for background inputs to change comparisons between policies substantially. For example, an apparently modest change in rates of household formation can substantially influence growth rates in energy consumption since possibilities for substitution and technical change are largely concentrated in new construction. More commonly, however, background variables have a relatively uniform impact across policies, and thus tend to cancel out in cross-policy comparisons. Consequently, while the quality of forecasts of background variables may be critical to the accuracy of individual policy forecasts, it is less essential for policy comparisons. Of course, simulation over a historical period for purposes of validation should use observed values for exogenous variables.

Input of foreground variables raises a problem of consistency between the policy scenario and the implicit (or explicit) model being used to generate these forecasts. For example, simulation of energy demand is often carried out using energy price forecasts as exogenous inputs. This is consistent with shifting demand patterns only if energy is in perfectly elastic supply; an assumption that is inconsistent with the known technology of energy production. The alternatives are

1. To proceed with the analysis of policy scenarios under the elastic supply assumption, treating the results as statements about demand structure rather than as forecasts of market equilibrium outcomes.
2. To introduce simple models of the left-out side of the market, such as constant elasticity forms, and carry out a few iterations to approximate the equilibrium levels of foreground variables for each policy.
3. To restructure the simulation models so as to make key foreground variables endogenous.

The first alternative may be quite useful in identifying the patterns of policy impacts, but can be quite misleading if improperly interpreted as forecasts of actual outcomes. The second alternative may yield more realistic forecasts. The accuracy of the simple model of the left-out side of the market may, however, become the constraint limiting forecast accuracy. The third alternative is the most defensible. However, it greatly expands the modeling, calibration, and simulation tasks which must be carried out by the model builder.

The final objective of policy simulation is to evaluate the impacts of specific alternative policies of interest and to lay out a realistic description of these impacts. An intermediate objective is to explore the general characteristics of ranges of policy alternatives and the operating characteristics of the simulation system. These two objectives suggest different choices of policy scenarios. Final policy simulations require full articulation of a limited number of realistic policy alternatives which may differ in complex ways and may require substantial preparation. The intermediate objective, on the other hand, is best met by considering policies as alternative treatments in an experimental design. These treatments may be chosen to stress the model, determine its sensitivity to specific inputs, or map a response surface; that is, the individual treatments need not in themselves be realistic policies. The intermediate objective is usually more useful to modelers in evaluating system performance. It is also sometimes valuable to policy makers, since simulation results are often used as a guide to the formulation of reasonable policy alternatives rather than as a means of ranking specified policies.

Given base-year and exogenous inputs, a calibrated simulation model can be run to produce outputs of the variables of primary interest for policy as well as a variety of secondary variables. Analytic or numerical perturbation of the model can then be used to investigate sensitivity to specific parameters and to calculate error transmission and confidence bounds. If the model operation involves stochastic components, as in the case of Monte Carlo simulation of microeconomic decision units, an analysis of the sampling procedures intrinsic to the system can provide sampling variance. Otherwise, it is possible to obtain sampling variance numerically by repetitions of the simulation.

For complex simulation models, preparation of specific policy scenarios may be a lengthy process and model outputs may confound the contributions of various aspects of the policy, acting in interaction with exogenous variables. For purposes of studying model characteristics, as well as a guide to the formulation of policy, it is useful to give a broader view of the structure of response to policy and to isolate specific impacts. One way to achieve this is to "model the model," treating the complex system as a black box whose operating characteristics can be approximated by a simpler reduced-form econometric system relating model outputs to model inputs. Such a response surface methodology can be used to interpolate or extrapolate from the list of policy alternatives studied in detail and, in addition, allows judgments on the locus of undominated or optimal policies. It can also be used to infer the partial impacts of each input on each output, permitting model operating characteristics to be summarized in terms of multipliers and elasticities. Furthermore, the fitting of response surfaces can in itself be viewed as a classical experiment in which various input "treatments" are applied to the complex system and responses are observed. Thus, the principles of experimental design and statistical analysis can be applied to the construction of the response surface.

H. Policy Analysis

The basic objective of policy analysis is to identify and quantify the consequences of policy alternatives. Simulation models provide a method for achieving this quantification, including consistent treatment of indirect effects and feedbacks, provided the policy alternatives can be translated into model inputs. It should be recognized, however, that simulation models are essentially complex accounting systems which build in assumptions, it is hoped well grounded on historical observation, with respect to the behavior of economic actors. Simulation models will tend to do well what a traditional policy analysis can do well, e.g., make short-run baseline forecasts under familiar conditions and do less well what traditional analysis does poorly, e.g., make long-run forecasts of response to drastic policies having little or no historical parallels. The primary benefits of simulation systems are to speed up the analyst's work, enforce logical consistency in the analysis, provide a uniform format for outputs, and allow analysis of more complex problems.

The use of econometric simulation models in policy analysis can be compared conceptually to the running of a laboratory experiment. In both cases, the primary question typically posed is of the kind, "What happens if . . . ?" In laboratory experimentation, we are interested in observing the effects upon one set of variables following or resulting from given changes in a second set of variables, while keeping constant the influence of a third set of other important environmental variables. The observed responses in the first set of variables can then be attributed to the initial changes in the second set of variables, permitting quantitative measurement of the underlying causal relationships involved. Econometric models, once constructed, can also be used to provide answers to economic questions of the kind, "What happens if . . . ?" Thus, we can change the exogenous variables affected by a given policy and then use the econometric model to give a set of conditional predictions or forecasts for endogenous variables of interest. The result is a pseudo-experimental analysis in which the variables of interest do not actually have to be changed, something which is typically either impossible or highly expensive in the case of economic experiments. Of course, the validity of the resulting model forecasts will depend in large part upon the ability of the model to accurately specify the structure of the underlying technological and behavioral relationships involved.

Econometric models, like laboratory experiments, can also be quite complicated in terms of such dimensions as the number of variables involved, the level of disaggregation used, and the complexity of the structural relationships assumed. Beyond some point, however, additional complexity may not be desirable in terms of yielding either additional insight or more accurate forecasts. Furthermore, more complex models are likely to be more costly, to both build and operate, so that any additional gains in model performance may be more than offset by the additional costs involved. Of course, the issue of the best econometric model to use for any given policy analysis will ultimately depend upon the nature of the policy issues involved and the kinds of questions which must be answered.

A final point which should be made follows from a basic tenet of economic analysis, namely, that the validity of any analysis should be judged primarily in terms of the predictive accuracy of the results and not in terms of the reasonableness or unreasonableness of the assumptions used. Since all economic analyses abstract from reality to some extent, some variables are inevitably omitted and other conditions simplified by assumption. Similarly, in policy analysis it is important that the results not be judged solely in terms of the assumptions used, including the specific structure of the assumed policy scenarios. Such scenarios can never capture the totality of any given policy; rather, the trick, as in all economic analyses, is to focus upon the most important variables and relationships. The result is that simulation models used in policy analysis must be judged in terms of such criteria as the internal consistency of the model, the reasonableness of the predictions, and ultimately, the ability of the model to predict or forecast accurately.

II.2. THE PROBLEM OF MODELING RESIDENTIAL ENERGY CONSUMPTION

A. The Nature of Energy Consumption

We consider the classical economic model of consumer behavior, preference maximization subject to a budget constraint. Decisions about levels of energy consumption are broadly similar to those on other commodity use, such as food, housing, and health services; and forecasts should generally show similar responses to changes in prices and income. Energy consumption has, however, three special features which need to be considered in a full description of behavior, particularly the dynamics of consumer response.

First, energy is consumed as an input to a household production process, to provide heat, cooling, lighting, and other needs. The level of energy consumption is then determined by the household technology as well as behavioral decisions on utilization. For example, energy consumption for heating is not usually controlled directly by the consumer, but is determined indirectly by behavior (thermostat setting), technology (furnace efficiency), and exogenous conditions (weather and energy prices). One implication of this structure is that the rational consumer is choosing an *ex ante* energy consumption policy rather than *ex post* realized consumption levels, so that the marginal conditions characterizing choice apply *ex ante* rather than *ex post*.

Second, the household technology for energy consumption is largely embodied in the characteristics of the dwelling and in durable equipment. Much of the behavioral response in energy consumption operates through choice of dwelling and equipment portfolio and choice of equipment characteristics such as size, energy source, and efficiency. Consequently, replacement and retrofit decisions will depend on energy price expectations, and responses to unanticipated price shifts may involve long lags.

Third, energy costs are normally billed to households periodically for all uses combined. Consequently, the marginal energy cost of behavioral policies may be unclear to the consumer. Aggregation of uses, the presence of complex billing features such as connect charges and block rate structures, and the effect of exogenous factors such as weather and fuel price adjustment factors in energy bills all obscure the linkage from policy to cost. As a result, even highly rational consumers may make decisions based on simple models of cost inferred from historical experience.

One implication of the special features of residential energy consumption is that neither purely technological nor purely behavioral models are likely to provide satisfactory forecasts of energy demand. Technological components are necessary to capture the physical constraints on energy conversion and use, particularly for equipment in place, and may help to characterize the domain of feasible technologies. Behavioral components are necessary to explain consumer expectations and their influence on equipment choice and to explain the influence of energy prices on energy consumption policy.

A complete model of the technology and behavior of energy consumption will involve extreme detail on the physical characteristics of dwelling and equipment and a very difficult dynamic stochastic optimization problem for the consumer. Any practical model for use in policy simulation will substantially compromise this ideal. Nevertheless, there are advantages to starting the modeling process with a dynamically optimizing consumer facing a technology for using energy to meet household needs. The heuristics and stylizations necessary to reach a practical model can then be assessed in terms of their fidelity to the core features of the ideal model.

B. Models of Consumer Behavior

The consumer faces decisions on the type and features of the dwelling he inhabits, including the portfolio of appliances used, characterized by fuel and efficiency, and levels of utilization. The dynamic structure of the decision process is that the consumer considers initial costs and expected future costs in choosing a dwelling and appliances. He then utilizes this stock of durables taking into account realized prices. At future times, the characteristic of the stock may be modified by retrofit or replacement. A particular consequence of this dynamic structure is that the characteristics of the dwelling shell and appliance portfolio—level of thermal integrity, appliance capacities, efficiencies, and fuels—are fixed at the date of construction and are

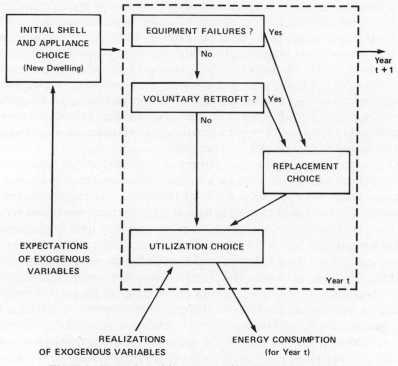

Fig. II.4 Dynamic decision structure in energy consumption.

unchanged by realized events until a retrofit or replacement is made. Utilization decisions are made conditional on realized events and the characteristics of durables in place.

Many replacement decisions are involuntary and are due to equipment failures which may be stochastic. However, voluntary retrofit and replacement decisions occur and may even be anticipated. This suggests the dynamic decision structure in Fig. II.4.

One implication of this structure for modeling is that shell and equipment decisions in new dwellings should be handled in one submodel. Then in existing dwellings, replacement and retrofit decisions should be placed in a second submodel and utilization decisions should be placed in a third submodel. Of course, the fully rational consumer will be aware of the linkages between these decisions, imposing common taste parameters across the submodels and utilizing downstream submodels to aid the formation of upstream expectations.

First we consider the design of new structures. One important question is whether this decision can be treated as that of a buyer – occupant who is making dynamically optimal choices or that of a contractor – seller who may have a different objective function. It is clear that in a new single-family structure built to order, the consumer has full discretion. This is not obvious for single-family structures built to stock or multiple-family structures. In these cases, the consumer faces a market in which the prices of new units of various characteristics are determined by the balancing of supply and demand. Under the realistic assumption of a large number of buyers, each consumer will have available a full array of alternatives at prevailing market prices and will have full discretion in choosing among these alternatives. The primary question for modeling is then whether the structure of supply and demand is such that sellers act de facto as agents for the buyers, so the distinction between construction to order and construction to stock disappears.

An initial issue regarding the behavior of *sellers as agents* arises even for construction to order. Perfect fidelity of the agent to clients' objectives can be expected only if the client can costlessly monitor or audit agent behavior. For example, if a contractor can increase his profits by cutting corners on hidden construction which is not readily detected by the buyer, he may do so in spite of buyer preferences. This is more of a problem in construction to stock where a specific buyer is not identified. In fact, it may create a *lemons* problem where buyers find that they are unable to verify *above-market quality* construction claims in dwellings built to stock and are thus unwilling to pay the premium necessary to induce contractors to provide such construction. In the following discussion we assume that quality of dwellings can be audited at negligible cost, so problems of agent fidelity and *lemons* are absent. We note, however, that these information problems are one plausible explanation of the apparent fact that consumers are attracted to energy-efficient dwellings or appliances only at rates of return considerably larger than their market cost of funds.

The technology for supply of residential dwellings appears to have roughly constant returns, so market prices faced by buyers will equal these constant supply costs plus a net rent reflecting the "monopoly power" of suppliers of each dwelling type. Note that monopoly power may occur because there are small numbers of suppliers and barriers to entry or there are time lags in supply so that surprises in demand can lead to short-run excess demand or supply, and consequently, positive or negative rents to clear the market. In fact, the residential construction industry is quite competitive with low entry barriers, and mark-ups due to classical monopoly power are probably minor. The presence of short-run rents in the market is, however, an important issue. An unanticipated change in, say, relative prices of fuels, will shift consumer demand toward structures with heating – ventilating – air conditioning (HVAC) systems using the reduced-cost fuel. Then, in the short run with a fixed supply of dwellings with the different HVAC systems, market prices will increase for structures with the economical system and fall for other structures, until demand and supply are balanced. The suppliers of the economical HVAC system experience positive rents, those with other systems negative rents. In the longer run, these rents will induce a supply response. Since construction times for residential units are under a year, this supply response should be quite rapid. Hence, the error caused by ignoring short-run rents and assuming prices equal supply costs is to miss short-run lags of a year or less in observed demand response. In practice, since evolutionary changes in energy prices should be anticipated, the magnitude of this error should be small. In any case, it is feasible to bound the possible error: decompose energy price forecasts into trends which consumers are likely to anticipate and shocks which they are unlikely to anticipate. Then construct modified price forecasts in which shocks are delayed 1 yr and compare the demands produced by the original and modified price forecasts. These demand forecasts should bracket the demands produced by the market with short-run rents.

Empirical study of housing-market price behavior around major energy price shocks could permit explicit modeling of the appearance of net rents and of supply response to the presence of rents. Since good evidence on short-run supply response is not currently available, we shall assume hereafter that buyers face supply prices which equal supply costs. Given this assumption, we can now treat occupants of multiple-family and rental units symmetrically with occupants of single-family units — such consumers can, by *voting with their feet,* choose a multiple-family or rental unit with the structural characteristics they desire at a market price reflecting the supply cost of these features.

Note that even if the assumptions of full information on dwelling characteristics and no short-run rents are valid for new structures and therefore for old structures at their date of construction, there is *no* implication that the current price of old structures reflects their replacement cost. To the contrary, the price of these structures will include a net rent which for the marginal consumer equalizes their desirability to the desirability of the best available technology in new construction, given current price expectations. Thus, the high operating cost of obsolescent technologies in old structures will be offset by reduced initial cost, with the sellers of old dwellings absorbing the windfall loss associated with unanticipated adverse changes in energy prices. These conclusions imply that observations on sales of structures at the date of construction or on current prices of old structures, contain information on tastes and expectations, while observations on prices of new structures contain information on costs of equipment (unless short-term rents are significant).

Next we consider the questions of replacement and retrofit in existing structures. The simplest case is the owner-occupied single-family dwelling, where there are no complications in defining the decision maker's objective function. At every point in the life of existing equipment, the rational consumer will consider voluntary retrofit or scrappage and replacement. Equipment failure requires involuntary replacement. In either case, once a decision to replace has been made, the choice of fuel source, efficiency, capacity, and other characteristics is described by an optimization similar to that in new dwellings, except that equipment costs reflect piecemeal replacement in an old structure. The proportion of retrofits which are voluntary will depend on the nature of equipment durability and on changes in energy prices. If equipment has a lifetime of known duration or has sharply increasing maintenance costs or sharply decreasing reliability, then the savings in present value of initial cost associated with waiting until failure becomes small relative to the expected savings in operating costs. Then voluntary replacement is likely. On the other hand, if expected remaining life falls slowly and maintenance and reliability are relatively stable, then the equipment is likely to be operated until failure. Many residential appliances such as water heaters and HVAC systems appear to be of the second type.

Finally, we consider utilization decisions in owner-occupied dwellings. Given the characteristics of equipment in place, the rational consumer will choose utilization policy to maximize expected utility given realized energy prices and the distribution of operating costs generated by exogenous conditions such as weather. For some appliances such as refrigerators, the opportunities to modify utilization are minimal and energy consumption is effectively determined by equipment characteristics. However, for most equipment the opportunities to affect energy cost by changing utilization patterns are significant.

One question in the modeling of utilization is the quality of information on marginal energy costs available to the consumer, given the difficulty of disentangling the effects of multiple end uses and stochastic components in energy consumption and the complexities of utility rate schedules. It is wise in modeling this behavior to admit the possibility that the consumer responds to more general and readily observed information. For example, a consumer can rather simply model the total cost of an energy source and the incremental cost of weather-sensitive appliances using observations on seasonal utility bills. The marketplace and publications provide indices sufficient to form subjective impressions of total cost differences for different energy sources at typical utilization levels. It is much more difficult for the consumer to obtain reliable information on true marginal costs. Consumer experiments such as trial changes in thermostat settings are rarely sufficiently controlled to yield unambiguous results. Summarizing, there is little evidence in the information readily available to consumers, or in the discipline imposed on consumers by the market or by successful demonstrations of peers, to suggest that consumers will form sophisticated or accurate models of marginal energy cost.

Consider the linkages between dwelling and equipment design decisions, retrofit decisions, and utilization decisions. A fully rational consumer will consider these decisions jointly in a dynamic setting, taking into account, in design and retrofit decisions, the strategic possibilities for adjusting utilization and future replacements as conditions change. In practice, this problem is too difficult to solve analytically except for special cases.[1] It is possible that the representative consumer is successful at solving this problem by intuition or search. However, the *natural selection* arguments sometimes invoked to suggest that decision makers are nudged unconsciously toward optimal behavior, lack force when applied to household energy consumption. Dwelling and equipment decisions are sufficiently infrequent and idiosyncratic so there is little opportunity for learning by doing or by demonstration, and there is broad compass for sustainable behavior that is not obviously suboptimal. These observations suggest that rigorous adherence to the fully rational optimizing model for the consumer may have little advantage in predictive power over simpler models which adopt boundedly rational heuristics.

The decision process for energy consumption in rental housing, particularly multi-family structures, is less clear than in owner-occupied housing. In competitive rental markets, we would expect units with tenant-supplied utilities to have rental rates which equalize (across energy sources or dwelling characteristics) rental costs plus utility costs. Then landlords under such arrangements should have the incentive to act as agents for tenants, providing dwelling characteristics which maximize tenant preferences. The competitive landlord will in effect solve the same dynamic stochastic optimization problem as the owner–occupant. The limitations of this argument are primarily informational: Landlords may have difficulty certifying the quality of "above market quality" units and consequently may fail to achieve a market return equal to the value of these investments to tenants. This may be a particular issue for retrofit in existing units, where rent negotiations between landlord and existing tenants may be sheltered from the full discipline of the competitive market and marginal cost differences can be obscured by bargaining.

The competitive rental market will establish a rental differential between units with landlord-supplied utilities and units with tenant-supplied utilities which is equal to the expected utility bill in landlord-supplied units. This gives the landlord a profit motive to minimize the present value of initial and operating costs of equipment. However, in this arrangement there is an incentive incompatibility in that the tenant does not face, at least in the short run, the correct marginal cost of energy consumption, and the landlord does not face the correct marginal value of service. Consequently, tenant-controlled services are likely to be used more than is optimal, and landlord-controlled services are likely to be supplied less than is optimal.

In multiple-family rental units, there are additional incentive problems. First, there is a free rider problem in utilization of shared utilities because each decision maker bears only a fraction of the marginal cost of his decisions. Second, there may be both incentive and group decision problems in retrofit decisions in existing multiple-family structures.

Problems of incentive compatibility in multi-family units are recognized by energy suppliers, but we are unaware of systematic empirical studies of energy usage and retrofit decisions in single- and multiple-family housing units with alternative arrangements for control and payment for energy consumption. The usual assumption, that demand behavior for these units has a structure similar to that for single-family owner-occupied units, deserves testing.

C. Illustrative Models of Residential Energy Demand

The preceding subsection has outlined the principles of energy consumption behavior of households, including the dynamics of consumer decisions, the role of technology in constraining options, and the impact of exogenous factors. Next we consider a series of simplified models for rational consumers which are intended to illustrate these principles and to provide a *test-bed* against which boundedly rational heuristics adopted in practical simulation models can be judged. In all, we consider four examples dealing with:

1. utilization of an existing appliance whose energy consumption is under direct control,
2. utilization of a HVAC system controlled indirectly by thermostat,
3. equipment replacement decisions, and
4. design of a multiple-appliance system.

These examples are considered in the order in which they would be treated by a fully rational consumer solving a dynamic stochastic program to maximize utility. For analytic tractability and ease of exposition, we will, however, consider each example individually rather than as part of the overall decision problem and adopt heuristics where necessary.

The starting point for all examples is an instantaneous utility function of the generic form $u = U(z, s)$, where s is the service supplied by energy-using equipment and z is consumption of a composite commodity of all other goods. This utility function is assumed to satisfy the von Neumann–Morgenstern axioms so that the utility of a lottery equals the expected utility of its outcomes. The consumer's objective is to maximize expected present value of utility at any planning date θ,

$$(1) \qquad U_\theta = E_\theta \sum_{t=\theta}^{\infty} e^{-\rho t} U(z_t, s_t),$$

where ρ is a rate of impatience and E_θ is the expected value given the information available at θ, taking into account the strategic possibility of planning revisions. This optimization is constrained by a budget at date θ requiring that the expected present value of remaining expenditures not exceed expected remaining wealth. Note that this formulation already imposes a strong behavioral assumption that preferences are simultaneously additively separable over uncertain events and over time. We will also ignore some difficult modeling questions associated with either the assumption that consumers are infinitely lived or that they have fixed known lifetimes, as well as questions of how market arrangements enforce the budget constraint. An additional complication is that the individual actually consumes an array of services which requires energy inputs, and there will be interactions among these services. Except in the last example, we ignore this problem and treat each service as if it existed in isolation.

Example 1 (Utilization of directly controlled equipment). *Ex post* utilization decisions given equipment in place involve, first, an allocation of instantaneous expenditure between the services of energy-using equipment and other commodities and, second, an allocation of expenditures over time. The instantaneous problem for a service for which energy consumption is under direct control is

$$(2) \qquad \max_{z,s} U(z, s)$$

subject to

$$(3) \qquad y = z + psh,$$

where y is the instantaneous expenditure, p the price of energy, s the service level (utilization) of equipment, h the energy–service ratio (ESR), an equipment characteristic, and z the consumption of a composite of other commodities. Energy price and income are expressed in units of the composite commodity z.

The solution to problem (2) is characterized by an indirect utility function

(4) $$u = V(y, ph),$$

defined by

(5) $$V(y, \tilde{p}) = \max_s U(y - \tilde{p}s, s).$$

Roy's identity gives the demand for energy,

(6) $$x = sh = -hV_2(y, ph)/V_1(y, ph).$$

For example, suppose

(7) $$V(y, \tilde{p}) = [(y - A\tilde{p}^v)/B\tilde{p}^\eta]^{1-\alpha}/(1 - \alpha)$$

with $\alpha > 0$, $\alpha \neq 1$, $0 < v \leq 1$, $0 \leq \eta \leq 1$. This function is increasing in y, decreasing in $\tilde{p}$, and quasi-convex in $(y, \tilde{p})$ in a domain of positive $(y, \tilde{p})$, and hence is the indirect utility function of some direct utility function U. Further, the demand for energy satisfies

(8) $$x = (v - \eta)Ap^{v-1}h^v + \eta y/p,$$

so that η is an income effect and v is a price effect. For an appliance whose utilization is effectively fixed by initial characteristics, we will have v near one and η near zero. Where there is some flexibility in usage, v will typically be somewhat less than one and η somewhat greater than zero. In the second case, energy demand increases less than linearly in the energy–service ratio h. This implies that increasing appliance efficiency (reducing h) does not lead to a proportionate reduction in energy demand since the increased efficiency lowers the effective cost of service and stimulates more consumption.

Next consider the time allocation of expenditure. At this point we will not attempt a complete characterization of this problem which should include uncertainty about equipment failure. Instead we consider the problem in which current equipment remains in place over a planning period $t = 0, \ldots, L$. From (1)–(4), the consumer has at time 0 the objective

(9) $$\max_{(y_t)} E_0 \sum_{t=0}^{L} e^{-\rho t} V(y_t, p_t h)$$

along with the budget constraint that

(10) $$W_0 = E_0 \left[\sum_{t=0}^{L} y_t e^{-rt} + W_{L+1} \right],$$

where p_t is energy price in period t, r is an instantaneous interest rate, y_t is expenditure in period t, and W_{L+1} is set by a terminal wealth constraint. For simplicity, we take $W_{L+1} = 0$, and assume that above-subsistence expenditure programs exist which meet the terminal condition with certainty.

If there is no uncertainty, (9), (10) is an isoperimetric discrete-time optimal control problem. The solution to this problem is characterized by a marginal condition

$$(11) \qquad V_1(y_t, p_t h) = \lambda e^{-(r-\rho)t},$$

where λ is an undetermined multiplier. This problem is rather simple to solve and for some indirect utility functions yields analytic expressions for optimal expenditure patterns and energy consumption. When there is uncertainty regarding future energy prices or wealth, and the fully rational consumer takes into account the strategic possibilities for policy revisions in light of new information, the problem becomes a more difficult dynamic stochastic programming problem. We shall set up this problem and discuss some of its features. However, we believe that in many applications uncertainty will be small relative to anticipated changes, and consequently the solution to a *certainty equivalent* problem of the isoperimetric form in (9), (10) will approximate the solution to the fully rational consumer's problem.

In the case of uncertainty, assume prices and wealth have equations of motion

$$(12) \qquad p_{t+1} = p_t e^{g+\eta_t},$$

$$(13) \qquad W_{t+1} = (W_t - y_t)e^{r+\xi_t},$$

where η_t and ξ_t are random variables which are independent of each other and independent over time, g is a fully anticipated instantaneous trend growth rate in energy price, and r is a fully anticipated trend interest rate. For simplicity, we make g and r time independent; this is inessential as long as their time profiles are fully anticipated. Assume that at date t when y_t is selected, the random variables η_t and ξ_t are not yet observed. Let $J(W_t, p_t, t)$ denote the expected present value at date t of the optimized utility stream from t to L. This performance function satisfies

$$(14) \qquad J(W_L, p_L, L) = V(W_L, p_L h)$$

and the recursion relation

$$(15) \quad J(W_t, p_t, t) = \max_{y_t} \{V(y_t, p_t h) + e^{-\rho} E_t J(e^{r+\xi_t}(W_t - y_t), p_t e^{g+\eta_t}, t+1)\},$$

where E_t denotes expected value conditioned on information available at time t. This recursion implies that optimal expenditure y_t satisfies

$$(16) \qquad V_1(y_t, p_t h) = e^{r-\rho} E_{\xi,\eta} e^{\xi} J_1(e^{r+\xi}(W_t - y_t), p_t e^{g+\eta}, t+1).$$

The dynamic stochastic program (14)–(16) will not have a closed form solution for most utility functions, but can be solved numerically to obtain qualitative properties of the energy consumption stream. In the limiting case where η_t and ξ_t are zero, this problem reduces to the isoperimetric problem (9), (10). For small supports of ξ and η, the fully rational dynamic stochastic program (12)–(15) can be expanded around solutions to (9), (10) to obtain a system with linear equations of motion and a quadratic objective function in deviations from the optimal certainty state variables and controls. With sufficient curvature assumptions on the indirect utility function to ensure continuity of solutions, the correction to the certainty problem given by the solution to the linear-quadratic problem in deviations will approximate the fully rational optimal solution to the dynamic stochastic program.[2]

For the example [Eq. (7)] without uncertainty condition (11) becomes

$$(17) \qquad [y_t - Ah^v p_t^v]^{-\alpha}[Bh^\eta p_t^\eta]^{\alpha-1} = \lambda e^{-(r-\rho)t},$$

where λ is an undetermined multiplier. This implies

$$(18) \qquad y_t = Ah^v p_t + [Bh^\eta p_t^\eta]^{1-1/\alpha} e^{[(r-\rho)t/\alpha]} \lambda^{-1/\alpha},$$

and hence,

$$(19) \quad W = Ah^v \underbrace{\sum_{t=0}^{L} e^{-rt} p_t^v}_{P_1} + \lambda^{-1/\alpha} B^{1-1/\alpha} h^{\eta[1-(1/\alpha)]} \underbrace{\sum_{t=0}^{L} e^{[r(1-\alpha)-\rho]t/\alpha} p_t^{\eta(1-1/\alpha)}}_{P_2}.$$

Then

$$(20) \quad v_t = V(y_t, p_t h) = \frac{1}{1-\alpha}(Bh^\eta p_t^{\eta/\alpha} P_2)^{\alpha-1} e^{(r-\rho)(1-\alpha)t/\alpha}[W - Ah^v P_1]^{1-\alpha},$$

$$(21) \quad x_t = vAp_t^{v-1}h^v + \eta p_t^{\eta-1-\eta/\alpha} e^{(r-\rho)t/\alpha}[W - ah^v P_1]/P_2,$$

and

$$(22) \qquad \sum_{t=0}^{L} e^{-rt} p_t x_t / W = \eta + (v - \eta)Ah^v P_1 / W.$$

Typically, η is near zero and v is slightly less than one. Then the share of wealth used to purchase energy for the appliance, (22), is a concave increasing function of energy price and a convex decreasing function of wealth.

Example 2 (Utilization of a thermostat-controlled HVAC system). The starting point for an analysis of HVAC energy consumption is a thermal model of the dwelling. To a first approximation, the instantaneous net heat flow from a structure is linear in the temperature differential,

$$(23) \qquad\qquad Q = -\omega + q(T^C - T^e),$$

where Q is the heat flow in Btu/hr, T^C is thermostat setting, T^e is exterior temperature, and ω, q are coefficients specific to the structure. The primary component of ω is internal load, the heat generated by occupants and non-HVAC appliances. The coefficient q is proportional to the area of the shell of the structure and to the conductivity of the shell determined by construction materials and insulation.

Let $F(T)$ be the cumulative distribution function of external temperatures over the year. Assume for now that this distribution is known with certainty. Let T^b be a balance temperature for the structure satisfying $0 = -\omega + q(T^C - T^b)$ or $T^b = T^C - \omega/q$. Then the annual average hourly heating energy use is

$$(24) \qquad Q_H = \int_{-\infty}^{+\infty} \max(0, Q) F'(T)\, dT$$

$$= \int_{-\infty}^{T^b} [-\omega + q(T^C - T)] F'(T)\, dT$$

$$= q \int_{-\infty}^{T^b} F(T)\, dT.$$

If there is air conditioning, then the annual hourly cooling energy use is

$$(25) \qquad Q_A = \int_{-\infty}^{+\infty} \max(0, -Q) F'(T)\, dT$$

$$= \int_{T^b}^{\infty} [\omega + q(T - T^C)] F'(T)\, dT$$

$$= q \int_{T^b}^{\infty} [1 - F(T)] dT$$

Because of heat storage and build-up effects, the approximation for air conditioning is not as good as that for heating. In general, we would want to allow ω, q, and T^C to vary between heating and cooling; for simplicity we do not do this in the example.

The expressions

$$(26) \qquad D_H(T^b) = \int_{-\infty}^{T^b} F(T)\, dT,$$

$$(27) \qquad D_A(T^b) = \int_{T^b}^{\infty} [1 - F(T)]\, dT,$$

are the annual heating degree hours and cooling degree hours to base T^b, respectively, normalized by 8760 hr/yr. Thus HVAC energy consumption is proportional to degree-hours defined to the balance temperature base. The annual temperature distribution is fairly well approximated by a logistic,

$$(28) \qquad F(T) = (1 + e^{-\gamma - \delta T})^{-1},$$

where γ, δ are parameters specific to the location. Then

$$(29) \qquad Q_H = qD_H = q \log(1 + e^{\gamma + \delta T^b}),$$

$$(30) \qquad Q_A = qD_A = q \log(1 + e^{-\gamma - \alpha T^b}).$$

For the remainder of this example, assume air conditioning is absent. The instantaneous utility function has the form $u = U(z, T^i - T^*)$, where T^i is the actual interior temperature, T^* is *bliss* temperature, and z is a composite commodity of all other goods. Consider utility maximization over an annual climate cycle. We neglect the effect of discounting within a cycle. Let $z(T)$ denote consumption of the composite good when the exterior temperature is T, h denote the energy service ratio (Btu in/Btu out) of the furnace, and p the price of energy. If y is annual average expenditure per hour, the budget constraint is

$$(31) \qquad y = \int_{-\infty}^{+\infty} z(T)F'(T)\, dT + phQ_H.$$

Subject to this constraint, the consumer chooses T^C and $z(T)$ to maximize

$$(32) \qquad u = \int_{-\infty}^{+\infty} U(z(T), T^i(T) - T^*)F'(T)\, dT,$$

where $T^i(T) = \max(T^C, T + \omega/q)$ is the interior temperature when the exterior temperature is T, with q and h fixed by the *ex ante* choice of shell and equipment.

Rewrite (32) in the form

$$(33) \qquad u = \int_{-\infty}^{T^b} U(z(T), T^C - T^*)F'(T)\, dT$$

$$+ \int_{T^b}^{\infty} U(z(T), T + \omega/q - T^*)F'(T)\, dT$$

Then the first-order conditions for this problem are

$$(34) \qquad [U_1(z(T), T^C - T^*) - \lambda]F'(T) = 0 \quad \text{for } T \le T^b,$$

$$(35) \qquad [U_1(z(T), T + \omega/q - T^*) - \lambda]F'(T) = 0 \quad \text{for } T > T^b,$$

$$(36) \quad \int_{-\infty}^{T^b} U_2(z(T), T^C - T^*)F'(T)\, dT - \lambda phqF(T^b) = 0,$$

where λ is an undetermined multiplier. From (34), $z(T) = z(T^b)$ for $T \le T^b$. This implies in (36) that

(37) $$U_2(z(T^b), T^C - T^*) = \lambda phq.$$

Suppose, in particular, that

(38) $$U(z, T^i - T^*) = [z - \zeta(T^i - T^*)]^{1-\alpha}/(1 - \alpha),$$

where ζ is a function with a minimum at zero. Let $s = -\psi(x)$ be the solution to $-\zeta'(s) = x$, and define $\xi(x) = \zeta(-\psi(x))$. Then

(39) $$T^C = T^* - \psi(phq),$$

(40) $$T^b = T^* - \psi(phq) - \omega/q,$$

(41) $$\lambda = [z(T^b) - \xi(phq)]^{-\alpha},$$

(42) $$z(T) = \lambda^{-1/\alpha} + \zeta(T + \omega/q - T^b) \quad \text{for} \quad T > T^b$$
$$= \lambda^{-1/\alpha} + \xi(phq) \quad\quad \text{for} \quad T \le T^b,$$

(43) $$y = \lambda^{-1/\alpha} + \xi(phq)F(T^b)$$
$$+ \int_{T^b}^{\infty} \zeta(T + \omega/q - T^*)F'(T)\, dT$$
$$+ phq \int_{\infty}^{T^b} F(T)\, dt.$$

Equation (43) determines λ and hence $z(T)$. The effect of increasing phq (because p is higher, shell conductivity is higher, or appliance efficiency is lower) is to decrease T^C and T^b. For example, if

(44) $$\zeta(T^i - T^*) = A|T^* - T^i|^{\nu}$$

with $\nu > 1$, then

(45) $$\psi(phq) = (phq/\nu A)^{1/(\nu-1)},$$

(46) $$\xi(phq) = A^{-1/(\nu-1)}(phq/\nu)^{\nu/(\nu-1)}.$$

Further, $u = \lambda^{(1-1/\alpha)}/(1 - \alpha)$ falls and λ rises when phq increases. Substituting λ from (43),

(47) $$V(y, phq) = [y - \phi(phq)]^{1-\alpha}/(1 - \alpha),$$

where

(48) $$\phi(phq) = \xi(phq)F(T^b)$$
$$+ \int_{T^b}^{\infty} \zeta(T + \omega/q - T^*)F'(T)\, dT + phq \int_{-\infty}^{T^b} F(T)\, dT,$$

with T^b given by (37). In this form, the annual hourly average indirect

utility has the same general structure as the instantaneous indirect utility
function in Example 1. Hence, if the seasonal cycle operating decisions for
the HVAC system can be treated as occurring at a single point in time each
year, then the reduced-form weather-sensitive consumption can be analyzed
just like consumption under direct control.

Now consider the more likely case where the distribution of temperature is
uncertain. Assume that the thermostat setting and composite commodity
consumption must be chosen before the actual temperature distribution is
drawn and cannot be revised as the season progresses. Then expenditure
within a cycle must be a random variable. Suppose the consumer's problem
is broken into stages with expected seasonal expenditure as a policy variable. Suppose now that $F(T)$ in (31)–(48) is interpreted as the *marginal*
distribution of temperatures with uncertainty about year-to-year variations
integrated out. Then (31)–(48) characterize the optimal thermostat and
composite commodity demand policies as functions of the expected seasonal expenditure policy. Further, the budget condition (43) rewritten
using the *conditional* distribution of temperatures given the climate draw for
a particular year describes the realization of seasonal expenditure as a function of the expected expenditure policy. The optimal intertemporal problem is similar to that in Example 1, except that realized expenditure is a
random variable depending on consumption policy and on the distribution
of temperatures drawn in the current season. Reformulation of the terminal condition in light of this randomness will usually be required.

A final, more difficult, case occurs when thermostat and composite commodity consumption policies can be revised continuously as the season
develops and additional information becomes available on the temperature
distribution drawn. We shall not write down the dynamic stochastic program for this problem. However, note that in circumstances where weather
uncertainty can effectively be averaged out over the planning horizon of the
consumer, the thermostat setting and consumption policy will be quite
insensitive to realized weather patterns, and the solution to the preceding
case will be nearly optimal for this case.

In summary, the policies followed by consumers with indirect thermostat
control over HVAC systems will in most cases be very close to optimal
policies for a known weather distribution which margins out year-to-year
variations. Then *ex ante* marginal conditions for the thermostat setting and
composite consumption will be met.

Example 3. (Equipment replacement decisions): *Ex ante,* the consumer faces the problem of choosing the energy source and efficiency of an
appliance, taking into account expected utilization, initial equipment cost,
and downstream replacement alternatives. In general, there may be volun-

tary replacement of operating units, as well as replacement decisions following equipment failure. Aside from the range of opportunities and costs of
alternatives, there will be no difference between appliance choices in new
construction and appliance replacement in existing structures. The following analysis can be applied to either.

The formulation of this problem will depend on whether the life of the
appliance is certain or uncertain and the degree to which there are interdependencies beyond the overall budget constraint linking appliance replacements. A structure which covers the important cases assumes that an appliance is characterized by a vector (s, h, a) where s is the energy source, h is the
energy–service ratio, and a is age. Let p_{st} denote the price of energy source s
in period t. Assume that an appliance (s, h, a) which is surviving at period t
has a probability π_a of failing at the beginning of period $t + 1$, and that
expenditure policy in t must be set before survival is known. Let $C(s, h, t)$
denote the initial cost of an appliance at time t. If replacement occurs, its
cost is known before expenditure for the period is set. Let δ_t be a control
variable which is one if the appliance is replaced voluntarily, π_a otherwise.

In the notation of Example 1, remaining wealth satisfies

(49) $W_{t+1} = (W_t - y_t)e^{r+\xi_t}$ if no replacement,

          $= (W_t - C(s, h, t) - y_t)e^{r+\xi_t}$ if replacement.

Assume the consumer wishes to maximize expected present value of utility
and let $J(W, p, s, h, a, t)$ be a performance function giving the optimized
present value at t of utility from that time on. Let B denote the set of
available (s, h) designs. Assume the consumer has planning horizon L, and
that all surviving appliances are scrapped without salvage value at $L + 1$.
Let (s_t, h_t, a_t) denote the appliance operating in period t. Then the performance function satisfies the recursion relation

(50) $J(W_t, P_t, s_t, h_t, a_t, t)$

$$= \max_{\substack{y_t, \delta_t \\ (s,h) \in B}} \{ V(y_t, p_{s_t}h_t)$$

$$+ (1 - \delta_t)e^{-\rho}E_t J((W_t - y_t)e^{r+\xi_t}, p_{t+1}s_t, h_t, a_t + 1, t + 1)$$

$$+ \delta_t e^{-\rho}E_t J((W_t - C_t(a, h, t) - y)e^{r+\xi_t}, p_{t+1}s, h, 1, t + 1)\}.$$

In period L,

(51) $J(W_L, p_L, s_L, h_L, a_L, t) = V(W_L, p_{s_L L}h_L),$

so as before we can proceed by backward recursion to solve for J and the
optimal policy.

There are very few cases where this dynamic stochastic program has a simple solution. First we consider the case where there is no uncertainty, the appliance has known life (so $\pi_a = 0$ for $a < \theta$ and $\pi_\theta = 1$), all prices are constant, $r = \rho$, and $L = \infty$. Assume the indirect utility function has the additively separable form

(52) $V(y, ph) = \phi(y - \zeta(ph))$.

Note that in the absence of price changes, there is no incentive to scrap voluntarily. Consider a trial solution for the performance function,

(53) $J(W, p, s, h, a) = r^{-1}\phi[rW - (1 - e^{-r(\theta-a)})\zeta(p_s h)$

$$-\frac{e^{-r(\theta-a)}}{\theta}\min_{s',h'}\{C(s', h') + \frac{1 - e^{-r\theta}}{r}\zeta(p_{s'}h')\}],$$

with a stationary optimal appliance configuration (s^*, h^*) which minimizes

(54) $C(s', h') + r^{-1}(1 - e^{-r\theta})\zeta(p_{s'}h')$,

and a stationary expenditure stream which satisfies

(55) $y_0^* = rW + e^{-r(\theta-a)}\zeta(p_s h)$

$$-\theta^{-1}e^{-r(\theta-a)}\{C(s^*, h^*) + r^{-1}(1 - e^{-r\theta})\zeta(p_{s^*}h^*)\}$$

for $0 \leq t < \theta$, and

(56) $y^* = y_0^* + \zeta(p_{s^*}h^*) - \zeta(p_s h)$

for $t \geq \theta$. Using Roy's identity, $x = -hV_2/V_1$, (52) implies stationary energy consumption for $t < \theta$ and for $t \geq \theta$; in the latter range,

(57) $x^* = h^*\zeta'(p_{s^*}h^*)$.

If h can vary continuously, then the first-order condition for optimal h is

(58) $0 = r^{-1}(1 - e^{-r\theta})p_{s^*}\zeta'(p_{s^*}h^*) + C_2(s^*, h^*)$

or

(59) $0 = r^{-1}(1 - e^{-r\theta})p_{s^*}x^* + h^*C_2(s^*, h^*)$.

But this is simply the first-order condition for minimization of life-cycle cost (LCC) given the expected energy consumption stream and the marginal capital and operating costs of efficiency adjustments at the same service level. Of course, except in extreme cases, the service level is endogenous and determined jointly by the underlying utility maximization.

We can verify by substitution of the trial performance function (53) into the recursion (50) that this is the solution to the original dynamic programming problem.

It is possible for this case to draw out some qualitative implications of the optimal appliance choice. In (59), the longer the life of the appliance, the more efficient, other things equal. If *ex post* substitution is substantial, then decreasing h will less than proportionately decrease x. Then the first term in (59) is concave in h, and this equation will be solved for a more efficient appliance but higher consumption than would be the case in the absence of substitution.

A second tractable case of the problem (50) is a geometric failure time distribution with $\pi_a = \pi$ const., $L = \infty$, and stationary prices. For this problem there will be no voluntary scrappage and the performance function is independent of equipment age or chronological time,

$$(60) \quad J(W, p, s, h) = \max_{y,s',h'} \{V(y, p_s h) + (1 - \pi)e^{-\rho}J(e^r(W - y), p, s, h)$$

$$+ \pi e^{-\rho}J(e^r(W - C(s', h')) - y), p, s', h')\}.$$

Suppose (W, s, h, p_s) can be assumed, exactly or approximately, to be contained in a finite domain. Then (60) can be rewritten as a discrete-time, discrete-state Markov decision (with dimensionality equal to the number of states) which can be solved iteratively; see Howard (1960).

Next we consider nonstationary environments where the fully rational problem (50) is usually intractable. What heuristics might be reasonably adopted by the consumer or analyst? First, it may be adequate to ignore uncertainty in wealth or prices, so the only source of randomness is stochastic failure. Second, with a relatively high discount rate and long-lived appliances, it may be reasonable to ignore downstream replacements and the strategic considerations they introduce. Then the replacement unit is treated heuristically as having a life equal to the remaining life of the consumer. (Note that this approximation may distort the choice of efficiency for the replacement appliance.) Under these assumptions, the value of the performance function after replacement is given by a nonstochastic discounted sum of indirect utilities, and the choice of energy source and efficiency of the replacement will maximize this discounted sum subject to the budget constraint that remaining wealth at the time of replacement equal capital cost of the appliance plus present value of the expenditure stream. Given the replacement fuel and efficiency, the problem of allocating expenditure over remaining life, given wealth remaining after the purchase of the replacement, is identical to the isoperimetric problem (9), (10). If, in particular, the instantaneous indirect utility function has the form (7), then energy consumption satisfies (21) with W equal to net wealth after the appliance purchase. From (22), the LCC for the replacement (at date τ) satisfies

$$(61) \quad \text{LCC} = C(s, h, \tau) + \sum_{t=\tau}^{L} e^{-r(t-\tau)}p_t x_t$$

$$= C(s, h, \tau) + \eta[W_\tau - C(s, h, \tau)] + (v - \eta)Ah^v P_1,$$

where P_1 is defined as in (19), but with initial time shifted from 0 to τ. The value of the associated objective function is

$$(62) \qquad u = \sum_{t=\tau}^{L} e^{-\rho(t-\tau)} V(y_t, p_{st}h)$$

$$= (Bh^\eta)^{\alpha-1} P_2^\alpha [W - C(s, h, \tau) - Ah^\nu P_1]^{1-\alpha}/(1-\alpha),$$

This function is then maximized in (s, h). In the case $\eta = 0$ and $\nu = 1$, so that demand for service of the energy-using appliance is completely price and income inelastic, one has P_2 constant and $Ah^\nu P_1$ equal to the present value of energy costs. Then, (62) becomes

$$(63) \qquad u = Bh^{\alpha-1} P_2 [W - \text{LCC}]^{1-\alpha}/(1-\alpha),$$

and the optimal appliance among energy source and efficiency alternatives will minimize the LCC. However, in the case $\nu < 1$ with some price elasticity, the choice among alternatives is more complex, with the maximization of (62) taking into account the substitution response to operating cost differences. Note that so long as $\eta = 0$, the energy–service ratio enters (63) only through the LCC and hence the optimal efficiency minimizes the LCC. However for $\eta > 0$, optimal efficiency occurs at a *lower* level of efficiency than that which minimizes the LCC.

Finally in this example we can substitute (62) into the dynamic programming recursion equation (50) to obtain conditions for design of the first appliance and conditions for voluntary replacement. Again heuristics are needed to obtain closed form approximations. However, some qualitative properties of the solution can be noted. First, the possibility of voluntary replacement makes the design of the first appliance more sensitive to near-term prices compared to long-term prices. One cannot, however, conclude that with the possibility of voluntary replacement the efficiency of the first appliance will fall. Second, the core of the voluntary replacement decision will be a comparison of the utility gained from advancing the introduction of an appliance with optimal characteristics with the utility lost due to accelerated purchase of this appliance. The first gain comes from the use of a most appropriate energy source or efficiency level and will become large only if there are substantial trends or shocks in energy prices. The second loss will be small if the appliance is known to be near the end of its life or if it has high scrappage value so the net cost of the replacement is low. Third, in the case of perfectly inelastic demand for the service of the appliance, if replacement occurs in period t, then the condition must be met that the operating cost savings in t exceeds the present value of the savings associated with a one-period delay in the purchase.

Example 4 (Design of a multiple appliance system). The choice and utilization of multiple appliances may involve interactions through consumer preferences, through the household technology, and through the budget constraint. First, we consider the structure of preferences. There may be complex patterns of complementarity and substitutability among appliances. For example, the desirability of a clothes dryer is strongly linked to the presence of a clothes washer. In principle, the general instantaneous direct utility function considered in the preceding examples can be extended to a vector of services with a flexible functional form, and the corresponding indirect utility function depends on a vector of energy cost per service unit. However, practical measurement and forecasting are aided considerably by some separability between appliances, and in most cases an assumption of additive separability across services of the indirect utility function is a reasonable approximation. For example, the functional form (7) can be reinterpreted as applying to a vector of services, with all services other than the one under study swept into the composite commodity.

Interdependence of appliances in the household technology is particularly important for the elements of the HVAC system, where the thermal properties of the shell affect the ESR of both heating and cooling equipment, and where heating and cooling may share components. There is also interdependence in water heating use and services of dishwashing and clothes washing. The technological interdependence in HVAC systems and the thermal shell is most readily accommodated by considering this complex as a single system, as was done in Example 2. There is an added complication when the components of this system have differing lifetimes or failure time distributions, so that the decision to replace one component is influenced by strategic considerations for other components.

The final source of interdependence among appliances is the overall budget constraint, plus interactions in the initial or operating costs of multiple appliances. In the latter category are initial cost savings associated with shared technology, such as a common gas main or common oil storage, or associated with tied market arrangements such as discounts for all-electric homes, and operating cost savings associated with declining block rate structures. This interdependence is most significant for the HVAC system and is best analyzed by treating the components of this system as a single appliance.

At least formally, the dynamic programming problem (50) can be generalized to the multiple appliance case, with V displaying a joint or additively separable structure depending on tastes and on technological interdependence in utilization, replacement policy represented by a vector of decision variables δ_t, and initial costs representing the total for all replacements incorporating interactions.

[1] One class of dynamic stochastic programming problems which admit analytic solutions are those with quadratic objectives, linear state equations, and continuous controls; see Hansen and Sargent (1981).   However, discrete decisions on equipment replacement or energy source cannot be handled in this family.   It is possible to obtain fairly complete characterizations of replacement behavior in a stationary environment using renewal theory and Markov decision theory; see Rust (1983).   This approach does not, however, adapt to the nonstationary environments of interest in simulation.

[2] See Chow (1975).   An alternative approach is to reformulate (12)–(15) in continuous time with no price uncertainty and wealth following a diffusion process.   Merton (1978) has obtained explicit characterization of expenditure policy for this problem with indirect utility functions of the form (7).   This policy is linear in wealth and resembles the optimal policy for the certainty problem.

CHAPTER III

Residential Energy Demand Simulation Models

The basic purpose of this chapter is to present a detailed description of the two residential energy demand models used in this study: the Oak Ridge National Laboratory Residential Energy Consumption model and the Electric Power Research Institute Residential End-Use Energy Planning System model. Since both of these state-of-the-art microsimulation models are of recent origin and draw heavily upon previous research in this area, it may be helpful to start with a brief survey of historical developments in the area of econometric energy demand modeling.

III.1. HISTORICAL DEVELOPMENTS

Estimated energy demand functions, particularly for electricity, are among the earliest applications of econometric techniques to the estimation of economic relationships. This is particularly true in the case of residential

41

energy demand, probably because of the relative abundance of reasonably good data. A number of these studies, beginning with the early and pioneering study of Houthakker (1951), are listed in Table III.1 and have been classified in terms of two dimensions: static versus dynamic, where the latter refers to the explicit treatment of the short-run–long-run adjustment process and single fuel versus multi-fuel or interfuel substitution models. It should be emphasized that this list of previous studies of residential energy demand is not exhaustive, but it does serve to give the general flavor of much of this early work.[1]

Houthakker's study (1951) of residential electricity consumption in the United Kingdom is of interest for several reasons: First, it is one of the earliest studies of energy demand. Second, it takes into account the econometric implications of a two-part tariff by using marginal, rather than average, prices. Third, it considers the potential cross-price or substitution effect of natural gas on electricity demand. Houthakker's results, interpreted in terms of short-run elasticities, indicate an income elasticity greater than unity, an own-price elasticity for electricity of approximately −0.9 and a cross-price elasticity between electricity and natural gas of about 0.2. Thus, electricity demand even in the short run appears to be rather sensitive to both electricity and natural gas prices.

Wilson (1971), also one of the relatively early studies, analyzed the residential demand for electricity, as well as the demand for six different categories of electric household appliances, including space heating, air conditioners, and electric ranges. His results, based on cross-section data for U.S.

TABLE III.1
Residential Energy Demand Models

Type of model	Single fuel models	Multi-fuel models
Static	Houthakker (1951) Wilson (1971) Anderson (1972) Griffen (1974) Acton, Mitchell, and Mowill (1976) Halvorsen (1975, 1978)	Anderson (1973) Chern (1976) Pindyck (1979)
Dynamic	Fisher and Kaysen (1962) Balestra (1967) Houthakker and Taylor (1970) Mount, Chapman, and Tyrrell (1973) Houthakker, Verleger, and Sheehan (1974) Taylor, Blattenberger, and Verleger (1977) Berndt and Watkins (1977)	Erickson, Spann, and Ciliano (1973) FEA/PIES (1974) Baughman and Joskow (1975) McFadden, Puig, and Kirshner (1978)

cities, indicated that both the price of electricity and the price of natural gas were important determinants of the demands for electricity and electric appliances in general. Among other variables included were median family income, average number of rooms per household, and number of degree days, although these nonprice variables gave mixed results.

In a more recent study, Halvorsen (1978) attempted to break the correlation between supply and demand by using estimated, rather than actual, prices in his electricity demand equation. The estimated prices came from a separate pricing equation which was estimated first, yielding instrumental price variables for the demand equation. Although in principle Halvorsen could have used marginal prices, the specification he used did not yield different results (as between marginal and average prices) with respect to the resulting estimated price elasticities. Using a pooled set for states, Halvorsen's results indicated elastic demand for electricity and a sizable long-run income effect.

Although a number of innovative approaches have been tried within the confines of single-equation demand models, including differentiating between average and marginal prices and analyzing factors influencing household appliance ownership, these models are necessarily limited in terms of both structural specification and estimation efficiency. Pindyck (1979) is a good example of the use of multiple-equation demand models in order to overcome some of these single-equation problems. In this comparative study of the demand for energy across nine countries, Pindyck used the static translog indirect utility function to estimate expenditure share equations simultaneously for four different residential fuels — electricity, natural gas, fuel oil, and coal. His results indicated that long-run price elasticities of residential energy demand may be larger than many previous studies had found.

Although the estimated parameters produced by these, and other, static models of residential energy demand have been useful, these studies have all suffered from a general failure to include more dynamic elements within their models. Since capital in the form of energy-using household appliances is clearly an important factor in residential energy demand, it is likely that totally static models will fail to capture price and other economic effects either completely or accurately. For this reason, a number of researchers have carried out econometric analyses of energy demand using a variety of more dynamic models, a few of which are also listed in Table III.1.

Perhaps the best known, and clearly the most ambitious, of the early dynamic studies of residential energy demand is that by Fisher and Kaysen (1962). In this study, Fisher and Kaysen analyzed both the short-run and long-run demands for household electricity using a two-equation model. In the first equation, electricity consumption was estimated as a function of the stock and average utilization of electricity-using household appliances, while in the second, the long-run stock of appliances was related to appliance and fuel prices, as well as several structural variables. The long-run equations were estimated separately for five different classes of electric appliances — washing machines, refrigerators, irons, ranges, and water heaters. Their results indicated that income and population were among the more important determinants of long-run residential demand while the prices of both electricity and natural gas were less important. However, there were also significant differences in these general effects, especially the price effects, across regions.

A more recent dynamic study, Houthakker, Verleger, and Sheehan (1974), used marginal prices calculated from differences in typical electric bills and a flow-adjustment model to estimate long-run price and income elasticities. Using pooled state data for the period 1960–1971, their results indicated small short-run elasticities and rather substantial long-run elasticities, especially for income. They also found that the price elasticities were rather sensitive to the data used to construct the marginal prices, while those for income were less sensitive.

Finally, the study by Baughman and Joskow (1975) is representative of the multiple-equation approach based on the simultaneous estimation of fuel share equations. Their model utilizes a two-step procedure in which total energy consumption for the residential sector is estimated first, followed by a second step in which fuel share equations are estimated to capture interfuel substitution effects. Their results indicated that electricity demand is highly price sensitive, with a long-run elasticity of at least unity, while both aggregate energy consumption and the fuel shares are generally price sensitive. Income was more important in determining aggregate residential energy consumption.

These studies are interesting representations primarily in terms of reflecting both the strengths and weaknesses of previous econometric studies of residential energy demand. Among the major weaknesses are

1. the general failure to include the three major components of household energy choice — fuel type, appliance efficiency, and appliance utilization — within an appropriate theoretical choice framework;

2. the general lack of adequate disaggregation at the household level, including (at a minimum) energy demand specified by type of fuel by end use by type of housing by region; and

3. no role for new technologies in the form of more efficient household appliances and/or other energy conservation-related residential technologies.

In large part, the two microsimulation models examined in this study were designed with these particular weaknesses in mind. At the same time, their success owes much to the various contributions which previous research in residential energy demand modeling has produced.

III.2. THE OAK RIDGE NATIONAL LABORATORY MODEL

A. Objectives

The interests of policy makers are often focused on forecasts of residential energy use at aggregate national or regional levels. On the other hand, analysts want to study policies which are quite localized and heterogeneous in their impacts, such as mandatory insulation standards in new houses. To some extent, these objectives are incompatible, given the limits of contemporary data and modeling art. It is possible to carry out detailed engineering studies of the impact of policies such as insulation standards at the *test house* level. However, it is extremely difficult to project such impacts up to a regional level because of missing demographic and behavioral data. Alternatively, it is possible to develop fairly satisfactory aggregate-level models to forecast the impacts of policies whose impacts are relatively uniform, such as energy price shifts due to a tax on imported oil. However, it is difficult to assess the impacts of heterogeneous policies such as insulation standards within an aggregate model. To do so requires some assumption on how these effects aggregate. These assumptions tend to be ad hoc, and if incorrect may result in significant aggregation errors.

The Oak Ridge National Laboratory (ORNL) model is a compromise intended to satisfy the most pressing requirements for regional forecasts of the impacts of heterogeneous policies. The unit of analysis is aggregate — all consumers in a region. However, energy consumption is disaggregated by end use — refrigerators, gas water heaters, etc. The end-use disaggregation permits the assessment of policies which affect individual appliances. Aggregation problems are eased somewhat in the ORNL model by permitting some demographic segmentation.

We give a relatively abbreviated description of the Oak Ridge model, since it has now been discussed in some detail in the literature; see Hamblin (1981), Herbert (1980), Hirst and Carney (1978), Hirst – Goeltz – Carney

(1981), Lin–Hirst–Cohn (1976), Freedman–Rothenberg–Sutch (1981), McFadden (1982), and Weatherwax (1981). The version of the Oak Ridge model discussed below and used in our studies was the most recent available at the time our work was initiated in 1981. More recent versions of the model have now been released which are substantially modified to eliminate many of the shortcomings we point out in the version we used.

The primary output of the ORNL model is total and end-use residential energy consumption classified by fuel. The model can provide the demand detail necessary to drive a planning model for energy production, but does not produce all the outputs required to analyze the distributional effects of policy.

B. Inputs

The ORNL model forecasts changes from base-year energy consumption, taking into account changing demographics, economic conditions, and technological possibilities for conservation. Simulation inputs fall into three broad categories: base-year data on all variables (including variables which become model outputs in forecast years such as appliance saturation levels and energy consumption), rates of change for variables exogenous to the model (such as population and fuel prices), and behavioral and technological parameters which translate exogenous variable changes into model changes such as changes in energy consumption. Table III.2 lists the principal inputs. A crude count of dimensions gives 153 technological parameters, 971 behavioral parameters, 636 base-year values, and 8840 exogenous forecast values. In practice many of these values are redundant, because either they are not used in the model (e.g., because of excluded fuel–appliance combinations), are assumed to be zero or have common values or are obtained by a relatively simple interpolation as part of the preprocessing of the input files. There is an obvious ambiguity in the number of inputs depending on which stage in preprocessing they are counted. A rough estimate is that 500 behavioral and technological parameters, plus approximately 450 base-year data points plus inputs to preprocessed exogenous forecasts, must be determined by engineering or econometric study or by substantive judgmental assumption. Many of these values in the ORNL model have a significant judgmental component. This is inevitable in any attempt to construct a model of this complexity from existing data, but is also grounds for caution in applying model outputs.

Base-year values of variables and exogenous forecasts are readily obtain-

TABLE III.2

ORNL Model Inputs

Variable	Type[a]	Dimension
New equipment market shares, base year	BY	240
Air conditioning–space heat load reduction ratio	T	3
Appliance market share elasticity with respect to operating cost	B	400
Usage elasticity with respect to operating cost	B	160
Interest rates for PV cost minimization	B	320
Equipment market shares, base year	BY	120
Market share equation *slope* coefficient	B	80
New equipment technological parameter	T	32
Annual average energy use, new equipment, 1970	BY	120
Ratio of short- to long-run usage elasticities	B	1
A market penetration rate parameter	B	1
A horizon after which life-cycle cost is minimum	B	1
New construction technological parameters	T	12
New equipment prices, relative	F	3720
New equipment prices, base year	BY	120
Interest rate	BY	1
Retrofit technological parameters	T	3
Ratio of 1979 to 1970 usage factors	BY	4
Maximum saturation	B	8
Average equipment lifetimes	T/B	8
Lifetime of investments in thermal shell	T	1
New equipment installations, base year	BY	32
Real prices for fuels plus income	F	155
Fuel prices plus income, base year	BY	5
Average size of existing housing units	F	93
Average annual energy use, new equipment, before adjustment	F	3720
Thermal integrity of retrofit homes	F	24
Number of homes which are retrofit	F	93
Total number of occupied housing units	F	93
Total number of new housing units	F	93
Fractions of new homes with room–central air conditioning	F	2
Status quo new equipment energy use	F	72
Size of new housing units	F	31
Average thermal integrity, new structures	F	744

[a] Types are base-year data (BY), technological parameters (T), behavioral parameters (B), and exogenous forecasts (F).

able for many ORNL inputs. However, a number of the base variables in the ORNL model are not available in published data sources. In particular, base-year energy consumption by end use is not observed, even approximately, on any systematic basis. The ORNL model uses judgment and scattered end-use observations to fill these gaps.

C. Outputs

The ORNL model is designed to forecast annual residential energy consumption, classified by 5 fuel types, 3 dwelling types, and 8 end uses, for up to 30 years. Table III.3 lists the classification for which these forecasts are provided. Auxiliary outputs are expenditures on new equipment, classified by fuel, end use, dwelling type, and year; expenditures on retrofitting space heat in existing dwellings, classified by fuel, dwelling type, and year; expenditures on new dwelling thermal integrity classified by fuel, dwelling type, and year; retrofit fuel market shares classified by dwelling type and year; and total number of new equipment units installed, classified by fuel, dwelling type, end use, and year.

In addition, the model contains a number of variables used internally which could be obtained as outputs if needed, such as indices of efficiency and usage levels of equipment and structures. The model cannot provide disaggregation of outputs by subregional geography (e.g., urban–rural or climate zone) or by demographic group (e.g., young–old or rich–poor) without modification.

D. End-Use Approach

The ORNL model analyzes separately each of the eight end uses in Table III.3, e.g., the fuel choice on space heating is independent of the air conditioning decision, and the usage levels for hot water and other are independent. This may introduce some specification errors. For example, consumption of hot water is strongly affected by a dishwasher or clothes washer.

Energy consumption in each end use is modeled as the result of the number of units of equipment held, the efficiency of the equipment (measured in energy consumed per unit of service), and the intensity of utilization. The heart of the model is the accounting relationship

$$(1) \qquad\qquad E = N \times ESR \times U,$$

TABLE III.3

ORNL Classifications for Outputs

Fuel type	Electricity, gas, oil, other, none
Dwelling type	Single-family, multi-family, mobile home
End use	Space heating, air conditioning (room, central), water heating, refrigeration, freezing, cooking, lighting, other
Year	1970 to 2000

where E is the energy consumption for a specified end use, dwelling type, and fuel, N the number of units, ESR the average energy consumed per service unit, and U the average rate of utilization. If either ESR or U is constant over all units of equipment in the category, then this accounting relationship is valid. Otherwise, it is an approximation containing an aggregation bias due to the fact that the product of averages is not equal to the average of products. In general, we would expect a negative correlation between ESR and U, because *ex ante* a household anticipating heavy utilization will find it advantageous to purchase a more efficient appliance, and *ex post* the more efficient appliance will be more attractive to use. Then the model will tend to overpredict actual consumption. The ORNL model reduces aggregation biases somewhat by considering separate categories for existing equipment, retrofit equipment, and new equipment.

E. Structure

The ORNL model has a block recursive structure, illustrated schematically in Fig. III.1. Base-year data, exogenous variable forecasts, and behavioral parameters drive a housing submodel which produces forecasts of new construction by dwelling type and average size. The outputs of this model plus base-year data, exogenous base costs, and parameters drive the simulation model, which gives us output forecasts of energy consumption classified by fuel, dwelling type, end use, and year. The following sections describe the housing submodel, the module determining equipment efficiency, and the usage module.

F. The Housing Module

The housing module of the ORNL model forecasts number of households in a region, additions to housing stocks required to accommodate these households, and the average size of new dwellings. The structure of the module is outlined in Fig. III.2. First, number of households, classified by age group, is predicted for each region by multiplying population in the classification by predicted proportion which are heads of households. The latter prediction is obtained from a regression on national age-specific marriage and divorce rates and income. Second, households are allocated among three dwelling types (single-family, multiple-family, mobile home) in proportions determined by linear interpolation between existing 1970 housing-type shares and assumed year 2000 housing-type shares. Third, new construction of each dwelling type is assumed to equal demand determined

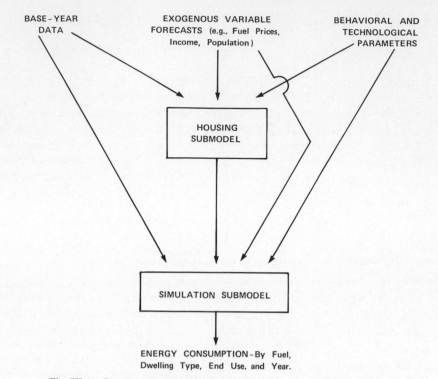

Fig. III.1 General structure of the ORNL model—a schematic outline.

by the allocation of households less the supply of existing dwellings of that type after retirement of an exogenously set fraction. Finally, size of a new single-family dwelling (in square feet) is forecast using a regression of square footage on income, persons per household, cost ($/ft²), and regional dummies. The method used to forecast size of multi-family and mobile home dwellings is not documented. However, inputs to the simulation module provided by ORNL contain the following representative values:

Percentage Increase in Square Footage over 1970

	Single family	Multiple family	Mobile home
1980	2.2	2.7	7.2
1990	7.6	9.1	21.8
2000	13.4	15.6	35.0

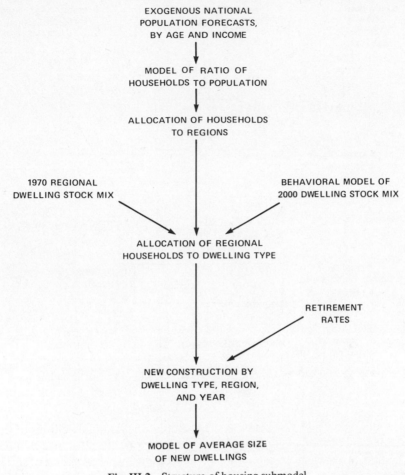

Fig. III.2   Structure of housing submodel.

A deficiency of the ORNL housing module from the standpoint of policy analysis is that it is insensitive to energy policy. In practice, both housing type and size decisions are likely to show some sensitivity to energy costs.

G. Efficiency Decisions

Figure III.3 gives a more detailed schematic diagram of the simulation submodel, to be discussed in this section and Section H. The ORNL model assumes that appliance efficiency is determined by life-cycle cost minimiza-

52   III. Residential Energy Demand Simulation Models

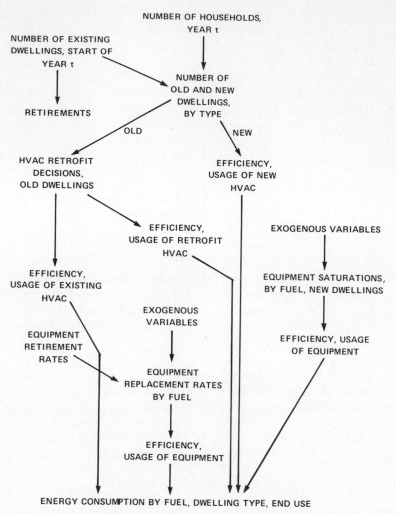

Fig. III.3   Structure of simulation submodel.

tion, taking into account the trade-off between capital and operating cost for
various levels of efficiency.   The key ingredients of this analysis are the
schedules of efficiency versus cost, postulated to be available in the market,
and assumptions on household discount rates and expectations about future
energy prices, durability, and intensity of use.

   The system forecasts the efficiency of the equipment in each end use and
the thermal integrity of the housing shell.   In principle, the calculation is
straightforward: consumers are assumed to choose efficiency to minimize
life-cycle cost, with some partial adjustment introduced to capture market

imperfections. The life-cycle cost calculation takes into account expected usage, which in turn depends on energy prices. Hence, this approach is consistent with the utility-maximizing behavior discussed in Chapter II. However, it does not consider optimization with respect to capacity, voluntary replacement decisions, or *ex post* usage optimization.

The efficiency calculations for heating, air conditioning, and the thermal shell are interrelated. Efficiency decisions for the remaining end uses are assumed to be made independently. Since the latter calculations are simpler, they will be discussed first. For concreteness, consider water heaters. For each fuel type, the life-cycle cost of a new water heater is the sum of initial cost and present value of operating cost. Initial cost is expressed as a simple function of the ESR, h,

$$(2) \qquad C(h) = c_0 + b\left(\left(\frac{1 - h_0}{h - h_0}\right)^{1/a} - 1\right),$$

where in the base year h is normalized to one and c_0 is the new equipment price. Equipment capacity, service quality (e.g., recovery rate), and durability are assumed fixed and not subject to choice. The parameters a, b, and h_0 are fitted to engineering data on the material and fabrication costs of achieving alternative energy service ratios. The assumption is then made that this also gives the locus of market prices. Several features of manufacturing behavior suggest that the connection of manufacturing cost and price is less simple: Consumer equipment manufacturers are relatively concentrated and appear to follow mark-up pricing rules to cover development and administrative overhead at anticipated production levels. As a consequence, the mark-up over cost is least on *popular* models and the engineering analysis may underestimate the cost of moving to efficient but historically low demand models. The present value of operating cost, PVOC, is defined by

$$(3) \qquad \text{PVOC} = \text{PWF} \times \text{P} \times \text{ESR} \times \text{U},$$

where PWF is a present worth factor defined assuming fixed equipment life and an interest rate which is individualized for each end use, P the fuel price, ESR the energy service ratio, and U the expected usage.

Several features of this formula deserve comment. First, equipment survival curves in reality have ogive shapes which could be incorporated into the PWF calculation. This still does not address the choice problems posed by stochastic survival or voluntary retirements. Economic theory would suggest a common interest rate for most consumer decisions (an exception may be distinctions between portable appliances and those attached to the dwelling, since the latter may share some of the tax and credit benefits of home mortgages); the alternative assumption in the ORNL model needs examination.

Second, fuel price is taken at the date of purchase, corresponding to the assumption that consumers expect no future changes in real price. Maintenance costs are not included in operating cost.

Third, expected usage is taken to equal average base-year usage from the appliance, an input to the program. This excludes joint determination of efficiency and usage level of the sort treated in Chapter II and suggests that in the later years of a simulation or for extreme policy scenarios the model may calculate efficiency choice on the basis of assumed usage which differs markedly from actual usage. An easy partial remedy would be to set expected usage equal to one-year-lagged actual usage (net of last year's ESR). A full remedy would require efficiency and usage to be determined jointly.

The optimal ESR is determined by minimizing life-cycle cost and can be derived analytically. The ORNL model assumes this optimum will be attained gradually. Two partial adjustment mechanisms are introduced (in sequence). First, due to *market imperfections,* consumers are assumed to purchase less than optimally efficient equipment. The equation representing this partial observation requires iterative solution: *Observed* efficiency levels in the base year when compared to the computed optimal level implies a difference (D) in observed and optimal life-cycle cost. This difference is assumed to persist into the future, possibly attenuated when fuel costs rise or time passes. The second adjustment assumes adaptive adjustment in ESRs to the level determined by the first stage,

$$(4) \qquad\qquad h_n = 0.25h^* + 0.75h_{n-1},$$

where h_n is the ESR in year n and h^* is the ESR determined in the first stage.

There would appear to be an advantage to replacing the adjustment mechanism just described with something computationally simpler. First, consumers appear to utilize relatively high interest rates when evaluating alternatives. This may be due to credit constraints, uncertainty about the effectiveness of promised energy efficiency, or the inability of mobile consumers to capture the full value of efficient appliances in imperfect second hand markets. This could be captured in the model simply by minimizing life-cycle cost with a correspondingly low PWF. The second adjustment could be retained if it is realistic to argue that there are significant delays in delivering equipment with desired efficiency levels to the market. We have *not* made these adjustments in the version of the model used in this study.

The determination of the efficiencies of heating and air conditioning equipment and the thermal integrity of the shell follows the same pattern as the water heater calculation, with the added complication that the decisions are interrelated by the effect of thermal integrity on heating and air conditioning operating cost. The most logical way to carry out this computation would be to write down the joint life-cycle cost of these three decisions and optimize jointly. This could be done by solving for the equipment efficiencies as functions of the level of thermal integrity, substituting these expressions back in to get joint life-cycle cost as a function of thermal integrity alone, and finally optimizing in this decision variable. Note that since the dwelling and equipment have different assumed lives, it is necessary to make some adjustments to the life-cycle cost formula to express all costs to a common horizon. This in turn requires assumptions on how the prospect of future decisions affects current choice, making the problem, in principle, a dynamic programming problem. A simpler and perhaps adequate approach would be to assume stationary expectations so that joint life-cycle cost (LCC) can be written as

$$(5) \qquad \text{LCC} = \sum_{k=0}^{2} C_k(h_k)/(1 - e^{-rL_k}) + p_f(h_1 h_0 u_1 + h_2 h_0 u_2)/r,$$

where LCC is the joint life-cycle cost including present value of replacement cost (to an infinite horizon), h_0 the ESR (inefficiency) of the thermal shell, h_1 the heating ESR, h_2 the air conditioning ESR, $c_k(h_k)$ the capital cost, P_f the fuel price, U_k the expected usage in end use k, L_k the equipment life, and r the interest rate. This formulation has the unrealistic feature that surviving equipment is assumed to move when the dwelling is replaced. Alternatively, we could consider LCC only for dwelling life and assume premature scrappage of surviving equipment,

$$(6) \qquad \text{LCC} = C_0(h_0) + C_1(h_1) \sum_{t=0}^{t_1} e^{-rtL_1}$$

$$+ C_2(h_2) \sum_{t=0}^{t_2} e^{-rtL_2}$$

$$+ p_f(h_1 h_0 u_1 + h_2 h_0 u_2)(1 - e^{-rL_0})/r,$$

where t_k is the largest integer less than L_0/L_k. For $L_0 = 25$ and values of r around 0.1, these formulas will have virtually identical solutions.

The computation actually carried out by the ORNL model differs from the procedure outlined above in several respects. First, the computation is done sequentially rather than jointly. Heating and air conditioning equipment efficiencies are calculated by minimizing their respective life-cycle costs, with thermal integrity set at its value in the previous period. Capital and operating costs in these calculations are defined and computed in the same manner as the water heater calculation discussed earlier and the earlier comments on the limitations of the procedure apply. An additional factor in the definition of expected usage of heat and air conditioning is dwelling size, which is appropriate. However, heating and cooling equipment capacity is assumed to be independent of dwelling size. In the presence of growing dwelling sizes, this leads to an underestimate of capital cost. For example, an increase of 13.4% in the size of single-family homes by the year 2000 can be expected to cause an increase in air conditioning equipment cost of 5.2% (at the historical elasticity of cost with respect to capacity of 0.4). As for other equipment, a two-phase partial adjustment mechanism is introduced for short-run response and the effect of *market imperfections.*

Once heating and air conditioning efficiencies are calculated, the thermal integrity of the shell is computed by minimizing the expression

$$(7) \qquad \text{LCC} = \text{CT} + \text{PWF}_H \times P_H \times \text{ESR}_H \times U_H$$
$$+ \text{PWF}_C \times P_C \times \text{ESR}_C \times U_C,$$

where CT is the initial cost of thermal improvements, subscripts H and C denote heating and cooling, PWF is a present worth factor, P the fuel price, ESR the energy service ratio, and U the expected utilization. In this formula, PWF is calculated for an assumed dwelling life of 25 yr. The thermal ESR for cooling is assumed to vary from its 1970 base as a fraction of the variation of the ESR for heating. Fuel prices are taken at the date of construction, with no adjustment for expectations. Expected usage quantities are set to 1970 values. Dwelling size does *not* enter expected usage in this formula.

This calculation has several deficiencies. First, unless cost of thermal improvements is proportional to dwelling size, the term for dwelling size will enter the determination of optimal thermal ESR. Further, this term should enter life-cycle cost difference calculations if the first partial adjustment mechanism of the ORNL model is utilized. Second, fixing expected usage at base-year levels excludes the trade-off between usage and efficiency of the sort considered in Chapter II and implicit in the usage elasticities permitted later in the simulation model. This will tend to lead the model to forecast too high a level of optimal efficiency.

Third, the ORNL calculation excludes the present value of future heating and cooling equipment replacements in the life-cycle cost, which biases downward the cost of added efficiency. For simplicity, ignore the difference in heating and cooling ESR. The first-order conditions for optimization of (6) are

$$(8) \qquad C_0'(h_0) + p_f[h_1 u_1 + h_2 u_2](1 - e^{-rL_0})/r = 0,$$
$$(9) \qquad C_k'(h_k)\sigma_k + p_f h_0 u_k(1 - e^{-rL_0})/r = 0, \qquad k = 1, 2,$$

where $\sigma_k = \Sigma_{t=0}^{t_k} e^{-rtL_k}$. For the assumed equipment lifetimes, $L_0 = 25$, $L_1 = 15$, $L_2 = 10$, and $r = 0.06$, we have $1 - e^{-rL_0} = 0.777$, $\sigma_1 = 1.41$, and $\sigma_2 = 1.85$. In comparison, the first-order conditions for the optimization in the ORNL model are

(10) $\qquad C_k'(h_k) + p_f h_0 u_k (1 - e^{-rL_k})/r = 0 \qquad k = 1, 2,$

(11) $\qquad C_0'(h_0) + p_f [h_1 u_1 + h_2 u_2](1 - e^{-rL_0})/r = 0,$

where we ignore the modest error caused by solving Eq. (7) using lagged h_0 rather than solving the system simultaneously. For the assumed lifetime, we obtain $1 - e^{-rL_1} = 0.593$ and $1 - e^{-rL_2} = 0.451$. For the system (10), (11) to give the same solution as the correct jointly optimized system (8), (9), it would be necessary to increase C_1 by 7.6% and C_2 by 7.4%. This error and the previous two errors in the ORNL calculation all go in the direction of underestimating the relative capital cost of increasing efficiency.

Finally, it should be noted that the introduction of the partial adjustment mechanisms in the determination of equipment efficiencies leads in the second step to the calculation of an *optimal* thermal ESR which is lower than would result from joint optimization of life-cycle costs. The partial adjustment toward this solution may then be going too far relative to the true joint optimum.

H. Appliance Saturation Models

The starting point of the ORNL appliance model is an econometrically estimated model of equipment ownership, classified by type of equipment and fuel type, as a function of equipment and fuel prices. The estimation is done principally on 1970 Census data at the state level, and is described in Lin–Hirst–Cohn (1976). The specification is of the form

(12) $\qquad \log(s_i^k/(1 - s_i^k)) = \alpha_i^k + \beta_i^k X + \epsilon_i^k,$

where s_i^k is the share of fuel i among appliances of type k, X is a vector of income, fuel prices, and appliance prices, and α, β are parameters. This is estimated as a multivariate system across fuels by three-stage least squares subject to the parameter restrictions

(13) $\qquad \sum_i \bar{s}_i^k (1 - \bar{s}_i^k) \beta_i^k = 0,$

where $\bar{s}_i^k$ is the 1970 *national* share of fuel i. The purpose of this restriction is to ensure that *on average* the fitted shares will sum to one. In the estimation, the $\bar{s}$ are treated as arithmetic rather than random variables.

When the fitted share equations are used in the simulation program, they are normalized so that the shares in any region and year sum to one.

Consequently, the model finally used to forecast appliance saturations is

(14) $s_i^k = [1 + \exp(-\alpha_i^k - \beta_i^k X)]^{-1} \Big/ \sum_j [1 + \exp(-\alpha_j^k - \beta_j^k X)]^{-1},$

where α, β are the estimated parameters.

The final forecasting model (14) is, in fact, a multinomial logit model

(15) $s_i^k = e^{V_i^k} \Big/ \sum_j e^{V_j^k},$

where the scale function V_i has the unconventional nonlinear form

(16) $V_i^k = -\ln[1 + e^{-\alpha_i - \beta_i X}]$

rather than the standard linear in-parameters form

(17) $V_i^k = \theta_i^k + \gamma_i^k X.$

Lin–Hirst–Cohn claim that their model is based on the conditional multinomial logit model of discrete behavior developed by McFadden (1974), modified to relax restrictions on cross-elasticities imposed by the multinomial logit form. However, McFadden's treatment emphasizes the derivation of the multinomial logit model from individual preference maximization and leads to scale values V_i^k which are functions solely of attributes of alternative i and household characteristics. It is this last property which restricts cross-elasticities. The standard multinomial logit functional form (15), with scale values (17) which depend on attributes of all alternatives, imposes no cross-elasticity restrictions. It is unnecessary to adopt the non-linear form (16) to achieve flexible cross-elasticities.

One issue concerns the empirical identification of the model. The authors do not have linearly independent equipment prices, and therefore they fit equipment price parameters by imposing judgmental restrictions on β's, choosing a set of restrictions which yield *reasonable* elasticities. This procedure lacks a statistical foundation.

The authors use equipment and operating cost coefficients to calculate appliance- and fuel-specific implicit interest rates which are used subsequently in determining life-cycle cost. We are aware of no behavioral studies which suggest varying discount factors for different purposes; theory would suggest the contrary. Implicit in this model is the assumption that equipment has a fixed lifetime, whereas in simulation the assumption is made that there is a geometric failure rate for each appliance.

Finally, there are some problems in variable specification in (12). Fuel type is expected to be sensitive to life-cycle costs which depend on efficiency and intensity of use. For some appliances, utilization is weather-sensitive; this enters the model only through possibly unrepresentative base-year utilization rates. A more subtle problem here is that level of utilization and fuel type are jointly determined. Then using actual utilization as an explanatory variable may create a simultaneous equations problem, while using *repre-sentative* utilization may cause an errors-in-variables problem.

The shares model is transformed in the simulation system to forecast shares in retrofit and new construction, in the following steps:

1. Base-year data on market shares by fuel and dwelling type of existing appliances are expanded to a classification by fuel, dwelling type, and old or new dwellings, by assuming the shares in each subclassification are the same. The program has the capacity to alter this assumption parametrically.

2. Next the nonlinear multinomial logit model (14) is used to forecast new equipment shares. The program does this by a series of indirect steps. The econometric model coefficients are translated into elasticities evaluated at national means of explanatory variables. These elasticities are input to the simulation model and then translated back into model coefficients. This permits judgmental changes in elasticities. However, the second translation is carried out at the values of shares and explanatory variables prevailing in the region of application and year of simulation. This double translation introduces an inconsistency between calibrated equations and the equations used in simulation.

The ORNL appliance model assumes all scrappage is involuntary, with a geometric survival curve for each appliance. Consequently, the model fails to capture the effects of prices on voluntary retrofit.

In summary, what are the primary differences between the ORNL appliance model and the theoretical choice scheme outlined in Chapter II? First, capacity, efficiency, and vintage detail are limited in the ORNL model, introducing some aggregation biases. Second, no possibility of voluntary scrappage, based on economic behavior, is included. Third, the choice model for new equipment fuel shares is awkward. Fourth, the capacity and efficiency decisions are not analyzed as part of a joint appliance decision. Of these differences, the first and fourth are intrinsic to the architecture of the ORNL model and cannot be easily changed.

I. Validation

Complex models such as the ORNL model tend to have systemic characteristics which are not detectable in calibration. For example, a complex model with a dynamic structure may compound negligible misspecification errors at the individual equation level into unstable transients which cause forecasts after some period of time to become totally unrealistic. On the other hand, such a system may have a *dynamic imperative* which makes the system quite insensitive to some specification errors. Thus, it is quite important to carry out an extensive model validation.

The usual method of validation is to forecast, or backcast, outside the calibration period and compare the forecast error with an absolute standard of accuracy or with alternative models using the same information. The most critical and interesting test is the ability of the model to make long-term forecasts using only the base-year information, since this most closely parallels policy applications.

A second validation procedure examines the sensitivity of forecasts to variations in model parameters or equation specifications. When there are classical or Bayesian measures of precision associated with model parameters, it is possible to formalize this and establish confidence bounds on the model forecasts.

The ORNL model has not been systematically validated. Hirst–Carney (1978) report on a within-calibration-period validation for 6 yr starting in 1960. The model parameters are tuned to reproduce historical experience through this period, so this is more a test of the completeness of the tuning than a validation test. The tuning problem is greatly compounded by the methods used to supply missing base-year values. The authors adjust these inputs *until the model's predictions for the first few years after the simulation begins are reasonably accurate.* A better validation test, but still within calibration period, has been carried out by Freedman, Rothenberg, and Sutch (1980). They find that a 5 yr forecast from 1970 by the ORNL model is more accurate for electricity consumption, but less accurate for consumption of other fuels, than a naive model that forecasts 1970 consumption levels to remain *constant.*

In some ways, the preceding result is too stringent a test of the ORNL model. First, in building a complex policy model like the ORNL model, we are probably willing to sacrifice baseline predictive accuracy in order to obtain reasonable predictions of *relative* impacts of alternative policy scenarios. Second, the place where a nonlinear dynamic system will work best is in long-run forecasts where substantial exogenous changes and long-run responses can be anticipated. For example, if we could run a 1960 base naive forecast against the ORNL model for the 17-yr period until 1976, with the latter model initialized using 1960 data, it is likely the ORNL model performance would look better. However, the apparent failure of the ORNL model to pick up short-run responses to price shocks in the early 1970s in the Freedman analysis may indicate that the ORNL model underestimates short-run impacts.

Hirst–Carney (1978) have also done a limited sensitivity analysis of se-

TABLE III.4

Sensitivity Analysis for Conservation Impact

Year 2000	Low parameters			Average parameters			High parameters		
Consumption (10^{15} Btu)	Base	Conser-vation	Impact	Base	Conser-vation	Impact	Base	Conser-vation	Impact
Electricity	16.0	14.1	1.9	17.0	14.5	2.5	18.2	14.8	3.4
Gas	4.6	3.8	0.8	5.0	4.1	0.9	5.8	4.6	1.2
Oil	1.7	1.6	0.1	1.9	1.7	0.2	2.1	1.8	0.3
Total	23.0	19.8	3.2	25.0	20.6	4.4	27.0	21.2	5.8

lected model parameters. They argue that forecasts attenuate fairly strongly the percentage impact of changes in key parameters. However, such a conclusion is very sensitive to the base chosen for the comparison. For example, a more relevant quantity for policy analysis may be the forecast of the relative reduction in consumption due to a conservation program, and this may be quite sensitive to parameter changes. Using the Hirst–Carney forecasts in the year 2000, we obtain Table III.4. In this table the effect of a variation of 25% in the key parameters to give the low and high cases chosen by Hirst–Carney implies variations of 30% in the predicted policy *impact* of the conservation program. By this policy-relevant standard, the model is rather sensitive to parameter specification.

III.3. THE RESIDENTIAL END-USE ENERGY PLANNING SYSTEM

A. Objectives

The Residential End-Use Energy Planning System (REEPS) is a proprietary model of the Electric Power Research Institute. The REEPS model is designed to provide end-use specific forecasts of energy consumption at the household level. It is a system which works by generating a simulated sample of households. Energy consumption forecasts for the sample, or a subsample corresponding to a particular population segment, are obtained by tabulation.

We give a fairly complete description of this model, since the principles underlying its design have not previously been described in the literature. The version of REEPS used in our analysis was the latest available when this study was initiated. More recent versions correct some of the shortcomings we identify in the version we used.

The range of policy issues which can be studied using REEPS includes not only those with impacts which are distributionally and geographically homogeneous, such as oil import taxes, but also policies which have highly heterogeneous impacts such as *lifeline* utility rates for the poor or building standards which vary by community. The microsimulation structure provides the flexibility necessary to describe the incidence of these policies or tabulate their impact on selected groups without unacceptable aggregation errors. A particular advantage of microsimulation is that it can be adapted quickly to the study of different populations and geographical areas and can be focused on groups of special interest. The cost of this approach compared to more aggregate models is increased computation time and an increased burden on the user in preparing program inputs and tabulating and interpreting outputs.

The sample enumeration technique is also appealing because it copies directly the process by which aggregate residential energy patterns are established. Households with diverse characteristics under various economic conditions make different decisions on appliance energy use. At the individual household level, families in new dwellings install space heating systems and other appliances which are utilized at a given level of intensity. The choices of appliance operating characteristics and utilization rates are influenced by the household and dwelling attributes, costs, weather, and other geographical features. These vary across households, and they result in different choices. Energy consumption, in turn, depends on these operating characteristics and utilization patterns. Over time, a household may wish to change its energy consumption patterns, but its flexibility is significantly constrained by the historical appliance decisions. Moreover, when a household moves and occupies an existing dwelling, it acquires a set of attached appliances whose characteristics have been determined by previous occupants and will significantly influence energy consumption patterns by the current occupants. Thus at any point in time, energy usage for a particular household is significantly influenced by a sequence of past decisions made under different circumstances. Aggregate residential sector energy consumption is simply the sum of individual household rates.

The sample enumeration technique traces through the sequence of household decisions on appliance installations and utilization patterns. This is performed by predicting the probabilities of the alternative decisions conditioned on the attributes of the household and the characteristics of the options. Then a decision is *made* through a random drawing based on the predicted probabilities. All of these decisions are made in response to different incomes, family sizes, relative and absolute energy prices, and other factors. By simulating many decisions for a group of households that repre-

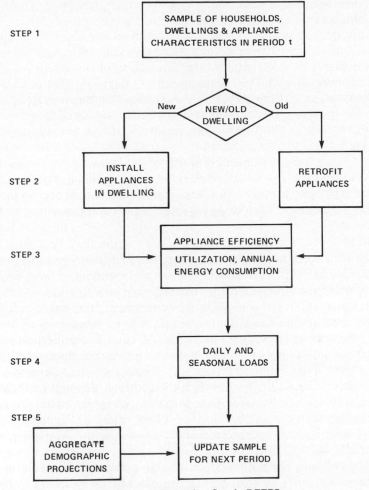

Fig. III.4   Information flow in REEPS.

sent the diversity of economic and demographic conditions in the United States, total or average behavior can be inferred in a given year by summing over the households in the sample.   From period to period the distribution of historical decisions on operating characteristics by location and building type is maintained and used along with the simulations of current period decisions to determine energy usage.

A diagram of the major components of the simulation model and the information flow between them is presented in Fig. III.4.   The model predicts four categories of energy-related decisions: appliance investment decisions in new dwellings, retrofit appliance investments in existing dwellings, appliance operating efficiencies, and annual energy consumption. Appliance choices are treated in detail because of their central role in determining total household energy consumption. This stems from the derived structure of residential energy demand wherein gas and electricity are inputs along with consumer durables in the production of household services. The number and operating characteristics of appliances *fix* the production technology for these services. Moreover, many consumer durables turn over at a very slow rate, implying that housing and appliance choices continue to exert a significant influence on energy consumption patterns for many years after they are made.

The simulation model predicts appliance and consumption decisions recursively with appliance choice dependent on previous appliance and housing decisions and anticipated usage and energy consumption dependent on appliance holdings. Each component is described briefly below.

STEP 1. As its initial input the model requires a recent historical sample of households with information on their socioeconomic attributes, appliance holdings and characteristics, the type and size of their residence, and various geographic and economic characteristics of the area in which they reside. For simulations at the national level, the model uses a synthetic sample which was constructed from the National Annual Housing Survey and other public sources. The synthetic sample was developed in the following manner. First, multi-way contingency tables of household and dwelling characteristics were tabulated for each Census Region from the 1977 Annual Housing Survey. These tables represent the correlation among the different explanatory variables in the model. These tables are adjusted for each subregion[2] so that they are consistent with aggregate information specific to that area. The adjustment procedure, known as iterative proportional fitting, preserves the correlation structure among the variables while ensuring consistency with the subregional aggregates. For each subregion, observations of household and dwelling characteristics are created by random drawings from these tables.

STEP 2. The simulation model forecasts purchases and installations of space heating, water heating, central air conditioners, room air conditioners, stoves, and dishwashers. Three categories of appliance purchase decisions are distinguished in this component of the simulation model:

1. physically attached appliances in new housing construction,
2. attached appliances in existing housing, and
3. other appliances.

Included in the first two categories are space heating systems, water heaters, central air conditioners, and stoves. These appliance categories are separated because they exhibit quite distinct structures. Installed equipment costs for attached appliances are considerably lower in new construction than in existing units. For this and other reasons, appliance decisions appear more price-sensitive in new housing than in old housing. The difference is not believed to be important for nonattached appliances; therefore no distinction is maintained. Whether a house is equipped with a particular appliance is determined according to the sampling procedure described previously. Because some appliance choices exhibit a large degree of interdependence (e.g., gas water heaters tend to be installed with gas space heating), they are modeled jointly. The probability that a housing unit installs a given appliance combination is calculated as a function of their installed capital costs, operating costs, and performance characteristics, as well as household and housing attributes. The costs themselves are dependent on utility rate structure, operating efficiencies, and building structural characteristics. As such, the impact of changes in utility tariffs, appliance efficiency markets, or building insulation standards can be examined through their relation to costs and finally to appliance installation probabilities.

STEP 3. This component of the simulation system calculates annual energy consumption by fuel type given the appliance portfolio and the household, dwelling, and geographical characteristics. Energy consumption is associated with each of the major appliances whose ownership is predicted in the model plus a residual category representing the remaining appliances. Energy consumption of the given appliance is determined as the result of two distinct but closely related decisions. In the first, the household selects the appliance operating efficiency. This decision is made initially in the year of purchase in response to planned utilization patterns, energy prices, and appliance costs. After the unit is installed, the household has little or no flexibility to change the efficiency so that its ability to modify energy consumption is significantly restricted. In the second decision, a household decides on how intensively to utilize the appliance. This decision is made in response to operating costs and household and geographical attributes. Utilization can change every period in response to unanticipated changes in operating costs or other variables. Given the appliance efficiency and utilization decisions, annual energy consumption is determined directly.

STEP 4. After the appliance and energy usage decisions are simulated for the current period, a new sample is created for the subsequent period simulation. Aggregate projections of housing stock and construction by building type as well as socioeconomic variables are used to adjust the distribution of household and dwelling characteristics for each subregion. The results of the appliance choice simulations from the previous period are used to adjust the distribution of the stock of appliances in existing dwellings by location, household and dwelling characteristics. Then a sample of observations is drawn from these distributions in a manner similar to the procedure described in Step 1. This sample is the input for the next period.

In each period of simulation, REEPS requires as input a sample of households with information on the respective location, socioeconomic and demographic attributes, and dwelling structural characteristics for each observation, as well as their appliance holdings at the beginning of the period. If REEPS is simulated for a recent historical period, the results of an actual household survey can be used as the input. Such an application of REEPS would be useful to estimate the short-term impact of a proposed energy policy on a population of households whose characteristics are representative of current attributes. However, in its most common application, REEPS will be used to forecast the long-term impacts of energy policies on a population whose characteristics change over time, reflecting projected demographic and economic growth.

The long-term forecasting application of REEPS requires successive samples of households in future years. Obviously, these samples are not real, but must be created synthetically in a manner which projects the distribution of household and dwelling characteristics into the future. Various techniques could be used to project this distribution. At one extreme, one could take a *bottom–up* approach in which disaggregate structural models of demographic, economic, and housing decisions are used to simulate a panel survey of households into the future. Appropriate models of household formation and dissolution would ensure that the representativeness of the sample is maintained over time.

REEPS takes an alternative *top–down* approach to project the distribution of household and dwelling characteristics by several multi-way cross-tabulations. In the current application, these tables are constructed from a recent National Annual Housing Survey data file. The cross-tabulations are constructed for various overlapping subsets of household and dwelling characteristics reflecting assumptions regarding the structure of the interdependence among the explanatory variables.

In each period, the tables are adjusted so that they are consistent with aggregate projections of household and dwelling characteristics and with the results from the previous period simulation.

Based on the adjusted table, a sample of households is created with infor-

TABLE III.5

Household Record Data

Household record as output from SAMPLER
Annual household income
Household size
Age of head of household
Dwelling unit building type
Dwelling tenure
Dwelling size — number of rooms
Dwelling vintage
Dwelling location

Appliance portfolio for the first period
Space heating system and fuel
Water heating fuel
Air conditioning system
Cooking fuel

---

mation on demographics, dwelling features, etc., for the respective observations. This sample is *drawn* in the following manner. First, a proportional sample is selected from a table representing a set of *core* variables. The distribution of these core variables from the table is represented exactly in the sample. Then for each observation in the sample, secondary characteristics are appended by random drawings from the other tables *given* the core characteristics. A limitation is that any impacts of energy policy on basic demographic and household stock projections must be supplied outside the simulation system.

B. Exogenous Variables and Sample Characteristics

As input in each period, REEPS requires a representative sample of households, with the household record data described in Table III.5. The categories used for these variables are defined in Table III.6. The dwelling location [3] is used to index several geographical variables, such as energy prices and weather, which are homogeneous within a given region. In addition, for the base year of simulation, REEPS uses information on the portfolio of appliances in existing dwellings, as listed in Table III.5. Algebraic transformations of the variables describing household – dwelling characteristics, geographical conditions, and base-year appliance holdings are used in the structural models to predict appliance investments, efficiency, and utilization decisions. Some of these transformations are complex. For example, annual space heating operating cost, an explanatory variable in the choice

TABLE III.6

Household – Dwelling Category Definitions

Building type
1. single-family detached
2. single-family attached/multi-family with less than 5 units
3. multi-family structure with 5 or more units
4. mobile home

Age of head of household
1. less than 30
2. 30–44
3. 45–60
4. greater than 60

Vintage
1. existing structure
2. new construction

Number of rooms
1. less than 4
2. 4
3. 5
4. 6
5. more than 6

Size of family
1. 1
2. 2
3. 3
4. 4
5. 5
6. more than 5

Tenure
1. own
2. rent

Income
1. less than $5,000
2. $5,000–$10,000
3. $10,000–$15,000
4. $15,000–$25,000
5. $25,000–$45,000
6. more than $45,000

Location — state of residence

model, is a function of the space heating alternative, and dwelling type and size, annual heating degree days, and energy prices.

C. Sample Projection Technique

The procedure used in REEPS to generate a synthetic sample in each forecast year is summarized in Fig. III.5. The major steps of the sampling procedure are described in detail below.

STEP 1. Construct contingency tables. The process of constructing the multi-way contingency tables begins by redefining all of the explanatory variables in discrete terms. For example, a naturally continuous variable such as household income is specified in terms of the ranges "less than $5,000," "$5,000 – 10,000," etc. The categories for the household and dwelling characteristics are presented in Table III.6. (In simulation, the midpoints of each range for categorical variables are used to transform them back to continuous ones.) Given these definitions, multi-way contingency tables of overlapping subsets of the explanatory variables are specified. The tables are intended to capture the critical interactions among the explanatory variables. A list of the cross-tabulations is presented in Table III.7. Note that the process of categorizing continuous variables and then using category midpoints in functions of the continuous variables introduces some grouping bias. This bias could be reduced by an additional step in which the original empirical distribution of the continuous variable is adjusted to be consistent with the contingency table cell frequencies.

Both the categorical definitions and contingency table specifications embody certain assumptions about the structure of interdependence among the variables. If, for example, we specify cross-tabulations of household income

TABLE III.7

Cross-Tabulations of Explanatory Variables

Income × building type × vintage × region
Age of head × income × building type × region
Family size × age of head × income × building type × region
Tenure × age of head × income × building type × region
Rooms × family size × building type × region

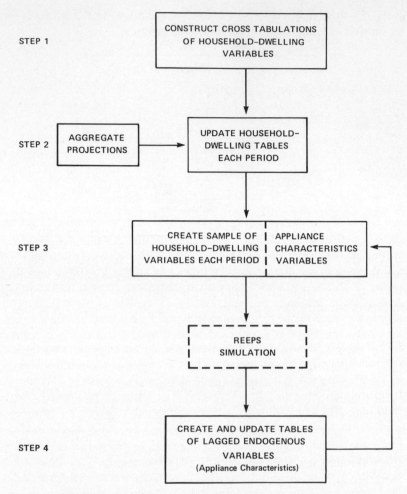

STEP 1   CONSTRUCT CROSS TABULATIONS
          OF HOUSEHOLD-DWELLING
          VARIABLES

STEP 2   AGGREGATE   UPDATE HOUSEHOLD-
          PROJECTIONS   DWELLING TABLES
                           EACH PERIOD

STEP 3   CREATE SAMPLE OF | APPLIANCE
          HOUSEHOLD-DWELLING | CHARACTERISTICS
          VARIABLES EACH PERIOD | VARIABLES

          REEPS
          SIMULATION

STEP 4   CREATE AND UPDATE TABLES
          OF LAGGED ENDOGENOUS
          VARIABLES
          (Appliance Characteristics)

Fig. III.5 Sample construction for exogenous variables.

by age of head and age of head by family size to represent the possible
interactions among these variables, then by assumption income is correlated
with size only by virtue of its common association with age. This relation is
known as conditional independence. Such assumptions are implicit in the
tables. Their validity can be tested statistically and modifications can be
made where necessary. However, the REEPs documentation indicates that
this has not been done systematically.

Given the contingency table specifications, the frequencies for each cell
are tabulated from a recent historical survey. In the version of REEPS used

TABLE III.8
Cross-Tabulations of Income
by Building Type

	Income		
Dwelling type	Low	High	
Base-year			
SF	350	350	700
MF	250	50	300
	600	400	1000
Updated			
SF	336	464	800
MF	314	86	400
	650	550	1200

in this study, the 1977 National Annual Housing Survey was used to construct the tables for each Census Region. Approximately 77,000 households were surveyed and information was collected on all of the explanatory variables in the simulation system.

STEP 2. Update the contingency tables. In each simulation period, the tables are adjusted to be consistent with projections of the marginal distributions of the respective household and dwelling variables. The marginal distributions are specified by the user. The adjustment procedure is described here and some of its properties are discussed. For a complete discussion of the algorithm see Bishop *et al.* (1975).

The procedure is illustrated by the following example. Suppose the correlation between income (with two values, high or low) and dwelling type (single family or multi-family) is represented by the contingency table in Table III.8.

The underlying correlation between income and dwelling type can be represented by the ratio of the product of the diagonal elements in the table, termed the cross product ratio (cpr). The value of the cpr in Table III.8 is

$$\text{cpr} = \frac{f_{11} \times f_{22}}{f_{12} \times f_{21}} = \frac{350 \times 50}{350 \times 250} = 0.2.$$

If income and dwelling type were completely uncorrelated then cpr equals one. Values different from unity mean the variables are correlated. Magnitudes increasing from one imply increasing positive correlation while those decreasing from one imply negative correlation of increasing magnitude.

Now suppose that we have projections of the marginal distributions of income and of building type and that we wish to produce a table consistent with those projections and with the above correlation structure. For example, assume we have the following projections of the number of households:

$$\text{low income} = 650,$$

$$\text{high income} = 550,$$

$$\text{single family} = 800,$$

$$\text{multi-family} = 400.$$

Under the iterative proportional fitting algorithm, the values of the cell entries are successively modified according to the formula.

$$f_{ij}^+ = f_{ij} \frac{f_{i.}^+}{f_{i.}},$$

where f_{ij}^+ is the new cell frequency, f_{ij} the previous cell frequency, $f_{i.}^+$ the *target* marginal frequency, and $f_{i.}$ the previous marginal frequency. This adjustment yields a table which is consistent with the marginal values of i (dwelling type), but inconsistent with the marginal values of j (income). The calculation is repeated using the marginal values of j (income), i.e.,

$$f_{ij}^{++} = f_{ij}^+ \frac{f_{.j}^+}{f_{.j}}.$$

This adjustment process continues until the table is consistent with both sets of marginal projections. In our example, the resulting cross-tabulation is shown in Table III.8. This table retains the correlation in the original table with the cpr of $(336)(86)/(314)(464) = 0.2$. This property generalizes to tables with more cells and higher dimensions: interactions of higher order than the marginal table of highest dimension remain invariant under the iterative proportional fitting adjustment. Thus, the interaction structure is preserved while the tables are modified to reflect the user-specified projections.

STEP 3.   Draw a sample of household–dwelling and base-year appliance characteristics. A sample with information on the explanatory variables is drawn from the updated contingency table. The sample is produced in two steps. The first step consists of drawing a proportional sample from a contingency table of *core* variables. In the current implementation the core variables are income, dwelling type, dwelling vintage, and dwelling location. The user can specify the total number of observations to be drawn from the table of core variables and can oversample household and dwelling characteristics of particular interest (with sampling weights to permit re-weighting to a representative sample). This facility is currently used to draw a disproportionate number of new dwellings each period. New dwellings are a particularly important segment of the residential energy market be-cause the major appliance installation decisions are made at the time of construction. The second step of the sampling process consists of drawing the other household – dwelling characteristics and base-year appliance hold-ings *given* the values of the core variables. This drawing is based on the updated cross-tabulation of the secondary variables versus the core vari-ables. The output of this step is a sequence of stratified synthetic samples for each simulation period, weighted to be representative of the population. The first period sample includes information on the stock of appliances. For samples in subsequent periods, the appliance stock variables will be assigned as a result of the energy simulation.

STEP 4. Sample future period appliance characteristics. The simula-tion system uses several appliance stock variables to predict investments in each period. To maintain consistency between the results of simulation and the inputs in subsequent years, appliance stock tables are maintained and updated in response to the simulation results each period. At the beginning of the following period, households in existing dwellings are assigned appli-ance holdings based on these tables. Given these stocks, the retrofit choice and related decisions are simulated.

D. Appliance Investment Decisions

This section describes the subsystem that simulates household appliance choices. This component predicts the purchases of the major energy-using household devices and their characteristics. These include household choices of space heating systems, air conditioning systems, water heaters, and other appliances. The simulation subsystem and the behavioral models that underlie it represent the appliance *investment* choices. It is important to address these investment decisions directly rather than the levels of long-run equilibrium ownership for a number of reasons. First, there is a tre-mendous inertia in these durable goods markets. Space heating, water heating, and central air conditioning are installed primarily at the time a house is built. Subsequent changes in space and water heating fuels are infrequent and often involve the technical obsolescence or physical breakdown of the previous system. In the 1975 Washington Center for Metropolitan Studies (WCMS) Energy Survey,[4] only 1% (32 of 3149) of the respondents said they had switched space heating fuel in the previous two years, and only a single case of these occurred in a house built since 1960. Instances of changes in water heating fuel were even less frequent.

Some of the reasons for this inertia are obvious. For physically attached appliances, the installation costs are considerably lower at the time the house is constructed than in subsequent periods. For example, one widely used construction cost estimating manual, the National Construction Estimator,[5] calculates the installed cost of central air conditioning units to be three times higher in existing houses than in new ones. In addition to costs, other factors such as the physical building design constrain retrofit choices more than new construction decisions. As a consequence, appliance choices are more flexible in new housing, and most changes in overall market saturation of such items as space heating or water heating systems occur by virtue of changes in installation rates in new construction.

The second major consideration in specifying an investment model is its policy relevance. Many proposed or adopted conservation measures are focused on new construction. These include building thermal standards for new units and recent embargoes on natural gas service hook-ups. Whereas a stock model cannot distinguish between new housing versus retrofit decisions, an investment model addresses them directly.

The overall appliance subsystem logic, presented in Fig. III.6, is straightforward. Using the list of households and their dwelling characteristics as input, the subsystem first distinguishes between new dwelling units and old ones. Initially the new units have no physically attached appliances. These appliances are now assigned. Based on probabilistic choice models described in later sections, the probabilities of installing the various appliance portfolios are calculated. The probabilities themselves depend on various cost and performance characteristics of the available appliance alternatives, as well as the household and dwelling attributes. The calculated probabilities are used to define a multinomial distribution from which a random drawing is made to determine the specific appliance portfolio installed in the new building to be occupied by a synthetic sample household.

If the dwelling is an old one, the subsystem determines what, if any, retrofit decisions on appliances are made in the current period. First, for each of the major end-use categories the subsystem determines whether the household currently owns a unit. In REEPS, all existing dwellings have space heating, water heating, and cooking. Thus, this check is only important for central and room air conditioners and dishwashers. If the dwelling currently does not own a unit, then the respective decisions to install one are simulated

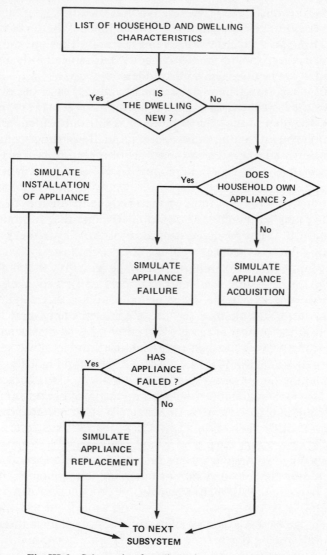

Fig. III.6 Schematic of appliance investment subsystem.

according to probabilistic choice models and the Monte Carlo procedure previously described.

Next, the appliance subsystem addresses the replacement retrofit of physically attached appliances. Currently, the subsystem assumes that a replacement is made only if the current unit fails. Failures are simulated based on physical decay probabilities. The subsystem could easily accommodate less restrictive assumptions on failure and replacements if deemed appropriate.

If the current appliance unit fails, the decisions on the operating characteristics of its replacement are simulated. The subsystem is designed to accommodate complete behavioral models of appliance retrofit choices; however, the current version has no behavioral response, but assumes replacement units never switch fuels.

The implementation logic of the appliance subsystem is complicated by the diversity of appliance purchase decisions and important structural considerations surrounding each of them. In the version of the simulation model we use, five major generic appliance categories — space heating, water heating, air conditioning, cooking, and dishwashing — are enumerated. For each of these, both first-time and replacement investment decisions are simulated as well as unit failures. Additionally, first-time central air conditioning and dishwasher purchase decisions in new construction are distinguished from those in existing dwellings. For each of the household investment decisions, specific assumptions are made regarding the choice setting, i.e., the circumstances under which a decision is simulated and the alternative set from which the household chooses.

These assumptions are imposed to reflect important policy considerations, such as the impact of natural gas embargoes or interdependence of appliance choices, as well as constraints on the behavioral model specification required by data limitations. All of the behavioral models that are the bases for the simulations are discrete choice models. That is, they describe the selection of one alternative from a limited set of appliance options. The major assumptions in the simulation restrict the number and types of alternatives from which the household selects. The full sets of alternatives for each appliance category are listed in Table III.9.

The respective alternative sets are reduced for specific households given natural gas unavailability and various other appliance choices. The major instances of restricted alternative sets are

1. When natural gas is unavailable to the dwelling, the gas alternatives for all appliances are excluded.
2. When the space heating alternative is non-oil, oil water heating is excluded.
3. When the space heating alternative is electric heat pump, other central and room air conditioning alternatives are excluded.
4. When the central air conditioning alternative is *nonheat pump,* the room air conditioning purchase alternative is excluded.
5. When the space heating alternative is nongas, the gas cooking range alternative is excluded.

TABLE III.9

Appliance Investment Alternatives

Space heating system
    Natural gas, forced air[a]
    Natural gas, central hot water[a]
    Natural gas, noncentral[a]
    Fuel oil/other, central forced air
    Fuel oil/other, central hot water
    Fuel oil/other, noncentral
    Electric, central forced air
    Electric, central hot water
    Electric, noncentral
Water heating
    Natural gas[a]
    Fuel oil/other
    Electric
Central air conditioning
    Yes, electric, nonheat pump
    No
    Yes, electric heat pump
Room air conditioning
    Yes
    No
Cooking range
    Electric
    Gas[a]
Dishwasher
    Yes
    No

---

[a] Feasible alternative only if natural gas service is available to dwelling.

  6. When the space heater, water heater, central air conditioner, or cooking range fails in an existing dwelling, it is replaced by an equivalent system.

  7. In existing housing equipped with central air conditioning, room air conditioner purchases are excluded.

  8. In existing housing with room air conditioning, additional acquisitions are feasible.

While all these prohibited combinations in REEPS are uncommon in reality, their exclusion in the model may introduce small biases. For example, in the Northeast, older houses often have gas cooking combined with oil heat (converted from coal).

Both in terms of energy consumption and policy significance, the most important household appliances are those physically attached to the dwelling unit. These include the space heating system, water heater, central air conditioning system, and to a lesser extent cooking range and dishwasher. These appliances account for almost eighty percent of all residential energy consumption (excluding transportation); see Hirst and Carney (1977). Moreover, they are the household energy activities most significantly affected by recent policy initiatives. Building thermal standards as well as solar and insulation tax credits will affect both space heating and central air conditioning energy patterns. Appliance efficiency targets affect all of the major appliance categories.

Beginning with the market for appliances in new housing, the model structure is described. Initially, the focus is on the choice of space heating system, water heater, and air conditioning. Cooking range and dishwasher choices are presented afterwards.

Given the breakdowns in Table III.9, there are 108 conceivable combinations of space heaters, water heaters, and air conditioning systems. However, some of these combinations are rare. For example, households with central air conditioning rarely have noncentral heating systems. Such cases are extreme examples of the high degree of interdependence among the respective appliance decisions. Cross-tabulations of WCMS survey data indicate the high correlation between space heating and water heating choices. This seems quite reasonable in view of the substantial shared costs for many of the combinations. In contrast, water heating and air conditioning decisions appear relatively independent based on WCMS cross-tabulations *given* space heating choice. This suggests a model in which the probabilities of air conditioning choice conditional on space heating systems is independent from that for water heater conditional on space heater, but where space heating choice takes into account air conditioner and water heater options.

To capture the structure of interdependence among appliance choices and the conditional independence of water heat and air conditioner choices, we write the probability that a newly built house is equipped with a given combination of space heating, water heating, and air conditioning in the form

(18) $P_{ijkl} = P_i \times P_{j|i} \times P_{k|i} \times P_{l|k},$

where i denotes space heating system (nine types), j denotes water heating fuel type (three types), k denotes central air conditioning (yes/no), and l denotes room air conditioning (number). Note that the product $P_{ijkl} = P_i \times P_{j|i} \times P_{k|ji} \times P_{l|jki}$ always holds by definition of conditional probabilities. Then the only substantive assumption in Eq. (18) is the conditional independence of water heat and air conditioning given space heat: $P_{k|ji} = P_{k|i}$ and $P_{l|jki} = P_{l|ki}$.

Appliance choice behavior is determined empirically by specifying the four probabilities in (18) as parametric functions of the cost and performance of the alternative appliances. These functions are influenced by the characteristics of the household and dwelling and by interactions between different types of appliances. The parameters in these functions are calibrated by fitting to the observed investment decisions of a national sample of households.

The choice of functional forms for the choice probabilities has been guided by several considerations. First, the functions must be computationally tractable, so that calibration and simulation on relatively large populations is possible. Second, the forms must be sufficiently flexible to adapt to the patterns of substitution and complementarity found in the data, without restrictive a priori assumptions. Third, households are assumed to be motivated to minimize the life-cycle cost of achieving specified levels of service, and more generally to weigh the desirability of energy-consuming services against other commodities in allocating their incomes. The functional forms for the choice probabilities should be consistent with such behavior. A family of functional forms for choice probabilities which meet these criteria and are therefore selected for our analysis are termed *nested logit* models. The most important features of these models are summarized below.

A nested logit model is a generalization of a form called the multinominal logit (MNL) form, which we define first. Suppose a household faces a choice among N alternatives, indexed $n = 1, \ldots, N$. For example, these might be alternative water heater fuels. Associated with each alternative is a list of attributes such as capital cost, operating cost, and measures of the convenience and quality of service of this particular appliance. These attributes can be combined into an overall measure of the desirability of the alternative. The multinomial logit model results from assuming first that desirability is measured by exponentiating a weighted sum of attributes. The weights are parameters of the functional form. This assumption is not very restrictive since the attributes may be complex transformations of the raw data, including interactions with household characteristics. Second, the probability that an alternative is chosen is assumed in the MNL model to be proportional to its desirability,

$$(19) \qquad \text{Prob}(j) = e^{V_j} \Bigg/ \sum_{n=1}^{N} e^{V_n},$$

where j and n index alternatives, $\text{Prob}(j)$ is the probability that a household chooses alternative j, and e^{V_j} is the desirability of alternative j with

$$(20) \quad V_j = \text{weight}_1 \times \text{attribute}_{1j} + \cdots + \text{weight}_k \times \text{attribute}_{kj}.$$

Note that the probability that an alternative is chosen is proportional to its desirability and that the probabilities sum to one. The weights in (20) are parameters. The attributes are transformations of the features of the alternative and characteristics of the household. If the choice being analyzed is conditional on other choices made previously, then the levels of the attributes may depend on the previous choices. On the other hand, if the alternatives in the choice being analyzed are compound, representing selection of a set of more elementary alternatives among which further choices will be made later, then the attributes summarize the *aggregate* features of the set. Generally, the attributes entering (20) for a specific alternative j depend solely on features of this specific alternative and not on features of other alternatives. In this case the multinomial logit model is said to have the property of *independence from irrelevant alternatives* (IIA).[6] However, it is possible for V_j to depend on interactions between features of alternative j and other alternatives, in which case the MNL model does *not* have the IIA property. For example, if in water heater fuel choice the attributes for alternative j are simply the capital and operating cost of this alternative, then the IIA property holds. On the other hand, if the attributes for alternative j are the *ratios* of capital and operating costs for V_j relative to the least cost alternative, then the IIA property does not hold.

If choice is described by an MNL model in which the IIA property holds, then at the level of the individual household a structural restriction is placed on cross-elasticities of choice probabilities with respect to the attributes of other alternatives: the cross-elasticity of P_j with respect to an attribute of alternative n is the same for all j not equal to n. This does *not* imply a restrictive pattern of cross-elasticities at the level of market demand, which is the result of aggregation over many different households facing different attributes. In particular, if the desirabilities of different alternatives tend to be fairly sharply differentiated for most households, the market cross-elasticities are primarily determined by the distribution of households and are virtually independent of whether the household choice probabilities have the IIA property or not. Furthermore, the MNL functional form is rather robust empirically in that it will often describe observed choice behavior adequately even when the forces underlying that behavior are theoretically inconsistent with the IIA property (see McFadden *et al.*, 1977).

The preceding arguments suggest that the MNL model is a satisfactory functional form for many applications. It is easy to work with computationally, permits addition or deletion of alternatives in a simple way, and is

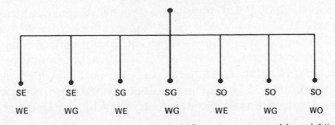

Fig. III.7   A simplified space–water heat choice structure—multinomial "comb."

consistent with an underlying view of households as life-cycle cost minimizers or preference maximizers. Within limits, the IIA property is unobtrusive and the form is sufficiently flexible to accommodate observed choice patterns. However, when the set of alternatives is very large, with clear subgroupings, then there are advantages to adopting functional forms in which the IIA property is not imposed across subgroup boundaries. For example, consider a simplified appliance choice for space heat and water heat, with the alternatives given in Fig. III.7. A multinomial logit model of joint water and space heater fuel choices which has the IIA property will at the household level imply equal cross-elasticities of the all-electric (SE, WE) alternative and the oil space, electric water (SO, WE) alternative with respect to the capital cost of an oil water heater. However, common sense suggests that substitutability between (SO, WE) and (SO, WO) which have a common space heating system will be higher than substitutability between (SE, WE) and (SO, WO).

One way of capturing this idea of greater substitutability within groups of similar alternatives is a hierarchical structure as in Fig. III.8, with similar alternatives grouped on the same branch of the tree, and choice probabilities specified so that discrimination is sharper (e.g., substitution is easier) within a branch than between branches. The *nested multinomial logit* model

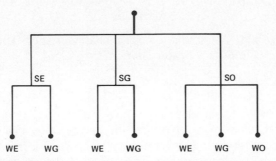

Fig. III.8   A simplified space–water heat choice structure—nested multinomial logit hierarchy. S, space heat; E, electricity; G, gas; W, water heat; O, oil.

achieves this result by describing choice at each level and branch of the tree
by a standard MNL model, with the attributes of upper level groups determined by an appropriate *weighted aggregate* of the attributes of the lower
level alternatives within the group.   Specifically, in the example of Fig. III.8,
choice of water heat fuel *conditioned* on space heat fuel is described by a
standard MNL model.   The attributes of the alternatives are the capital and
operating costs of the available water heaters, which may depend on the
given space heat system.

At the upper level of the tree, choice among space heating systems is also
described by an MNL model.   The attributes of the alternatives entering this
model are the capital and operating costs of the space heat system and an
attribute which summarizes the desirability of the water heating alternatives
below each branch.   In the nested MNL model, these summary measures of
desirability are defined to equal the logs of the sums of the desirability indices
for the water heater choices in each branch.   The nested MNL model for the
example in Fig. III.8 is written

$$(21) \qquad \text{Prob}(j|i) = e^{V_{ji}} \Big/ \sum_{n=1}^{N_i} e^{V_{ni}},$$

$$(22) \qquad \text{Prob}(i) = e^{W_i} \Big/ \sum_{n=1}^{3} e^{W_n},$$

where j indexes water heat choices, i indexes space heat choices, n ranges over
the set of available alternatives at each level, $\text{Prob}(j|i)$ is the water heat
probability given space heat, $\text{Prob}(i)$ is the space heat probability, and

$$(23) \quad V_{ji} = \text{weight}_1 \times \text{attribute}_{1ji} + \cdots + \text{weight}_K \times \text{attribute}_{Kji},$$

$$(24) \quad W_i = \text{weight}_{K+1} \times \text{attribute}_{K+1,i} + \cdots + \text{weight}_{K+L-1}$$

$$\times \text{attribute}_{K+L-1,i}$$

$$+ \text{weight}_{K+L} \times \log\!\left(\sum_{n=1}^{N_i} e^{V_{ni}} \right).$$

Attributes $1, \ldots, K$ are water heater characteristics, attributes $K + 1$,
$\ldots, K + L - 1$ are space heater characteristics and

$$(25) \qquad \text{attribute}_{K+L,i} = \log\!\left(\sum_{n=1}^{N_i} e^{V_{ni}} \right)$$

is the summary measure of the desirability of the water heater alternatives
under space heat type i.   This summary measure is termed the *inclusive
value* of the water heater alternatives for this space heat type, and the corresponding weight is termed the *inclusive value coefficient*.   This coefficient
should be positive, with a magnitude which is inversely proportional to the

degree of substitutability between the water heaters in the branch. As this parameter approaches unity, the nested logit model approaches the standard structure illustrated in Fig. III.7 where patterns of substitutability are not differentiated by group.

The nested MNL model has several attractive features. First, it shares the computational advantages of the standard MNL model, making it practical for large-scale calibration and simulation. The hierarchical structure has the particular advantage of limiting the number of alternatives which must be analyzed at one time. Second, this model allows alternatives to be added or dropped easily. Third, this model is consistent with an underlying theory of preference maximizing consumers. Fourth, the hierarchical structure can easily be expanded to more complex trees with multiple levels and different degrees of similarity on different branches.

For the appliance choice model developed in REEPS with the alternatives defined in Table III.9, a four-level hierarchy is assumed corresponding to the choices of:

1. space heat type,
2. water heat type given space heat,
3. central air conditioner given space heat, and
4. number of room air conditioners given space heat and the central air conditioner decision.

These levels correspond to the decomposition of the joint choice probabilities for these appliances into four conditional probabilities in (18). Figure III.9 illustrates this hierarchy. For compactness, this figure excludes the branches for space heating types EF and GN which are like the ER branch, and for types OW and OF which are like the ON branch. There are 78 possible appliance portfolios in this figure (59 if installation of one or more room air conditioners is aggregated into a single category).

To systematize the notation associated with a nested MNL of this complexity, it is useful to introduce a generating function for the choice probabilities. Suppose for the moment that alternatives are indexed by a single running index, $r = 1, \ldots, R$. Suppose $(y_1, \ldots, y_R)$ are positive measures of the desirability of the alternatives and $G(y_1, \ldots, y_R)$ is a positive linear homogeneous function whose mixed partial derivatives alternate in sign as their order increases, with $\partial G / \partial y_r > 0$, with the limiting property that if $y_r \to +\infty$, then $G \to +\infty$. Then $P_r = \partial \ln G / \partial \ln y_r$ defines a choice probability model. This model is consistent with an assumption that households maximize utility $u_r = \ln y_r + \epsilon_r$, where the disturbances ϵ_r have a joint type I extreme value distribution $F(\epsilon_1, \ldots, \epsilon_R) = \exp[-G(e^{-\epsilon_1}, \ldots, e^{-\epsilon_R})]$. The generating function $G(y_1, \ldots, y_R) = (y_1^{1/\theta} + \cdots + y_R^{1/\theta})^\theta$,

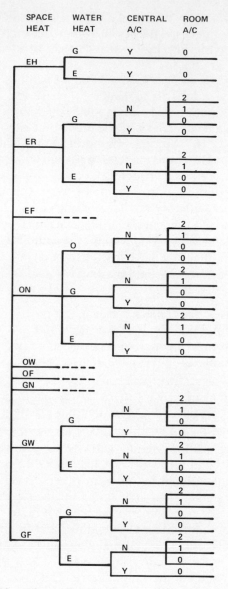

Fig. III.9 The REEPS appliance choice hierarchy. EH, electric heat pump; ER, electric resistance; EF, electric central forced air; ON, oil or other noncentral; OW, oil or other hydronic; OF, oil or other forced air; GN, gas noncentral; GW, gas hydronic; GF, gas forced air; G, gas; E, electric, Y, yes; N, no; 0, 1, or 2, number of room air conditioners.

$0 < \theta \le 1$, yields the standard MNL model. Nested MNL models are generated by taking G to be a composite, or recursive, function of this first type. For example, the model given in (21)–(24) is generated by

$$(26) \qquad G = \sum_i G^i \quad \text{and} \quad G^i = \left(\sum_j y_{ij}^{1/\theta} \right)^{\theta},$$

where $\ln y_{ij} = W_i + \theta V_{ji}$. When the generating function has a composite form such as $G = G^0(G^1, G^2, \ldots, G^M)$, the corresponding choice probabilities decompose into a product of marginal and conditional probabilities,

$$(27) \qquad P_{ij} = \frac{\partial \ln G}{\partial \ln y_{ij}} = \frac{\partial \ln G^0}{\partial \ln G^i} \frac{\partial \ln G^i}{\partial \ln y_{ij}} = P_i \times P_{j|i}.$$

If $P_{j|i}$ does not depend on i, then the choices of i and j are independent. This happens in the nested MNL structure if in the composite generating function $G^0(G^1, \ldots, G^M)$ all the second level functions $G^1, \ldots, G^M$ have exactly the same functional form and the desirability of ij can be written as a product $y_{ij} = x_i \times z_j$. Then,

$$(28) \quad G^0(G^1([y_{1j}]), \ldots, G^1([y_{Mj}])) = G^0(x_1 G^1([z_j]), \ldots, x_M G^M([z_j]))$$

$$= G^0([x_i])G^1([z_j]),$$

where $[y_{1j}]$ is the vector $(y_{11}, y_{12}, \ldots, y_{1N})$. The joint choice probability derived from this generating function is the product of the probabilities of choosing i and choosing j. This characterization of independence also extends to conditional independence, where the components x_i and z_j may both depend on a given choice in a third dimension k, and $P_{ijk} = P_{i|k} \times P_{j|k} \times P_k$.

The generating function for the full appliance choice model can now be written out. Let y_{ijklmn} denote the desirability of an appliance portfolio, where i is the space heat type, j the water heat fuel, k the central air conditioner (yes/no), l the number of room air conditioners, m the cooking fuel, and n the dishwasher (yes/no). The conditional independence assumptions on the model imply

$$(29) \qquad y_{ijklmn} = y_i^1 \times y_{ji}^2 \times y_{kli}^3 \times y_{mi}^4 \times y_n^5$$

so that, conditional on space heat, the desirabilities of the various appliances are multiplicative. The generating function for the model then has the form

$$(30) \quad G([y_{ijklmn}]) = \sum_i y_i^1 \times \sum_n y_n^5 \times \sum_m [(y_{mi}^4)^{1/\lambda}]^{\lambda} \times \sum_j [(y_{ji}^2)^{1/\theta}]^{\theta}$$

$$\times ((y_{10i}^3)^{1/\mu} + ((y_{00i}^3)^{1/\sigma_0} + ((y_{01i}^3)^{1/\sigma_1}$$

$$+ ((y_{02i}^3)^{1/\sigma_2} + \cdots)^{\sigma_2/\sigma_1})^{\sigma_1/\sigma_0})^{\sigma_0/\mu})^{\mu}.$$

The parameters λ, θ, μ, σ_0/μ, σ_1/σ_0, . . . , in this form are inclusive value coefficients. The components of the desirability measure y_i^1, y_{ji}^2, . . . , are related to the estimated weighted sums of attributes appearing in the text as follows:

1. $\ln y_n^5$ the weighted sum of dishwasher attributes.
2. $(1/\lambda) \ln y_{mi}^4$ the weighted sum of cooking fuel attributes, given space heat type i (denoted C_{mi}).
3. $(1/\theta) \ln y_{ji}^2$ the weighted sum of water heater attributes, given space heat type i (denoted W_{ji}).
4. $(1/\mu) \ln y_{10i}^3$ the weighted sum of central air conditioner attributes, given space heat type i, excluding inclusive value terms (denoted A_i).
5. $(1/\sigma_0) \ln y_{0li}^3$ for $l = 1, 2, \ldots$, corresponding to no central air conditioner and l room air conditioners, satisfies a difference equation

$$\ln y_{0li}^3 = \ln y_{0,l-1,i}^3 + \sigma_{l-1} z_{l-1} \ln(1 + e^{z_l}),$$

                    where the z_l are the weighted sum of attributes entering the binomial logit model for purchasing a room air conditioner given $l - 1$ held.
6. $\ln y_i^1$ the weighted sum of space heater attributes, excluding inclusive value terms (denoted S_i).

An inclusive value term of the form $\text{IV} = \ln(1 + e^{z_0})$ enters the central air conditioning model with a coefficient σ_0/μ. The space heater model contains three additive inclusive value terms, so the overall desirability of alternative i is determined by

$$(31) \qquad S_i + \lambda \ln[e^{C_{1i}} + e^{C_{2i}}] + \theta \ln \sum_j e^{W_{ji}} + \mu \ln[e^{A_i} + e^{(\sigma_0/\mu)\text{IV}}].$$

The impact of cooking choice on space heating is negligible, so the λ term is excluded in empirical analysis.

Water Heating Choice. The general form of the probability model for water heating, conditioned on choice of space heating system, is multinomial logit. The choice probability has the form given in (21) and (23). For the water heating model, the desirability measure V_{ji} is specified as a linear function of the operating and capital costs of the water heater alternative j and fuel specific performance characteristics. Operating costs (q_j) are defined as

$$(32) \qquad\qquad q_j = P_j \times \text{eff}_j \times G(\text{PERSONS}),$$

where P_j is the price per unit of fuel, eff_j is the efficiency of the water heating system defined in terms of the fuel units required to heat a gallon of water, and G(PERSONS) is the annual hot water requirements of the representative household, depending on the number of persons.

The water heater capital cost variable represents the price of the equipment and its installation, including service connection and the flue for gas or oil. It is assumed that when the water heating and space heating fuels are the same, the service connection and flue costs are shared, reducing the installed cost of the water heater.

A special case of shared equipment costs occurs when the space heating system is oil hot water. In that case, water from the space heater is often drawn for domestic use, eliminating the need for a separate water heater. This is represented in the empirical model by a binary variable equal to one when the water heating alternative is oil and the space heating choice is oil hot water.

Finally, the fuel-specific performance characteristics of each alternative, such as recovery rate or reliability, are captured by binary variables equal to one if the alternative is j, zero otherwise.

Room Air Conditioning Choice.   The room air conditioning choice model given no central conditioner represents decisions in both new and existing housing units. The only distinction between the two choice settings is made through the inclusion of an explanatory variable reflecting the age of the dwelling.

The choice of number of room air conditioners is described by a binary logit model giving the probability of purchase of an additional unit as a function of the number of units previously held. The probability that a room air conditioner is added has the form

$$(33) \qquad P_{mki} = 1/(1 + e^{-Z_{mki}}),$$

where i indexes the space heat type, $k = N$ indicates the no central air conditioner alternative, m indicates the number of room air conditioners previously held, and Z_{mki} is a weighted sum of attributes of a room air conditioner, including the number of units previously held. If, for example, a household previously holds no units, then the probabilities $P_{l|mki}$ that it will purchase and hold exactly l units satisfy

$$(34) \qquad P_{0|0ki} = 1 - P_{0ki},$$

$$(35) \qquad P_{1|0ki} = P_{0ki}(1 - P_{1ki}),$$

$$(36) \qquad P_{2|0ki} = P_{0ki}P_{1ki}(1 - P_{2ki}),$$

and so on, while the corresponding probabilities if the household previously held one unit (which does not require replacement) are

(37) $P_{1|lki} = 1 - P_{1ki},$

(38) $P_{2|lki} = P_{1ki}(1 - P_{2ki}),$

and so on. In practice, addition of more than one air conditioner in a year is rare and can usually be neglected. This choice probability structure is a generalization of a negative binomial distribution and reduces to a negative binomial distribution when the functions Z_{mki} are the same for all m. This structure is consistent with the nested logit model when attributes of alternatives are structured appropriately, and hence is consistent with household preference maximization.

The following explanatory variables are included in the specification: annual cooling degree days, dwelling tenure, age of the head of the household, the number of previously held room air conditioners per room, household income, vintage status of the dwelling (new or old), and a purchase alternative dummy. Some of the parameter estimates are noteworthy. The tenure variable coefficient indicates that home ownership exerts a strong, significant impact on room air conditioner purchase decisions. Also, the age of the household head is an important factor, with purchase decisions more likely in the earlier years of the household life cycle than later. The income coefficient estimate is negative, suggesting that room air conditioners are inferior substitutes for central units.

The effects of operating costs on room air conditioner purchases were examined and found to be negligible.

Central Air Conditioning Installations. The next decision examined is central air conditioner installations in new housing given the space heating system. The household desirability of central air conditioning is specified as a linear function of the marginal price of electricity, annual cooling degree days, household income, a purchase alternative dummy, and variables representing the interdependence of central air conditioning decisions with space heating and room air conditioning. The first interdependence variable is a term meant to capture the capital costs shared by central air conditioners and forced-air space heaters by virtue of their common ductwork. The second is a term referred to as the inclusive value of room air conditioning, which in this context measures the attractiveness of room units relative to central ones. Characteristics of room units that make them highly attractive in a given situation (i.e., increase their inclusive value) are expected to diminish the probability of a central unit. The inclusive value term is defined as

(39) $IV = \log(1 + e^{-Z_{mki}}),$

where Z_{mki} was defined in (33) as a measure of the desirability of purchasing a room air conditioner, given m room units previously held, space heating type i, and k indexing the alternative of no central air conditioner.

As expected, cooling degree days and household income are major determinants of central air conditioning purchases in new housing. The price of electricity exerts a very small effect, if any, according to the statistical results. This is consistent with the findings for room air conditioners.

Space Heating System Choice. The space heating system choice in new housing is probably the most significant decision in the entire simulation model. The fuel consumption from space heating alone accounts for over 50% of total residential energy use. The decision on fuel type — gas, oil, or electricity — has significant implications for energy loads. In the simulation model, the space heating system choice continues to exert a major effect on usage patterns for many time periods after the decision is made. This reflects the substantial inertia in durable-goods investment decisions discussed previously.

The probabilistic choice model which is the basis for the space heating simulations is the most complex of the models in REEPS. The probabilities themselves depend on the cost and performance characteristics of the space heating alternatives, household attributes and regional variables, and inclusive value terms for water heating and air conditioning which reflect the interdependence among the appliance decisions.

The space heating model cost variables are specified to represent the derived structure of appliance demand. Under this structure, households respond to the cost-per-unit-service output in selecting their appliances. In the case of space heating, there are the costs of maintaining a house at some specified internal temperature. These depend on the physical characteristics of the house, the climate, and the system operating efficiency, as well as the cost of the energy input. To reflect this, an engineering thermal load model is used to calculate the system capacity and annual heating requirement for each house in the sample. These are used with estimates of system efficiencies and equipment and energy price data to calculate the capital and operating costs of each alternative for the sampled house.

Energy and equipment price data corresponding to the year of construction were used to reflect the prevailing conditions at the time. REEPS does not explicitly model the role of expectations in the assessment of heating system cost and performance (or in the other appliance models). However, it is useful to note the effect expectations will have on the estimation and interpretation of model parameters. Suppose households face an interest rate r, and expect capital and fuel prices to grow at rates g_k, g_f respectively. For simplicity, suppose the household and dwelling are infinitely lived, the heating system has a fixed life, and the rate of utilization x is fixed. Then the present value of capital and operating cost over the infinite horizon is

$$(40) \qquad C = \frac{P_k}{1 - e^{-(r-g_k)L}} + \frac{P_f x}{r - g_f},$$

where P_k and P_f are initial capital and fuel costs. If in the nested logit choice model for space heat the capital cost P_k and operating cost $P_f x$ at date of construction are entered as attributes, then their weights absorb the average effect of expectations. The estimated capital price coefficient provides an estimate δ of the implicit expectations-adjusted rate of interest, or discount rate, used by households. In the example,

$$(41) \qquad \delta = \frac{r - g_f}{1 - e^{-(r-g_k)L}};$$

for instance, if $r = 0.10$, $g_k = 0$, $g_f = 0.02$, $L = 20$, then $\delta = 0.093$.

If expectations are stable, then the estimated weights for P_k and $P_f x$ will correctly reflect expectations and behavior will be forecast correctly in simulation. If expectations are stable in the estimation period, a plausible assumption for the period 1960–1974 from which the observations are drawn, but if expectations change in the forecast period, then Eq. (41) suggests how weights should be modified to assure accurate forecasts. In the absence of an explicit model of expectations formation, this requires user judgment on expected growth rates of prices.

The installed equipment cost variables for both the space and water heating models are based on data provided in various editions of the National Construction Estimator (NCE). This publication lists equipment and installation costs for various system types and capacities.

In estimating the capacities for space heating systems, ASHRAE design guidelines were used along with information on system efficiency and oversizing practices provided by the National Association of Home Builders (NAHB). The capacity estimates were then applied to the equipment price data to yield the installed capital cost for each space heating alternative. When the estimated capacity requirement was less than the minimum size unit listed in NCE, the price of the minimum-sized unit was used. This reflects some indivisibilities in the capital costs for fuel-fired units.

In addition to the capital and operating cost variables, several regional and climatic shift variables are included in the space heating model. Alternative-specific dummies are also specified to reflect performance and noncost characteristics. Finally, inclusive values for water heating and central air conditioning are estimated based on the results from those empirical models. The inclusive value terms measure the respective attractiveness of water heating and air conditioning for each space heating alternative. This attractiveness varies across alternatives because the features of water heating and air conditioning depend on the space heating system.

The estimated model indicates that capital and operating costs substantially influence space heating system installations. The coefficients of the inclusive values suggest a significant interdependence in appliance decisions.

Installed capital cost enters the model divided by annual household income. The rationale for this variable is the following: The *typical* utility of space heating is $W = B_{EC} \times EQCOST + B_{OC} \times OPCOST + \ldots$, where EQ denotes equipment and OP operating cost. Then an offsetting change in equipment and operating costs which would leave a consumer indifferent is

$$(42) \qquad -\frac{\Delta\, OPCOST}{\Delta\, EQCOST} = \frac{B_{EC}}{B_{OC}}.$$

Now, assume that the rate at which consumers are willing to discount future operating cost savings relative to capital investments is inversely proportional to income, i.e., higher income households have lower discount rates. This relation reflects changes in credit availability and other opportunity costs of investments as income changes. Then $B_{EC}/B_{OC} = \alpha/\text{income}$, implying

$$(43) \qquad W = B_{EC}^{*} \times \frac{EQCOST}{\text{income}} + B_{OC} \times OPCOST + \cdots,$$

where $B_{EC}^{*} = \alpha \times B_{OC}$.

The estimation results indicate that income significantly affects the implied capital cost – operating cost trade-off in space heating system choices. (These are consistent with findings by Hausman, 1979 in examining room air conditioner purchases and by Goett, 1978 in examining space and water heating choice.)

Cooking Fuel Choice. The model for cooking fuel choice probabilities in new housing is a binomial logit of the same general form as previous models. The two alternatives in the model are electric and nonelectric which includes gas and propane. The cooking choice probabilities depend on the space heating fuel. However, in contrast to the air conditioning and water heating models, the characteristics of the cooking fuel alternatives do not affect space heating choice. This one-way dependence is represented in two ways. First, based upon cross-tabulations of the 1977 National Annual Housing Survey, it is assumed that new dwellings with electric space heating always install electric stoves. According to these cross-tabulations, this is true for almost 99% of electrically heated dwellings built in the previous two years. Second, interaction terms representing the increased likelihood of gas stoves in gas heated dwellings and electric stoves in oil heated homes are included in the specification. In addition to these terms, the explanatory variables are the prices of natural gas and electricity interacting with their respective alternatives, certain regional variables, and an alternative dummy for the gas option.

The estimated values confirm that prices are significant determinants of cooking fuel choice in new dwellings. Curiously, the interaction terms are both small in magnitude and statistically insignificant, indicating that this effect is smaller than simple one-way cross-tabulations would suggest. There do appear to be some moderate region-specific effects, with relatively large nonelectric penetrations in the Northeast. Finally, electricity is clearly the preferred cooking fuel in new housing, even after accounting for the other factors which influence fuel choice.

Appliance Retrofit Installations in Existing Housing. The second major type of appliance purchase decision consists of retrofit installations in existing houses. These are broken down into two major categories — first time installations and replacement installations. Only central air conditioning systems and dishwashers fall in the first category under the current model structure, since space heating, water heating, and stoves are always installed in new dwellings. All of the major physically attached appliances fall into the second category and are subject to failure and replacement. However, under the current system, the failure and replacement models are quite simple. Failures occur with a fixed probability whose value is inversely proportional to the average appliance lifetime. Appliances are replaced by units with the same fuel. Nonetheless, the architecture of the subsystem can accommodate behavioral models once the necessary survey data on such decisions become available for estimation.

The dishwasher installation model is a binomial logit which predicts the probability of installing a unit given that the household does not currently own one. The purchase probability is expressed as a function of household income, the price of electricity, household size, and an alternative dummy.

Retrofit installations of central air conditioners account for a major share of the overall market penetration of these units. According to the 1977 Annual Housing Survey, almost a third of the central systems installed since 1970 were placed in existing dwellings. The simulation model explicitly considers these retrofit decisions. The probability model is a binomial logit in which the dependent variable is the decision to install a central air conditioner in an existing dwelling given that there is none currently. The probability depends upon several household, dwelling, and climatic characteristics. These include household income, age of head of household, tenure, cooling degree days, the presence of a central forced air heating system, and the number of currently held room units.

E. Fuel Availability

If the space heating, water heating, and cooking fuel choice probability models were applied directly to predict market penetration rates in new housing, they would tend to overpredict natural gas and oil shares. This is because the models implicitly assume that all of the alternatives are available to the dwelling. Often this is not the case. Local or regional supply conditions frequently restrict the availability of given fuel forms including electricity. For example, natural gas is simply not a feasible alternative in many locations because of the limited coverage of the distribution system. In recent years, regulatory commissions have restricted additions of new natural gas customers because of uncertainties regarding long-term supplies. Similarly, a number of electric utilities and regulatory commissions have limited electric heating service to new customers. In the case of fuel oil, historical competitive conditions have often restricted the development of markets for residential uses. As a consequence, present-day households in many areas would have difficulty obtaining reliable service even if they preferred oil heating. These regional and local supply conditions for all of the major fuel forms are not adequately reflected in current or projected energy prices.

The simulation system addresses the impact of regional nonprice supply conditions upon appliance fuel choice in two ways. First, regional shift parameters are specified for all of the major appliance alternatives. These shift parameters are intended to capture the effects of supply conditions which are not picked up by the price and socioeconomic variables. In addition to these, other regional variables are derived through a calibration of the appliance models on historical data. Under this calibration process the appliance choice models are simulated on a sample of households for a recent historical period. The *predicted* appliance penetration rates are compared to observed market saturations. Regional shift parameters are then calculated and added to the appliance choice models. The magnitudes of these parameters ensure that the choice models exactly predict the recent historical appliance market penetrations for each region.

Over and above these regional shift parameters, the simulation system accounts explicitly for natural gas supply conditions in each region. Two sources of natural gas unavailability are identified. The first is due to the limited local coverage of the distribution system. In each state, only a given percentage of households has access to natural gas service either because they are located in rural areas or because service has not been extended to their neighborhood for historical competitive reasons. The second source of unavailability is mandated embargoes of new service hookups. In recent years, regulatory commissions and gas utilities in many states have severely restricted new service connections. These restrictions have been prompted by significant uncertainties regarding long-term supplies. These uncertainties have caused utilities to limit new connections to guarantee uninterrupted service to existing customers. In certain regions, these service restrictions have been very large. For example, a 100% embargo was imposed in all of the mid-Atlantic states during the period 1975–1977. In recent years, however, these restrictions have been relaxed as long-term supply conditions improved.

The impacts of both limited gas distribution system coverage and mandated restrictions are represented by probability tables in the simulation system. The probability that a newly built dwelling is located within the distribution system depends on the state and period of simulation. An equivalent table is specified for gas restrictions. The overall probability of gas unavailability is simply the product of the first and one minus the second. Given the overall probability, the *event* gas availability is simulated. If the dwelling has natural gas available to it, then the space heating, water heating, and cooking fuel choice models are simulated with the full sets of alternatives available to the household. If natural gas is not available, then the models are simulated with a restricted alternative set which excludes the natural gas systems.

For simulation, the base-year gas restrictions are specified at recent historical levels reported by the American Gas Association. The future restrictions are projected by assuming that they fall to zero by 1982. It must be emphasized that these gas availability rates are exogenously specified policy variables. They depend upon supply conditions which are largely under the control of gas utilities and regulatory agencies. Alternative scenarios could be specified based upon a more detailed evaluation of future gas supply policies.

F. Usage

Given a dwelling and a stock of appliances, a household decides how intensively to operate these appliances, taking into account the cost of operation and the value of the services the appliances provide. When an appliance is purchased or replaced, the household selects among available models of different efficiencies by weighing the life-cycle operating cost and potential service provided by each. Energy policy and economic factors influence energy consumption by affecting the efficiencies of appliances purchased and the intensity of use of these appliances.

The energy consumption module of the simulation model determines annual electricity, gas, and oil consumption for six categories of appliances: space heating, central air conditioning, room air conditioning, water heating, cooking, and a residual category containing the remaining uses (e.g., lighting, refrigerator, freezer, dishwasher, clothes washer, clothes dryer, TV). This disaggregation isolates the weather-sensitive appliances which are important factors in summer and winter system peaks, plus water heating, as these are likely to be particular targets of appliance efficiency standards, load controls, and other energy conservation measures.

In REEPS the appliance not only includes the mechanical device, but also the dwelling physical characteristics which affect its performance. For example, a space heating system includes the equipment *and* the thermal characteristics of the dwelling. In that case a service hour of space heating is a unit of temperature differential for one hour. The amount of input energy required to provide one service-hour depends on the thermal characteristics of the dwelling. This modeling approach fails to utilize the engineering data on efficiencies which are more naturally measured separately for equipment and shell and makes it difficult to evaluate policies which affect equipment and shell separately. More importantly, REEPS treats heating and air conditioning efficiency decisions as independent, which ignores the joint impact of shell design.

The simulation model represents appliance-specific energy consumption as the result of two household decisions. In the first decision, a household selects the appliance operating efficiency measured in terms of service-hours per unit of energy. In the second decision, a household chooses how intensively to utilize its appliances, where utilization is expressed as service-hours per year. Energy consumption is then determined by definition as utilization divided by efficiency.

REEPS does not model the impact of a third dimension, capacity and service quality, assuming that it is technologically determined. From an empirical standpoint, we cannot distinguish between efficiency and capacity choices without data on the size of appliances owned by individual households. This omission is justified by absence of data on sizes and features of purchased appliances, but is nevertheless a limitation of the model which could bias some policy conclusions.

In REEPS, the appliance operating efficiency is determined when the unit is purchased and installed. The desired level of efficiency is calculated as a function of energy prices, household and dwelling characteristics, and geographical variables. Bounds on the range of efficiencies available in the market are specified to reflect the existing technology and mandated standards. If the desired efficiency level falls outside this range, then the household is forced to choose the boundary level.

After an appliance is purchased, the household's ability to change its efficiency is significantly restricted. In the simulation model, the efficiencies for room air conditioners, stoves, and water heaters are fixed at the time of installation and cannot change thereafter. For space heating and central air conditioning, efficiencies can improve, but only along a restricted frontier and only in response to quantum changes in energy prices or other variables. This reflects the significantly higher costs of retrofit efficiency changes and the restrictions on such changes imposed by the physical characteristics of the dwelling and equipment.

Given the level of efficiency, the simulation model determines the utilization rate in each period. Utilization is calculated as a function of operating costs and other variables. Operating costs in turn depend on energy prices and appliance efficiency. Thus, a mandated increase in efficiency would stimulate utilization by reducing operating costs.

The utilization rate changes each period in response to changes in price and other variables. However, the price responsiveness is generally small, reflecting the low propensity of households to modify their utilization patterns once the appliance is installed. The impact of a price change on energy use is invariably smaller in the short run when only utilization changes than in the long run when efficiency is modified.

A household selects appliance efficiency in a manner which trades-off incremental appliance purchase price against expected operating cost. This choice is made consistent with planned utilization patterns, which are themselves influenced by operating costs. This interdependence of efficiency and utilization implies a relation between the two decisions and a consistency in their long-run responsiveness to socioeconomic and policy variables. For example, if expected appliance operating costs rise due to a fuel price increase, then in the long run households will purchase more efficient units and utilize them less intensively to mitigate the operating cost impact. The amount of the efficiency and utilization changes will be balanced so that at the margin the incremental appliance costs and the reduced comfort just equal the perceived benefit of the operating cost savings. Conversely, if operating costs decrease due to an increase in efficiency, some of the technically feasible energy savings impact would be lost due to the change in utilization patterns.

This consistency between efficiency choice and utilization is represented in the simulation model in the following manner. The long-run relation between efficiency choice and appliance utilization and their mutual responsiveness to energy prices and other variables are derived from a model of household utility optimization. This relation in turn implies a long-run model of appliance-specific energy demand. By specifying the respective structures of household preferences and of the appliance purchase cost–

efficiency trade-off, the structural parameters of the efficiency choice and utilization models are expressed in terms of those for long-run energy demand. The magnitudes of the energy demand parameters are estimated from a statistical analysis of household survey data. In turn, these estimates are used to derive values for the utilization efficiency choice model parameters. Thus, REEPS takes the behavioral approach to consumption behavior discussed in Chapter II. However, the REEPS analysis does not develop an explicit model of expectations or develop fully the dynamic stochastic programming structure of the optimization problem of the household or the restrictions on functional forms for fuel choice and usage decisions which are implicit in this problem. Further, REEPS utilizes relatively simple functional forms for preferences and usage to facilitate estimation and simulation; these may be too restrictive.

The model of the efficiency–utilization choice quantifies the structural relationship between short-run energy consumption decisions given efficiency and longer run decisions in which efficiency levels are determined optimally. The REEPS formulation is a simplified version of Example 2 in Chapter II. In the notation we use H is the utilization rate defined as units of service provided by an appliance, e the efficiency of an appliance, measured in units of service per unit of energy consumed, E the energy consumption of the appliance, p the (marginal) price of energy, r the discount (amortization) rate, I the household income, R the number of rooms, N the number of persons, D the degree-days per month, a measure of thermal requirements for heating or cooling, P the purchase price of an appliance (including associated dwelling features for space heating and central air conditioning), and T the design temperature. Monthly energy consumption is simply utilization divided by efficiency or

$$(44) \qquad E = H/e.$$

The monthly operating cost of the appliance is then

$$(45) \qquad pE = Hp/e.$$

If the purchase price of the appliance is amortized over time, then the monthly cost of purchase is rP. The discount rate r includes interest, depreciation, and maintenance. The amortized monthly cost of ownership and operation of the appliance is then

$$(46) \qquad C = Hp/e + rP.$$

The household has tastes for the service provided by the appliance (H) and consumption of all other goods (Z) which can be summarized in a utility function $U(H, Z, R, N, D)$. Tastes may also depend on number of rooms, number of persons in the household, and thermal requirements measured by heating or cooling degree-days. The consumer faces a budget constraint that amortized monthly cost of the appliance plus consumption of all other goods must equal income,

$$(47) \qquad\qquad\qquad\qquad I = Z + C.$$

Note that this is a *steady state* assumption which excludes some of the intermediate-run dynamics of individual consumer behavior which are affected by equipment usage and household life cycle. In the short run when the efficiency level of the appliance is fixed, the household will choose the level of utilization H to maximize utility $U(H, (I - rP) - H(p/e), R, N, D)$, where the budget constraint implies $Z = I - rP - H(p/e)$. The optimal utilization H is then some function of $(I - rP)$, (p/e), R, N, and D. The precise form of this function depends on the shape of the utility function. However, the functional dependence of optimum utilization can be approximated to the first order by a constant elasticity form

$$(48) \qquad\qquad H = A(p/e)^{\beta_1}(I - rP)^{\beta_2}R^{\beta_3}B^{\beta_4}D^{\beta_5},$$

where A, β_1, β_2, β_3, β_4, β_5 are parameters.

The constant elasticity demand function (48) can be derived from the indirect utility function

$$(49) \quad V(I - rP, (p/e), R, N, D) = \frac{(I - rP)^{1-\beta_2}}{1 - \beta_2} - \frac{A(p/e)^{1+\beta_1}R^{\beta_3}N^{\beta_4}D^{\beta_5}}{1 + \beta_1}.$$

This function satisfies the properties of an indirect utility function imposed by economic theory provided $\beta_2 \geq 0$ and $\beta_1 \leq -\beta_2 s$, where $s = pE/(I - rP)$ is the share of disposable income spent on operation of this appliance. As a practical matter, the amortized monthly cost of an appliance is rarely more than a few percent of income, so the condition $\beta_1 \leq -\beta_2 s$ is almost always satisfied by empirical elasticities within the limits of statistical accuracy.

The short-run energy consumption implied by (49) is

$$(50) \qquad E = H/e = Ap^{\beta_1}(I - rP)^{\beta_2}R^{\beta_3}N^{\beta_4}D^{\beta_5}e^{-\beta_1-1},$$

$$(51) \qquad\qquad E \doteq Ap^{\beta_1}I^{\beta_2}R^{\beta_3}N^{\beta_4}D^{\beta_5}e^{-\beta_1-1},$$

where the approximation is usually acceptable because amortized monthly cost of an appliance is rarely more than a few percent of income.

In the long run when the household replaces the appliance or constructs or reconstructs a dwelling, it can vary both the level of service quality and the level of efficiency. The purchase cost of the appliance is a function of its efficiency and of the capacity of the unit. Capacity is assumed to be technologically determined, so the consumer optimizes only with respect to efficiency. An interesting issue whose quantification awaits suitable data is whether there are technological or market factors which induce a relationship between efficiency and capacity, and whether the consumer can substitute efficiency, capacity, and intensity of use to achieve the same level of service. Purchase price may be a complex function of appliance efficiency and capacity; however, this function is approximated to first order by a constant elasticity form

$$(52) \qquad P = P_0 e^{\alpha_1} R^{\alpha_2} T^{\alpha_3},$$

where the term $R^{\alpha_2} T^{\alpha_3}$ in number of rooms and design temperature is intended to index required capacity for space conditioning and P_0 is a constant. For nonspace conditioning end uses, α_2 and α_3 are assumed equal to zero.

The long-run optimization problem under *steady state* conditions can be written

$$(53) \quad \underset{H,e}{\text{Max}} U\left(H, I - rP - \frac{pH}{e}, R, N, D \right) = \underset{e}{\text{Max}} V(I - rP, (p/e), R, N, D).$$

From (53), we obtain two first-order conditions for optimization,

$$(54) \qquad \frac{\partial U}{\partial H} - \frac{p}{e} \frac{\partial U}{\partial Z} = 0;$$

$$(55) \qquad \frac{\partial U}{\partial Z}\left(-r\frac{\partial P}{\partial e} + \frac{pH}{e^2} \right) = 0.$$

The first of these conditions is the same as that for the short-run problem with e fixed, which had the (approximate) solution (51). Condition (55) holds when $-r(\partial P/\partial e) + (pH/e^2) = 0$. This is just the first-order condition for minimization of monthly amortized life-cycle costs $C = rP + pH/e$ in e for a fixed H. For the purchase price function (52), condition (55) becomes

$$(56) \qquad \alpha_1 r P_0 e^{\alpha_1 - 1} R^{\alpha_2} T^{\alpha_3} = pH/e^2.$$

Equations (56) and (48) can be solved for the long-run optimal values of e and H

$$(57) \qquad e = (A/\alpha_1 r P_0)^{\lambda} p^{(\beta_1 + 1)\lambda}(I - rP)^{\beta_2 \lambda} R^{(\beta_3 - \alpha_2)\lambda} N^{\beta_4 \lambda} D^{\beta_5 \lambda} T^{-\alpha_3 \lambda}$$

$$\doteq (A/\alpha_1 r P_0)^{\lambda} p^{(\beta_1 + 1)\lambda} I^{(\beta_2 \lambda)} R^{(\beta_3 - \alpha_2)\lambda} N^{\beta_4 \lambda} D^{\beta_5 \lambda} T^{-\alpha_3 \lambda}$$

and

$$(58) \qquad H = A(A/\alpha_1 r P_0)^{-\beta_1 \lambda} p^{\beta_1 \alpha_1 \lambda}(I - rP)^{\beta_2(1 + \alpha_1)\lambda} R^{((\beta_1 \alpha_2 + \beta_3)(1 + \alpha_1))\lambda}$$

$$\times N^{\beta_4(1 + \alpha_1)\lambda} D^{\beta_5(1 + \alpha_1)\lambda} T^{\beta_1 \alpha_3 \lambda}$$

$$\doteq A(A/\alpha_1 r P_0)^{-\beta_1 \lambda} p^{\beta_1 \alpha_1 \lambda} I^{\beta_2(1 + \alpha_1)\lambda} R^{(\beta_1 \alpha_2 + \beta_3)(1 + \alpha_1)\lambda}$$

$$\times N^{\beta_4(1 + \alpha_1)\lambda} D^{\beta_5(1 + \alpha_1)\lambda} T^{\beta_1 \alpha_3 \lambda},$$

where $\lambda = 1/(1 + \alpha_1 + \beta_1)$ and the approximations are acceptable when amortized purchase price is less than a few percent of income. Combining these equations gives the optimal long-run energy consumption of the appliance,

$$(59) \qquad\qquad E = H/e = K_0 p^{\gamma_1} I^{\gamma_2} R^{\gamma_3} N^{\gamma_4} D^{\gamma_5} T^{\gamma_6},$$

where

$$K_0 = A(A/\alpha_1 r P_0)^{-(1-\beta_1)\lambda},$$
$$\gamma_1 = (\beta_1\alpha_1 - (1 + \beta_1))\lambda,$$
$$\gamma_2 = \beta_2\alpha_1\lambda,$$
$$\gamma_3 = (\beta_3\alpha_1 + (1 + \beta_1)\beta_2)\lambda,$$
$$\gamma_4 = \beta_4\alpha_1\lambda,$$
$$\gamma_5 = \beta_5\alpha_1\lambda,$$
$$\gamma_6 = (1 + \beta_1))\alpha_3\lambda.$$

Formulas (47)–(59) can also be obtained starting from (49) with the indirect utility function. The second-order condition for utility maximization implies $\lambda > 0$.

Equations (57) and (58) imply a systematic relation between efficiency choice and utilization patterns in the long run. For example, the coefficient of income I in utilization is $(1 + \alpha_1)$ times the value in efficiency choice. The coefficients themselves indicate the responsiveness or elasticity of the efficiency and utilization decisions with respect to changes in the explanatory variables. Given the general structure of preferences specified in (49) and the price–efficiency trade-off in (52), these elasticities are constant regardless of the levels of the explanatory variables except for the small adjustment to income. In particular, the elasticities do not depend upon the discount rate r. This implies that a change in, say, energy prices will induce a given long-run percentage change in efficiency and utilization rates, irrespective of the actual discount rate. This feature of the specification is used in simulation to avoid any explicit assumption regarding consumer discount rates. However, the discount rate is implicit in the base-year efficiency levels.

Equation (59) provides the key to deriving numerical estimates of the efficiency choice and utilization elasticities from a statistical analysis of observed household energy consumption patterns. The parameters of (59) can be estimated using nonlinear regression and individual household cross-section data on total energy consumption, socioeconomic characteristics, prices, and other geographical variables. Then given engineering estimates of the purchase price – efficiency trade-off parameters in (52), the efficiency and utilization elasticities can be calculated. For example, the elasticity of demand for efficiency with respect to income is simply

$$(60) \qquad \epsilon_1^e = \beta_2 \lambda = \gamma_2/\alpha_1,$$

where γ_2 is the statistically estimated coefficient of income and α_1 is the engineering cost parameter.

In simulation, the structural models of efficiency choice (57) and energy demand (59) with the numerical estimates of their coefficients are used in the following manner. In the year that an appliance is purchased, its efficiency is determined according to (57). However, for all appliances, it may be the case under some simulation scenarios that efficiency levels deemed optimal by a particular consumer will lie outside bounds imposed by standards or market availability, $e_{min} \leq e \leq e_{max}$. When formula (57) gives a value outside these bounds, efficiency is set equal to the nearest bound, and (51) evaluated at this bound gives consumption.

Normally, once the appliance efficiency is determined, it will remain fixed for the service life of the unit. However, for an appliance whose efficiency is influenced by dwelling characteristics, it is possible to introduce short-run modifications in e. The purchase cost of these modifications will generally be higher than equivalent modifications in new construction. To capture this effect, REEPS assumes that the purchase cost function (52) has a higher coefficient P_0 in retrofit than in new construction, and is otherwise the same for both. REEPS also assumes that once a given level of efficiency is attained, it is never decreased by short-run modifications. The short-run behavior for these appliances can be described as follows: In each period, an optimal efficiency level is computed using (57) with P_0 reflecting the higher cost of retrofit. If the optimal e exceeds the efficiency attained in the past period, the modifications are made and consumption is determined by (50) calculated at the new efficiency. If the optimal e is less than the efficiency of the last period, then no modifications are made, the old efficiency prevails, and (50) evaluated at the old efficiency determines consumption.

Energy usage can change from period to period as a result of changes in prices and other variables. In general, these changes will be different from those which would occur in the long run. The short-run price elasticity is smaller than the long-run value because households have limited flexibility in mitigating the impacts of operating costs. For the very same reason, the short-run elasticity with respect to weather is greater than the long-run value. That is, in the short run, households have less flexibility to mitigate the impacts of weather changes in heating requirements so a change in weather has a large impact on usage in the short run and a smaller impact in the long run.

REEPS estimates of coefficients of (59) are obtained using the 1972–1973 Consumer Expenditure Survey of the Bureau of Labor Statistics. Since this survey was taken after an extended period of relatively stable and predictable energy prices, observed behavior in this national cross-section is assumed to incorporate long-run adjustments in appliance efficiencies.

The estimation method requires only total energy consumption levels, available from utility bills, for a cross section of households. A statistical analysis recovers the consumption attributable to each appliance and the sensitivity of the appliance energy usage to economic and demographic variables.

To begin the analysis write (59) in the general form

$$(61) \qquad\qquad E_i = A_i Z_1^{\gamma_{1i}} \cdots Z_k^{\gamma_{ki}},$$

where $i = 1, \ldots, 6$ indexes the appliance and end use, $Z_1, \ldots, Z_k$ are explanatory variables, and γ_{ki} is the elasticity of energy usage for appliance i with respect to the explanatory variable k. The list of explanatory variables affecting energy use is expected to be large and will vary among appliance end uses. Nonetheless, this analysis focuses on those variables which have a major impact on consumption and are likely to shift as a result of the passage of time or as a result of energy policy. The reason for these decisions on model architecture is to simplify the simulation system as much as possible in those aspects which are not critical for realism in forecasting and policy analysis. The constant elasticity specification can be interpreted as a first-order approximation to the true function, and the intercept parameter A_i will incorporate the average impact of omitted variables which do not shift with energy policy or time. Thus, these fitted energy consumption forms will be relatively robust representations of the policy sensitivity of real usage.

Define a dummy variable D_i which is one if a household has an electric appliance i and is zero if the household does not have the appliance or has a nonelectric appliance. Then electricity consumption of a household is given by

$$(62) \qquad \text{KWH} = \sum_{i=1}^{6} D_i E_i + \epsilon = \sum_{i=1}^{6} D_i A_i Z_i^{\gamma_{1i}} \cdots Z_i^{\gamma_{ki}} + \epsilon,$$

where KWH is the electricity consumption (in kWh), ϵ a random disturbance, and E_i the consumption of appliance i. This approach is similar to that taken by several previous researchers (see McFadden *et al.*, 1978; George, 1979; Parti and Parti, 1980).

Equation (62) is estimated by nonlinear least squares. The model is quite effective in explaining overall electricity consumption of households. The impact of explanatory variables on energy consumption are of anticipated sign, except that electric water heat and electric cooking are found to be insensitive to price. Price and income elasticities are generally relatively large. In large part, this reflects long-run adjustments of appliance efficiency and capacity in response to economic conditions. However, several other factors may amplify elasticities. An empirical correlation between higher electricity prices and average age of dwellings across the country (with price and average age both highest in the Northeast) will attribute technologically limited lower consumption in older dwellings to a price response. A high income elasticity of energy use for electric cooking may reflect the tendency of new suburban dwellings to be predominantly electric and to have a large portfolio of minor appliances. The price elasticity of room air conditioner energy consumption is particularly large and may reflect an empirical correlation between price and the extent of use of multiple room air conditioners.

Differences in household life-style or other unobserved factors may cause households to differ in planned usage of particular appliances and consequently may influence the household choice on whether to acquire the appliance or what energy source to use. Consequently, the appliance dummy variables in (62) may be correlated with the disturbance, causing nonlinear least squares to yield biased coefficient estimates. A procedure for testing for this bias, and for correcting bias if it is found to exist, has been developed by Dubin and McFadden (1984). It was not possible to apply this method to the Consumer Expenditure Survey data because it omits required variables. Nevertheless, it would be very desirable to check this aspect of the REEPS specification.

REEPS obtains simulation parameter values for electrical appliances from the econometric analysis of the Consumer Expenditure Survey and from engineering calculations of purchase price elasticities from Oak Ridge National Laboratory studies.

Assuming observed usage levels are in long-run equilibrium in 1972–1973, the coefficients of (59) are matched to estimated elasticities, and then solved for the underlying parameters. Base year efficiency is normalized to one for each appliance. Nonelectrical appliances are assumed to have usage equations identical to their electrical analogues, except for adjustments for the relative technical efficiency of the fuels. This is a strong assumption which precludes the possibility that alternative fuels may alter usage patterns. An obvious case is noncentral electrical heat which is much more easily zoned than central oil or gas sytems. This aspect of REEPS deserves more careful empirical study.

The REEPS model uses judgment to modify estimated parameters which are considered implausible or inconsistent. Some use of prior information is essential in constructing a complex simulation model from limited data. However, further empirical study is needed to test the plausibility of these judgments.

G. Validation

The only systematic validation of the national version of REEPS is based on forecasts from the 1977–1978 base year using Energy Information Administration price forecasts and historical prices for the year 1980. REEPS forecasts have been compared to actual experience for the first few years in which observations are available and to other long-term forecasts. The results indicate that REEPS is quite accurate in the first few years, taking into account some national deviations in exogenous variables. However, this test is confounded by the fact that REEPS coefficients of dummy variables have been *tuned* to match appliance penetration rates in the period 1975–1977.

More extensive validation studies have been done on the use of REEPS at regional and local levels. Goett (1984) reports estimates of model parameters based on data from the 1979 Annual Housing Survey and on data from the Pacific Northwest. He finds substantial agreement between these data sets on price and income response, but considerable variation in coefficients of dummy variables, suggesting significant regional variations in supply conditions or tastes. Goett also finds some variations between the model coefficients estimated from the Annual Housing Survey and those using the WCMS data. The version of REEPS employed in this study used the WCMS data based coefficients.

H. Policy Forecast Procedures

The procedure used to calculate policy impacts on REEPS is simply to produce simulated samples under base conditions and under alternative policies and tabulate the differences. To reduce sampling variance in REEPS policy impact and growth rate estimates, the microsimulation sampling procedure *matches* households in different cases or periods. Schematically, a desired model output in period t under policy j has the form

$$(63) \qquad F(t, j) = \int f(t, j, x, \epsilon)g(x|\epsilon, t)h(\epsilon) \, d\epsilon \, dx,$$

where the integral is over household units, $f(t, j, x, \epsilon)$ is the household behavior function of observed variables x and unobserved variables ϵ, $g(x|\epsilon,t)$ is the population density of x given ϵ and t, and h is the population density of ϵ. The simulation procedure samples N household units (x_{nt}, ϵ_n) from the density $g(x_{nt}|\epsilon_n, t)h(\epsilon_n)$, and approximates $F(t, j)$ by the sample average

$$(64) \qquad F(t, j) = \frac{1}{N} \sum_{n=1}^{N} f(t, j, x_{nt}, \epsilon_n).$$

By using the same sample of unobservables $\epsilon_1, \ldots, \epsilon_N$ for different policies or periods, REEPS reduces the sampling variance in estimates of policy impacts, $F(t, j) - F(t, 1)$, or of time changes, $F(t + 1, j) - F(t, j)$. Further, stratified sampling of ϵ's without replacement is used to reduce the variance of F relative to random sampling. A *random tiler* due to McFadden is used to limit *excursions* in the sample: Assume $N = 2^K$ is a power of two, and assume (without loss of generality) that ϵ is distributed uniformly on the unit interval. The points $k/2^K$ for $k = 0, \ldots, 2^K - 1$ can be represented as binary fractions $0.i_1i_2 \cdots i_K$. The ϵ_n are drawn without replacement from this collection of points as follows: i_k is sampled randomly from 0, 1 on draws $n = 1 + j \times 2^k$ for $j = 0, \ldots, 2^{K-k} - 1$. In the block of 2^k successive draws starting with $n = 1 + j \times 2^k$, i_k remains fixed at the sampled value for the first 2^{k-1} draws, and then at the complement of this value for the remaining 2^{k-1} draws. This random tiler has several desirable features. The unconditional probability that a point in the set $A = \{k/2^K | k = 0, \ldots, 2^k - 1\}$ is selected on draw n is the same for each point. However, 2^k successive draws starting from $n = 1 + j \times 2^k$ always select exactly one point from each of the intervals $l \times 2^{k-K} \le \epsilon < (l + 1)2^{k-K}$ for $l = 0, \ldots, 2^{K-k} - 1$. Thus, each group of successive draws are spread *evenly* over the unit interval, reducing the sampling variance in F.

Forecasts from a simulation model are subject to at least five sources of error:

1. imprecision in estimated or judgmental parameters,
2. errors in base-year variables or external forecasts,
3. randomness in behavior,
4. sampling error, and
5. model misspecification.

It would be highly desirable to attach standard errors to impact estimates, so proper caution is observed in drawing policy conclusions. These are not provided by the version of REEPS used in this study.

Model misspecification errors are difficult to quantify except through validation against observed events. There are several feasible approaches to quantifying the remaining errors and tracking their transmission through the model to the forecasts. The most flexible and straightforward method is a Monte Carlo procedure in which parameters, external variables, and equation disturbances are drawn from their respective distributions, and independent sampling protocols are used for repeated runs of the simulation system. Then an empirical distribution of forecasts is obtained and can be used to calculate standard errors. The distributions of parameters and equation disturbances are the classical sampling distributions for statistical estimates, but must be Bayes distributions for judgmental parameters and other model elements generated by unknown statistical processes. The major drawback to this method is that it is extremely computer-intensive. A variety of Monte Carlo techniques may be used to reduce computation.

A second approach to error analysis is to linearize the system about *mean* forecasts, approximate the error distributions by normals, and use the standard theory of linear transformations of normals to approximate forecasts errors. In simple cases it may be possible to linearize the model analytically using Taylor's expansions. However, more commonly this must be done numerically by fitting a linear response surface to model inputs and outputs, including parameters and disturbances. This method provides a convenient calculus for identifying variance components and isolating major sources of error. However, it can be quite inaccurate in highly nonlinear models, particularly when true error distributions are badly skewed.

These two methods can sometimes be usefully combined, with the Monte Carlo procedure used to obtain the distribution of *differences* between model forecasts and approximate forecasts from the linearized response surface. Then the variance of the forecast is approximately the sum of the variance of the difference obtained from the Monte Carlo calculations and the variance of the linearized forecast. The principles behind this calculation can be described schematically as follows: let $y = G(z)$ denote the simulation model, where y is the forecast and z is a vector containing input variables, parameters, and disturbances. Let $h(z)$ denote the density of z. Let $\bar{z}$ and $\bar{y}$ denote the means of z and y, respectively, V_{zz} the variance of z, and V_{yz} the covariance of y and z. Then the linear response surface which minimizes squared deviations from the simulation model approaches $\tilde{y} = \tilde{G}(z) = \bar{y} + (z - \bar{z})'V_{zz}^{-1}V_{zy}$, with $\mathrm{Var}(\tilde{y}) = V_{yz}V_{zz}^{-1}V_{zy}$. The variance of the forecast then satisfies $\mathrm{Var}(y) = \mathrm{Var}(y - \tilde{y} + \tilde{y}) = \mathrm{Var}(y - \tilde{y}) + \mathrm{Var}(\tilde{y})$ since the least squares construction of the response surface implies $\tilde{y}$ and $y - \tilde{y}$ are orthogonal. If $\tilde{y}$ is a good approximation to y, then the component of variance which must be approximated by Monte Carlo sampling is small and the sample size needed to achieve specified precision is reduced.

III.4. A METHODOLOGICAL COMPARISON

A. Aggregation and Sampling Errors

   This section identifies the major architectural similarities and differences in the ORNL and REEPS simulation models. The final test of a simulation model is its practical usefulness in policy analysis, taking into account inaccuracy, flexibility, and ease of use and interpretation. Chapter VII compares the experience with these models applied to questions of national energy policy. The architecture of a simulation model does, however, tell a great deal about how the system will perform in policy applications.

   The most fundamental architectural difference in the ORNL and REEPS systems is choice of the basic unit of analysis. The ORNL design is aggregate, with behavioral equations describing the *average* behavior of households. One consequence of this design is that the ORNL system is simpler computationally, but more complex conceptually, than the REEPS system; i.e., ORNL requires fewer calculations and tabulations, but its equations are complicated by the need to incorporate the effects of aggregation over households.

   What are the relative merits of the aggregate and disaggregate approaches? When the objective of the analysis is aggregate forecasts and the policies under examination can be translated into inputs at the aggregate level, the primary criteria are accuracy and ease of use. The main impediment to accuracy of aggregate forecasts is incomplete treatment of the effects of aggregation across households. Thus, when households are either relatively homogeneous or vary idiosyncratically in ways which would remain unexplained in a disaggregate model, or when an adequate theory of aggregation can be built into the aggregate model, we would expect the aggregate approach to be as accurate and easy to use as the disaggregate approach. On the other hand, when heterogeneity is present, the aggregation errors in the aggregate approach must be balanced against the sampling errors in the disaggregate approach. One advantage is that sampling errors can in principle be controlled by increasing simulated sample size. There is no corresponding simple method of controlling aggregation errors.

   One argument sometimes made for the use of disaggregate models is that household models can be more readily formulated consistently with behavioral laws and estimated using the evidence generated by wide individual variation in explanatory variables, than can their aggregate counterparts. There are limits to this claim. First, behavioral theory may not provide a particularly strong foundation for household models, in which case there is relatively little loss of behavioral structure when a theory of aggregation is added to construct aggregate relationships. Further, under some conditions the separate contributions of individual behavior and aggregation will be identifiable from the aggregate relationship. Second, the apparent advantage from large sample sizes and widely varying explanatory variables in disaggregate data will be dissipated if much of the variation in individual response is unsystematic. Third, in principle, an aggregate model can use behavioral equations fitted to household data and then be adjusted to take into account the effects of aggregation.

A final comment is that while the design principles underlying the ORNL and REEPS models are, respectively, aggregate and disaggregate, this distinction begins to blur in the operational models. It is possible to modify the ORNL model to analyze specified subpopulations rather than the general population; such as the segmentation by income class used in this study. On the other hand, the version of REEPS used here does not achieve full disaggregation to the household level for all variables; e.g., only average fuel prices in the state of residence are used.

B. Complexity and Flexibility

Disaggregate microsimulation models have a clear advantage in flexibility over aggregate models, giving the user the ability to vary heterogeneous inputs or tabulate simulated sample outputs in a variety of ways. This is particularly useful when the policy analyst is interested in distributional as well as aggregate impacts. The cost of this flexibility is computational complexity and an additional burden on the user in the preparation of input files and processing of output files.

Comparing ORNL and REEPS input requirements, we see that REEPS requires an actual or synthesized sample of households in the base year, classified by state location and household and dwelling characteristics, as well as all external price and demographic variables at the state level. In addition policy inputs must be specified in REEPS at the household level. This is considerably more data than is required by ORNL; however, its preparation may not involve substantially greater effort. The REEPS sampling subroutine permits synthesis of a base-year sample from readily available Annual Housing Survey tables. Some price and demographic and policy variables can be assumed to be uniform across states. Heterogeneous variables require extensive collection and coding, but in this case aggregation of these variables into suitable inputs for the ORNL model may be as burdensome as preparation of the disaggregate input file.

REEPS and ORNL output similar information on appliance holdings and efficiencies and energy consumption by appliance, at the household and aggregate levels, respectively. REEPS then requires the additional step of tabulating over households to produce aggregate forecasts.

One minor difference in the ORNL and REEPS models is that changes in household composition and dwelling type and size are modeled explicitly in ORNL and required as external inputs by REEPS. In neither case are these housing variables sensitive to energy policy, a deficiency in both models. Given this recursive structure, we may as well treat the housing variables throughout as external inputs.

C. Adaptability

One question about the ORNL and REEPS system is the ease with which they can be modified to add new appliances or fuels, change variable or equation specifications, or broaden the range of policy dependence. In principle, the simpler the computational structure, the easier it is for the user to understand and change the system. Then, an aggregate model such as ORNL should be easier to modify. There are, however, several additional considerations. First, although REEPS is more complex computationally, much of this comes in the simulated sampling procedures. The behavioral core is then relatively clean and uncomplicated by aggregation effects. On the other side, the REEPS behavioral models are somewhat more integrated across decisions than is the case in ORNL, and the user must understand how to make modifications consistent with the overall decision structure. Second, the computer code for REEPS is written to facilitate modifications, with a modular design, and master files for parameters and variables which are easily changed. The last point is a question of software design rather than aggregate or disaggregate architecture; the ORNL model could be recoded using the same principles to improve its adaptability.

[1] Recent surveys of the energy demand modeling literature can be found in Taylor (1975), Hartman (1979), and Bohi (1981). Taylor includes only studies of electricity demand in his paper, while the latter two include all major fuel types as well as studies of all three demand sectors — residential, commercial, and industrial.

[2] In the current national applications of REEPS, the subregions are defined as Department of Energy Regions. In cases where the DOE Region overlaps a Census Region, an assignment is made based on population.

³ The current national version of REEPS distinguishes the 48 contiguous states as separate locations. The system can accommodate any level of geographical resolution for which the user can provide the necessary data and projections.

⁴ The 1975 WCMS survey interviewed over 3100 households. The survey asked detailed questions on household and dwelling characteristics, as well as energy usage patterns. The 1975 survey is used as the database in the statistical analysis of the appliance choice models described in this chapter (except dishwasher). The survey is described in "Report on Methodology, 1975 National Survey, Lifestyles and Household Energy Use," Response Analysis Corporation, Princeton, N.J., 1976.

⁵ "National Construction Estimator," 6th Ed., Solana Beach, California: Craftsman Book Company, 1978.

⁶ The term *independence from irrelevant alternatives* refers to the property that the relative odds of two alternatives are independent of the availability and attributes of other alternatives.

CHAPTER **IV**

Residential Energy Policy Analysis: The Alternative Policy Scenarios

IV.1. INTRODUCTION

A range of alternative energy policy scenarios—scenarios involving primary impacts on the consumption of residential energy—were used in the analyses reported in this book. These alternative scenarios were designed to reflect existing economic and energy problems, as of the 1981–1982 period, and to include a variety of alternative policy approaches to these problems. Since these problems arose primarily from historical events over the last two decades, a brief retrospective discussion of some of these events is in order. Our purpose is to provide some historical perspective for the specific policy analyses to follow. After this presentation, we then discuss the specific energy policy scenarios used in our analysis of residential energy demand.

111

A. Economic Activity and Residential Energy Demand, 1960–1981

Energy demand in all sectors, but especially in the residential sector, has undergone significant structural change over the past two decades, much of it due to the recent events of the 1970s. It is becoming increasingly apparent that the world oil price shocks of 1973–1974 and 1979 resulted not only in sizable disruptions in the short run, but more importantly they induced long-run shifts in the composition of capital stocks in all sectors of the economy towards more energy-efficient plant and equipment. In the residential sector, these structural changes have resulted in reduced utilization of existing stocks of energy-consuming appliances, a shift in household energy consumption towards less expensive fuels, and the purchase of new, more energy-efficient appliances.

Much of this story is reflected in the data shown in the accompanying tables. Table IV.1 illustrates several trends at aggregate levels of economic activity in terms of real growth in gross national product, personal consumption expenditures, and population. The single most important fact is that all three of these variables showed considerably lower annual growth rates during the decade of the 1970s as compared to the 1960s. In addition, real energy expenditures indicate that the share of energy expenditures in personal consumption expenditures began to increase in the early 1970s, reaching a level of almost 10% by 1980, primarily as a result of increasing energy prices.

The energy consumption figures shown in Table IV.2 give a more detailed picture of energy demand at the sectoral level. These figures indicate that total energy consumption grew at an average annual rate during the 1970s which was only about one-third of the growth rate during the previous decade and less than half of that for the 1950s. Indeed, four of the years between 1974 and 1981 show decreases in total U.S. energy demand. Looking at each of the three end-use sectors shown — residential and commercial, industrial, and transportation — the same general story is also evident. Interestingly enough, it appears that energy demand in the residential and commercial sector grew at an average annual rate during the 1970s which was approximately the same as the growth rate in total energy consumption, while the industrial and transportation sectors grew at somewhat lower and higher rates, respectively.

The annual energy consumption shares for the residential and commercial sector also reveal an interesting story. Table IV.2 illustrates that the energy share for this sector has steadily increased from approximately 30% in 1950 to a peak of 36.8% in 1975, after which it began to decline. However,

TABLE IV.1

Real U.S. Aggregate Economic Activity: 1950–1981[a,b]

| Year | Gross National Product | Personal consumption expenditures | | | Population (millions) |
		Total	Energy[c]	Energy share (%)	
1950	534.8	337.3	21.7	6.43	152.3
1951	579.4	341.6	22.0		154.9
1952	600.8	350.1	23.1		157.6
1953	623.6	363.4	24.4		160.2
1954	616.1	370.0	25.7		163.0
1955	657.5	394.1	28.1	7.13	165.9
1956	671.6	405.4	29.9		168.9
1957	683.8	413.8	31.1		172.0
1958	680.9	418.0	31.9		174.9
1959	721.7	440.4	32.9		177.8
1960	737.2	452.0	34.0	7.52	180.7
1961	756.6	461.4	34.2		183.7
1962	800.3	482.0	35.5		186.5
1963	832.5	500.5	36.4		189.2
1964	876.4	528.0	37.5		191.9
1965	929.3	557.5	39.4	7.07	194.3
1966	984.8	585.7	40.9		196.6
1967	1,011.4	602.7	42.1		198.7
1968	1,058.1	634.4	43.3		200.7
1969	1,087.6	657.9	44.7		202.7
1970	1,085.6	672.1	45.6	6.78	204.9
1971	1,122.4	696.8	47.2		207.1
1972	1,185.9	737.1	49.2		208.8
1973	1,255.0	768.5	51.7		210.4
1974	1,248.0	763.6	57.2		211.9
1975	1,233.9	780.2	60.8	7.79	213.6
1976	1,300.4	823.7	64.7		215.2
1977	1,371.7	863.9	68.3		216.9
1978	1,436.9	904.8	70.2		218.7
1979	1,483.0	930.9	78.9		220.6
1980	1,480.7	935.1	89.0	9.52	227.0
1981	1,509.6	959.1	89.3		
Average annual percentage change					
1950–1960	3.21	2.93	4.49		1.71
1960–1970	3.87	3.97	2.94		1.26
1970–1980	3.10	3.30	6.69		0.84

[a] Billions of 1972 dollars.

[b] Source: U.S. Dept. of Commerce, Bureau of Economic Analysis and Bureau of the Census.

[c] Personal consumption expenditures — energy includes expenditures on gasoline and oil, fuel oil and coal, and electricity and gas.

TABLE IV.2

U.S. Energy Consumption: Total and by End-Use Sector, 1950–1981[a,b]

Year	Total energy consumption	Residential and commercial		Industrial		Transportation	
		Total[c]	Share	Total[c]	Share	Total[c]	Share
1950	33.62	9.96	.296	14.71	.438	8.95	.266
1951	36.11	10.30		16.26		9.55	
1952	35.84	10.57		15.74		9.52	
1953	36.78	10.52		16.67		9.59	
1954	35.73	10.88		15.36		9.50	
1955	39.18	11.60	.296	17.35	.443	10.23	.261
1956	40.76	12.19		18.02		10.55	
1957	40.81	12.16		17.81		10.85	
1958	40.66	13.08		16.92		10.66	
1959	42.42	13.65		17.98		10.79	
1960	44.08	14.73	.334	18.83	.427	10.52	.239
1961	44.73	15.17		18.89		10.66	
1962	46.80	16.03		19.63		11.14	
1963	48.61	16.49		20.54		11.58	
1964	50.78	17.00		21.85		11.92	
1965	52.99	18.00	.340	22.66	.428	12.33	.233
1966	55.99	19.02		23.89		13.08	
1967	57.89	20.10		24.07		13.72	
1968	61.32	21.30		25.19		14.83	
1969	64.53	22.74		26.33		15.46	
1970	66.83	23.94	.358	26.82	.401	16.06	.240
1971	68.30	24.87		26.75		16.68	
1972	71.63	26.05		27.92		17.66	
1973	74.61	26.62		29.46		18.52	
1974	72.76	25.98		28.74		18.03	
1975	70.71	26.02	.368	26.51	.375	18.18	.257
1976	74.51	27.22		28.22		19.07	
1977	76.33	27.58		29.01		19.74	
1978	78.15	28.23		29.30		20.61	
1979	78.97	27.48		31.54		19.95	
1980	76.27	27.35	.359	30.29	.397	18.63	.244
1981	74.26	27.11	.365	28.95		18.19	

Average annual percentage change

1950–1960	2.71	3.91		2.47		1.62	
1960–1970	4.16	4.86		3.54		4.23	
1970–1980	1.32	1.33		1.22		1.48	

[a] Quadrillions (10^{15}) Btu.

[b] Source: U.S. Dept of Energy, Energy Information Administration, Annual Report to Congress, 1980, 1981.

[c] Includes energy consumption by electric utilities allocated on basis of electricity sales by privately owned Class A and B electric utilities.

for the last year shown, 1981, the share of residential and commercial energy consumption shows an increasing trend again as the result of relatively larger declines in energy consumption in the industrial sector. That is, absolute energy consumption in all three sectors over the last two years has decreased, but these declines have been largest in the industrial sector and smallest in the residential and commercial sector.

A detailed disaggregation of total residential and commercial energy consumption, broken down by type of fuel, is shown in Table IV.3 for the years

TABLE IV.3

U.S. Energy Consumption by the Residential–Commercial Sector: 1960–1981[a,b]

Year	Coal	Natural gas	Petroleum	Electricity	Total energy consumed[c] 10^{15} Btu	Annual percentage change
1960	0.98	4.27	4.92	4.56	14.73	7.9
1961	0.87	4.48	5.03	4.79	15.17	3.0
1962	0.87	4.85	5.23	5.08	16.03	5.7
1963	0.73	5.03	5.26	5.47	16.49	2.9
1964	0.61	5.34	5.19	5.86	17.00	3.1
1965	0.68	5.52	5.63	6.17	18.00	5.9
1966	0.68	5.95	5.77	6.62	19.02	5.7
1967	0.59	6.22	6.21	7.08	20.10	5.7
1968	0.53	6.45	6.13	8.19	21.30	6.0
1969	0.45	6.89	6.27	9.13	22.74	6.8
1970	0.43	7.11	6.45	9.95	23.94	5.3
1971	0.41	7.37	6.44	10.65	24.87	3.9
1972	0.39	7.64	6.67	11.35	26.05	4.7
1973	0.29	7.63	6.74	11.96	26.62	2.2
1974	0.29	7.52	6.14	12.03	25.98	−2.4
1975	0.24	7.58	5.79	12.41	26.02	0.2
1976	0.23	7.87	6.30	12.82	27.22	4.6
1977	0.23	7.46	6.25	13.64	27.58	1.3
1978	0.24	7.62	6.27	14.10	28.23	2.4
1979	0.21	7.89	4.73	14.65	27.48	−2.7
1980	0.17	7.65	4.11	15.42	27.35	−0.5
1981	0.16	7.39	3.83	15.73	27.11	−0.9
Average annual percentage change						
1960–1970	−8.24	5.10	2.71	7.80	4.86	
1970–1980	−9.28	0.73	−4.51	4.58	1.33	

[a] Quadrillions (10^{15}) Btu.

[b] Sources: Federal Energy Administration, Project Independence Report (Nov. 1974); DOE/EIA, Monthly Energy Review (February 1982).

1960–1981. These figures indicate that electricity consumption in this sector, including estimated electric energy losses, has virtually quadrupled over the 21-yr period shown, in spite of a general slowing down in the average annual growth rate. By 1981 the energy share of residential and commercial electricity consumption was almost 60%. The second most popular fuel in this sector was natural gas, which shows a similar growth pattern in demand over the period shown, although the average annual growth rates were substantially smaller than those for electricity, especially for the 1970s. By 1981, the natural gas share of total energy consumption was about 27%. Petroleum and coal account for substantially smaller shares and both indicate declining consumption over time although with quite different trend patterns. Coal consumption has declined steadily over the period from an energy share of about 7% in 1960 to less than 1% by 1981. In contrast, petroleum consumption in this sector grew rather steadily from 1960 to 1973 and then declined for several years. The upward trend resumed in 1975, but in 1979 petroleum consumption in this sector fell sharply and this downward trend has continued since then. By 1981, petroleum accounted for only 14% of total residential and commercial energy consumption, down from a figure of about 33% in 1960. Thus, during the last two decades, the residential–commercial sector has been characterized by substantial increases in the consumption of both electricity and natural gas, a reduced role

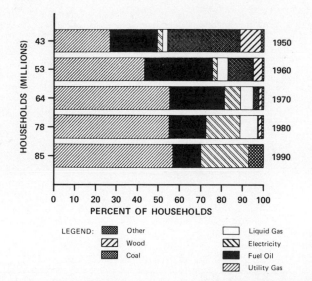

Fig. IV.1 Percentage of households by type of space heating fuel: 1950–1990. *Other* includes liquid gas, coal, wood, and other fuels. Source: Energy Information Administration, 1981 Annual Report to Congress, Vol. 3 (February 1982).

for petroleum and the virtual elimination of coal as an important fuel in this sector. Of the two major fuels, electricity and natural gas, electricity has clearly become the dominant source of residential energy. Similar trends for the household or residential sector are also portrayed graphically in Fig. IV.1, although in this case electricity consumption does not include losses so that the share of residential electricity consumption appears smaller.

The energy story over the same period with respect to energy prices is shown in Table IV.4. Annual percentage changes in the prices of heating oil,

TABLE IV.4

Annual Rates of Change in Selected U.S. Prices: 1960–1981[a,b]

Year	All items	All commodities	Food	Services	Energy	Heating oil	Natural gas	Elec- tricity
		Changes in consumer prices				Changes in residential fuel prices		
1960	1.6	0.9	1.0	3.3	2.6	—	—	—
1961	1.0	0.5	1.3	2.0	0.2	0.9	4.0	−1.1
1962	1.1	0.9	0.9	1.9	0.3	0.9	−2.9	−1.5
1963	1.2	0.9	1.4	2.0	0.3	1.8	0.0	−1.7
1964	1.3	1.1	1.3	1.9	−0.4	−0.9	1.0	−2.6
1965	1.7	1.2	2.2	2.2	1.8	0.0	0.0	−2.4
1966	2.9	2.6	5.0	3.9	1.6	1.8	−1.0	−2.4
1967	2.9	1.8	0.9	4.4	2.2	2.6	0.0	−1.4
1968	4.2	3.7	3.6	5.2	1.5	2.5	0.0	−2.0
1969	5.4	4.5	5.1	6.9	2.7	3.3	1.0	−1.4
1970	5.9	4.7	5.5	8.1	2.7	4.0	3.9	0.5
1971	4.3	3.4	3.0	5.6	3.9	5.4	4.7	4.1
1972	3.3	3.0	4.3	3.8	2.8	1.5	6.3	4.8
1973	6.2	7.4	14.5	4.4	8.0	16.5	5.9	3.9
1974	11.0	12.0	14.4	9.3	29.3	59.3	12.8	18.1
1975	9.1	8.9	8.5	9.5	10.6	8.9	19.9	13.4
1976	5.8	4.3	3.1	8.3	7.2	7.5	13.6	7.6
1977	6.5	5.8	6.3	7.7	9.5	14.9	18.8	9.7
1978	7.7	7.1	10.0	8.5	6.3	7.4	9.1	6.3
1979	11.3	11.4	10.9	11.0	25.2	30.5	15.6	8.0
1980	13.5	12.2	8.6	15.4	30.9	45.0	22.5	15.4
1981	10.4	8.4	7.9	13.1	13.5	22.5	21.5	15.2
Average annual percentage change								
1960–1970	2.65	2.07	2.56	3.80	1.41	1.54	0.55	−1.45
1970–1980	7.69	7.29	8.10	8.33	12.4	18.3	12.1	8.35

[a] Percent change.

[b] Source: Dept. of Labor, Bureau of Labor Statistics; Department of Energy, Energy Information Administration.

natural gas, and electricity for residential users are shown in the three columns on the right, while similar figures for aggregate consumer prices, and several basic components, are shown in the first five columns for comparison. The rates of average annual percentage change shown at the bottom of this table indicate substantially higher rates of price inflation during the 1970s as compared to the 1960s for each of the three major residential fuels. The figures for heating oil clearly dominate this story, as well as indicating the primary source of the underlying inflation, namely, the crude oil price shocks of 1973–1974 and 1979–1980.

The overall story here is of course quite familiar by now, with respect to both aggregate energy consumption and residential energy demand. Following the generally stable era of the 1960s, energy prices in all sectors of the U.S. economy escalated rapidly during the 1970s. This led, with some lag, to reductions in energy demand in all sectors, including residential consumption, and to significant changes in the structure of inter-fuel demands. For example, in 1950, over 45% of the houses were heated with coal or wood, while today coal has essentially disappeared as a source of energy for residential heating. Over the past 30 years, older homes have been converted to and new homes have been built with fuel oil, natural gas, and electric heating systems because of changes in both relative energy prices and fuel availability. In the residential sector more recently, electricity has clearly emerged as the dominant or preferred fuel, followed by natural gas.

In addition to this pattern of inter-fuel substitution, the residential sector has also experienced a significant decline in energy consumption per household as revealed in Fig. IV.2. After rising from 1960 to 1975, the total energy

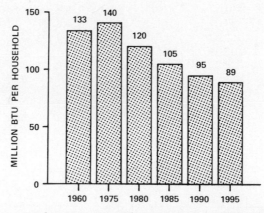

Fig. IV.2 Average annual energy consumption per household: 1960–1995. Source: Energy Information Administration, 1981 Annual Report to Congress, Vol. 3 (February 1982).

consumption per household in 1980 fell to about 90% of the 1960 level. This decline in household energy consumption is expected to continue as less efficient heating systems and energy-using household appliances are replaced by newer, more efficient units and as thermal performance is improved in both old and new homes.

Of course, whether these recent trends in energy consumption per household and residential inter-fuel substitution continue will depend in large part upon both future energy prices and future U.S. energy policy. Thus, there is a critical need for in-depth analyses of alternative policy options, particularly with respect to those policies impacting the residential or household sector.

B. The Energy Policy Scenarios — Selection and Design

Three alternative residential energy policy scenarios were used in the policy analyses which are discussed in the remainder of this book:

(i) a *base case* or existing status quo scenario which assumed no change in existing energy policy as of 1981;

(ii) an immediate or accelerated natural gas *deregulation* scenario which assumed total decontrol of natural gas prices by 1981; and

(iii) the use of mandatory thermal efficiency design *standards* for all new housing.

These three scenarios were selected in part to represent a broad range of alternative energy policies, each having a fundamental impact on energy demand in the residential sector, and in part to demonstrate the capabilities of each of the two models, REEPS and ORNL, for dealing with a variety of different energy policies.

According to the U.S. Department of Energy, most Federal energy programs can be placed in one of five general categories:

1. conservation programs — including automobile fuel, building energy and appliance energy efficiency standards; various tax incentive programs; and programs which limit the use of certain types of fuels by power plants and other industrial users;

2. supply programs — including support for research and development, and tax incentives for new technologies;

3. price controls—including regulatory programs, primarily at the Federal level, which affect the interstate prices of natural gas and electricity;

4. direct and indirect transfer payments—designed to cushion the effects of higher energy prices, especially on low-income groups; and

5. emergency programs—including the Strategic Petroleum Reserve, standby rationing authority and U.S. obligations under the International Energy Agency's emergency oil allocation programs.

If we broaden the definition of the third category, price controls, to include all price-related programs, i.e., both decontrol and regulatory programs, then most Federal energy policies primarily targeted at residential energy consumption would fall into the first, third, and fourth categories.

The three alternative residential energy policy scenarios adopted for the purposes of our analysis clearly fall into the first and third categories. Since one of the primary focuses of our analysis was the distributional impact of nontransfer policies, that is, policies not designed primarily to meet distributional concerns, programs included in the fourth category were specifically excluded. Thus, our analysis is designed to suggest, in part, the types and magnitudes of transfer programs which may be needed in addition to offset or supplement the unintended distributional consequences of other residential energy policies.

The first two scenarios, base case and deregulation, represent energy pricing policies, because the primary impact of these policies is on the prices of residential fuels, and hence on residential energy consumption, while the third scenario, standards, represents a nonprice policy in which minimum standards on new housing thermal efficiency are assumed. Thus, a broad range of possible energy policy options, including both price and nonprice strategies, are represented by the three scenarios used in our analysis. Furthermore, the two new policy scenarios, deregulation and standards, represent realistic current policy options and have both been given active consideration by Federal energy policy makers during the last several years.

The two residential fuel price scenarios, base case and deregulation, were based primarily on data and forecasts reported in the Energy Information Administration's (EIA) 1980 Annual Report to Congress (1981), which was the most recent and comprehensive set of EIA projections for the residential sector available at the time our analysis was carried out. The base case or existing policy scenario assumes that decontrol of newly discovered natural gas will take place in 1985 under the current provisions of the Natural Gas Policy Act (NGPA) of 1978. The residential fuel price projections used in this scenario were based upon the so-called "mid-range" projections of the EIA.

Alternatively, the deregulation or accelerated natural gas decontrol scenario assumes that decontrol occurs somewhat earlier, in 1981 rather than 1985 as currently mandated, resulting in higher natural gas prices for the period 1981–1985 relative to base case prices. The prices of the other residential fuels, primarily electricity and fuel oil, were assumed to be unaffected by accelerated natural gas decontrol so that these price projections are the same as those used in the base case scenario. Similarly, the residential fuel price projections assumed in the third policy scenario, standards, are the same as those used in the base case scenario, implicitly assuming that the implementation of mandatory appliance efficiency standards would not affect residential fuel prices.

IV.2. THE BASE CASE SCENARIO

Each of the two residential energy demand models used in this analysis, REEPS and ORNL, require information on four basic categories of model inputs: base- or initial-year variables, annual demographic and housing projections, annual fuel price projections, and various behavioral and technological parameters. The base-year variables include initial-year values for variables which are exogenous to the model, such as the real rate of interest, as well as initial-year values for all endogenous or forecast variables, such as energy consumption and appliance saturation rates. For our analysis, 1977 was used as the base year and the models were generally run for the period 1977–2000. The demographic and housing projections include annual estimates of population and number of households, broken down by income group, type of housing, and age of structure for each year in the analysis. The fuel price projections include forecasted residential fuel prices by type of fuel for each year. Finally, values for various behavioral and technological parameters used in the model must be supplied by the user.

A. Base-Year Variables

The base-year variables used in our analysis, and their sources, are listed in part A of Table IV.5. To start each of the models at the same point, it was necessary to use a set of model input values which were consistent at each of two different levels: total and by disaggregates or subgroups, i.e., by fuel–dwelling type–end-use–income group combinations. Our approach involved using national or aggregate data taken from version 7.1 of the ORNL

TABLE IV.5

Model Input Variables and Sources of Data

Variable	Data source
A. Base-year variables	
1. Average 1977 energy usage per household for each fuel–dwelling type–end-use combination	National ORNL data (version 7.1) broken into various subgroups using conditional probabilities from REEPS simulations based on Annual Housing Survey data.
2. 1977 market shares by fuel–dwelling type–end-use combination	
3. Market shares for new equipment installations in 1977 by fuel and end use, for existing and new structures	
B. Demographic–housing projections	
1. Per capita income	U.S. Census and U.S. Census projections
2. Stock of occupied housing units (in millions) by type by year	National ORNL data (version 7.1) broken into 6 income groups using conditional probabilities from SAMPLER program based on Annual Housing Survey data
3. New construction of occupied housing units (in millions) by type by year	
4. Number of retrofit units (in millions) by housing type by year	SAMPLER program, using conditional income probabilities given housing type based on Annual Housing Survey data
5. Average fraction of new homes with room-central air conditioning	REEPS simulation based on Annual Housing Survey data.

model. The required subgroup values were then computed using conditional probabilities from REEPS simulations based on 1977 Annual Housing Survey data. Applying these conditional probabilities to the national data resulted in the various subgroup totals. The resulting values, for both national and subgroup levels, were used to run each of the two models so that the data were consistent both across models and within each model, i.e., across subgroups. A real interest rate of 10% was assumed in both models for the purpose of modeling trade-offs between initial equipment and annual operating costs.

B. Demographic–Housing Projections

In addition to base-year variables, annual estimates of the number of households by type by income group, as well as per capita income, were required. These variables and the data sources used are shown in part B of Table IV.5.

Since one of the primary purposes of our analysis was to examine the distributional impact of residential energy policy by income group, it was necessary to run each of the two models at income group, as well as national, levels. For this purpose, the six income groups used by REEPS, and shown in Table IV.6, were adopted for use with both models. These six groups: 0–5000, 5000–10,000, 10,000–15,000, 15,000–25,000, 25,000–45,000 and over 45,000 dollars, respectively, were measured in terms of 1975 dollars, the common monetary denominator of both models. The population distribution in 1977 by income group, as well as the per capita income for each of the six income groups, are also shown in Table IV.6 and were obtained from the U.S. Census Current Population Report, "Money Income in 1977 of Families and Persons in the United States." The per capita income data for 1977 were deflated from 1977 to 1975 dollars using the consumer price index. This involved redefining the composition of each of the 1977 income groups to be consistent with income group definitions measured in 1975 dollars. The result was a set of income groups and per capita income estimates, measured consistently in terms of 1975 dollars.

Using these six income groups, another problem arose in terms of both the base-year variables and the demographic–housing projections since little of these data were available from published sources by income group. Accordingly, an alternative procedure was used to provide the necessary estimates on a consistent basis for use with each of the two models. This procedure involved using the results of the REEPS simulations to produce similar input data for use with the ORNL model on an income group basis, since REEPS includes household income as one of its dimensions. For example, the

TABLE IV.6

Income Group Characteristics[a]

	Income groups	Percentage of population: 1977	1977 per capita income (in 1975 $)
1	0–$5000	10.5	$ 1218
2	5000–10,000	19.4	2642
3	10,000–15,000	20.1	4081
4	15,000–25,000	28.9	5362
5	25,000–45,000	17.7	9780
6	over 45,000	3.4	13,317
N	aggregate	100.0	4,614[b]

[a] Source: U.S. Census Current Population Report, "Money Income in 1977 of Families and Persons in the U.S.," Table 23.

[b] This is average per capita income, i.e., weighted by the percentage of population in each of the 6 income groups.

average fraction of new homes with room versus central air conditioning and average 1977 energy consumption per household were obtained for each income group by fuel–dwelling type–end-use combinations by appropriate aggregation across the REEPS micro-level simulation outputs. This procedure produced a set of the necessary model input variables which were consistent between the two models.

The required housing stock variables, also shown in Table IV.5, were generated using the version 7.1 aggregate data from the national ORNL model and conditional probabilities by income group by dwelling type generated by the SAMPLER program, a component of REEPS. The function of SAMPLER is to produce a set of synthetic micro observations at the household level for further processing by REEPS, where this sample of households can be appropriately weighted to reflect true population distributions by such characteristics as region, income group, dwelling type, end use, fuel type, etc. Again, this disaggregated set of required model input values for the demographic–housing projections was used in both models.

C. Fuel Price Projections

Annual price projections for the major residential fuels were also required by each of the two models for the period of analysis. The residential fuel price projections used in the base case policy scenario are shown in Table IV.7 and Fig. IV.3, and were based on the so-called mid-range forecasts of the Energy Information Administration's 1980 Annual Report to Congress, published in March of 1981. These fuel price projections were the most recent forecasts available at the time the analysis was carried out. Actual fuel prices for the years 1965, 1973, and 1978–1980, and estimated fuel prices for 1985, 1990, 1995, and 2000, were taken directly from the EIA report, while the estimates shown for intermediate years were based on exponential interpolations between the appropriate pair of years for which EIA projections were available. All prices shown in Table IV.7 are in terms of 1979 dollars per million Btu.

Three residential fuels were used—electricity, natural gas, and fuel oil (distillate)—with the price for electricity reported in end-use rather than primary-use terms. That is, the energy content of residential electricity was assumed to be 3412 Btu/kWh rather than 11,500 Btu/kWh.

The EIA middle or mid-range residential fuel price projections were based on the set of assumed world oil prices for the 1980–2000 period shown in Table IV.8. These projections assume that the real price of crude oil approximately doubles over this 20-yr period. The alternative forecasts, low-range

TABLE IV.7

EIA Residential Fuel Price Projections[a]

Year	Fuel prices			Price trend factors		
	Electricity	Natural gas[c]	Fuel Oil	Electricity	Natural gas[c]	Fuel Oil
1965	14.86	2.27	2.44			
1973	11.09	1.98	2.52			
1977	12.35	2.52	3.58	1.000	1.000	1.000
1978	12.69	2.68	3.92	1.028	1.063	1.095
1979	13.77	3.18	4.33	1.115	1.262	1.209
1980	14.07	3.52	4.79	1.139	1.397	1.338
1981	14.60	3.81 (5.00)	5.28	1.182	1.512 (1.984)	1.475
1982	15.16	4.13 (5.06)	5.83	1.228	1.639 (2.008)	1.628
1983	15.73	4.47 (5.12)	6.44	1.274	1.774 (2.032)	1.799
1984	16.33	4.84 (5.18)	7.11	1.322	1.921 (2.056)	1.986
1985	16.95	5.24 (5.24)	7.85	1.372	2.079 (2.079)	2.193
1987	16.96	5.37	8.17	1.373	2.131	2.282
1989	16.97	5.49	8.50	1.374	2.179	2.374
1990	16.98	5.56	8.67	1.375	2.206	2.422
1991	16.97	5.69	8.99	1.374	2.258	2.511
1993	16.95	5.96	9.66	1.372	2.365	2.698
1995	16.94	6.25	10.39	1.372	2.480	2.902
2000	17.02	6.24	12.20	1.378	2.476	3.408
1980–2000[d]	+21.0	+77.3	+154.7			

[a] Source: EIA 1980 Annual Report to Congress (March 1981), Vol. 3, Tables 3.2, 3.9, and 4.4.

[b] 1979 $/10^6 Btu.

[c] Figures in parentheses refer to price projections used under the accelerated natural gas deregulation scenario.

[d] Percent change.

and high-range, assumed real price increases of 35 and 200%, respectively. This doubling of real crude oil prices for the mid-range case results in a decline in U.S. oil consumption, as a percentage of total free world oil consumption, from 35% in 1979 to an estimated 30% by 1990, primarily due to the substitution of coal for oil. At the same time, net U.S. oil imports are assumed to decline from about $6\frac{1}{2}$ million barrels/day in 1980 to 5 million barrels/day in 1990, and to 2 million barrels/day by the year 2000.

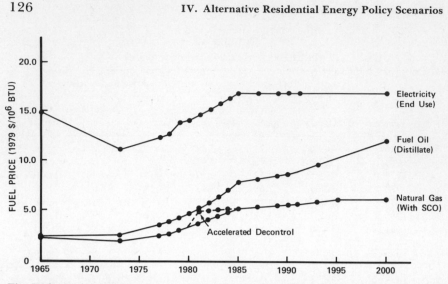

Fig. IV.3 Residential Fuel Prices: 1965–2000. Source: EIA Mid-Range Forecasts, 1980 Annual Report to Congress.

With respect to domestic energy policy, the current provisions of the Natural Gas Policy Act of 1978 are assumed to prevail under the base case scenario, resulting in complete decontrol of new natural gas by 1985 and generally reduced consumption after that. Substantial increases in coal consumption are assumed, due in part to the price advantage of coal and in part to the restrictions on oil and gas use imposed by the Powerplant and Industrial Fuel Use Act. This Act, and in particular its Systems Compliance Option (SCO), limits natural gas consumption for electric utilities by 1990 to

TABLE IV.8
EIA World Oil Price Projections[a,b]

	Nominal prices			Middle case real price[c]
Year	Low	Middle	High	
1979 (Actual)	$21.50	$ 21.50	$21.50	$21.50
1980	34.00	34.00	34.00	31.00
1990	77.00	98.00	117.00	41.00
2000	185.00	264.00	409.00	60.00

[a] In $/barrel.
[b] Source: EIA 1980 Annual Report to Congress (March, 1981), p. ix.
[c] 1979 dollars.

20% of the average annual amount used between 1974 and 1976 and pro-
hibits the use of natural gas to generate electricity after 1990. Thus, the
impact of the SCO is to reduce industrial demand for natural gas which, in
turn, results in slightly lower natural gas prices over the 1980–2000 period.
Since the 1981 interpretation of this provision by the Economic Regulatory
Administration (responsible for administering the Fuel Use Act) was that it
required the enforcement of the SCO, we used the "with-SCO" natural gas
price projections of the EIA.

The nuclear contribution to total U.S. primary energy supply is forecasted
to grow from 3.8% in 1978 to 9.2% in 1990, and to 13.5% by the year 2000.
This is a somewhat lower growth rate than that assumed in EIAs 1979 annual
report, due primarily to the impact of the Three Mile Island accident.

As shown in Table IV.7, the residential fuel price forecasts used in our
analyses assume that over the period 1980–2000 real prices for electricity,
natural gas and fuel oil increase by 21%, 77%, and 155%, respectively. These
EIA projections appeared reasonable in light of the 1981 energy situation,
although it may be that the assumed price increases for natural gas were a
little on the low side for a nonrecessionary economy. At any rate, these fuel
price projections were used to run both the ORNL and REEPS models so
that comparable results between the two models could be obtained.

Both models required that the annual fuel price series be measured relative
to 1977 prices. These relative price series, labeled price trend factors, are
shown in the last three columns of Table IV.7. The base-year (i.e., 1977)
fuel prices are shown in Table IV.9. Since the ORNL model uses Btu prices
while the REEPS model uses fuel prices expressed in terms of physical units
(i.e., kWh for electricity, therms for natural gas, and gallons for fuel oil), it
was necessary to convert the EIA Btu prices for 1977 into physical unit

TABLE IV.9

1977 Base-Year Fuel Prices[a]

Residential fuel	1979 \$/10^6 Btu	1975 \$/10^6 Btu	1975 \$/physical unit[b]
Electricity	12.35	9.53	.0325 (kWh)
Natural gas	2.52	1.94	.194 (therm)
Fuel oil	3.58	2.76	.383 (gallon)

[a] A 1975–1979 deflator of 1.296 was used, based on the U.S. GNP price
deflator—personal consumption expenditures.

[b] Physical unit conversion factors used: therm = 10^5 Btu, kWh = 3412
Btu, gallon = 13,869 Btu (based on 582,500 Btu/barrel)

prices. The conversion factors used for the three fuels are shown in the footnotes to Table IV.9 and were taken from the EIA report. It was also necessary to convert the base-year prices from 1979 to 1975 dollars, since both models use 1975 dollars as the nominal unit of accounting in their calculations. The personal consumption expenditure component of the GNP implicit price deflator was used to carry out the necessary deflation.

In addition, the ORNL model, but not the REEPS model, includes a fourth residential fuel type—other. Since neither data nor documentation describing this fourth fuel category were available, we used the same fuel price projections for it as used in version 7.1 of the ORNL model. "Other" fuel is primarily a residual category of secondary importance, and a more detailed treatment of it was not possible.

D. Behavioral – Technological Parameters and Model Standardization

One of the primary focuses of our analysis was to compare relative model performance between the two models, REEPS and ORNL, for each of the three alternative policy scenarios. Accordingly, we assumed the same values for all variables in the first three categories of model inputs for each of the models. That is, for any given policy scenario, the same values for the base-year variables and the demographic – housing and fuel price projections were used in each of the two models.

For the fourth category of model inputs, behavioral and technological parameters, we used the values supplied with the most recent (as of mid-1981) version of each model to be able to judge relative performance in terms of the existing models, rather than in terms of standardized versions modified to suit our own purposes. Since the existing versions are the models which are potentially available for use by policy makers, we felt that this assumption would result in a more accurate picture of actual, as opposed to ideal, model performance. Put another way, our fundamental interest was running one *black box* or model against the other, starting both at the same point or set of values, but without modifying or altering the internal structure of the models, including both architecture and assumed parameter values. A further consideration was that in many cases it would have been virtually impossible to compute a consistent set of parameter values due to fundamental differences in model specification between the two models.

IV.3 THE IMMEDIATE NATURAL GAS DEREGULATION SCENARIO

The purpose of this alternative fuel price policy scenario was to analyze the impact upon residential consumption of accelerated natural gas decontrol, that is, moving the decontrol date from 1985 to 1981. The current provisions of the Natural Gas Policy Act of 1978, assumed to be operational under the base case scenario, assume that complete decontrol of newly discovered natural gas takes place in 1985. An alternative policy, which has been given serious consideration by both the Carter and Reagan administrations, calls for moving this decontrol date forward in time by several years. Such a policy would have important incentive effects for suppliers of both old and new natural gas. In addition, we would also expect residential energy demand to be affected as households adjust appliance usage and installation decisions to a new regime of residential fuel prices.

Our assumption of complete decontrol of natural gas in 1981 required estimation of a new set of natural gas price projections for the period 1981 – 1985, a set which, at the same time, would also be consistent with the decontrolled natural gas prices projected by EIA for the post-1985 period. It was assumed that prices for the remaining two residential fuels, electricity and fuel oil, would not be affected by the accelerated decontrol of new natural gas, at least to a first approximation.

The deregulated natural gas fuel price series for 1981 – 1985 is shown in Fig. IV.3 and is also included in Table IV.7 as the parenthesized figures in the third column. These projections were based on the assumption that after the 1981 decontrol, the price of residential natural gas would increase at the same growth rate as the 1985 – 1990 deregulated prices, i.e., the base case or decontrolled natural gas prices for 1985 – 1990. Thus, the effect of accelerated decontrol was assumed to be an immediate price jump or *fly up* in 1981, followed by a steady increase out to the base case fuel price for 1985. The price of natural gas from 1985 forward was assumed to be unaffected by accelerated decontrol in 1981 since the base case projections for 1985 and later years already assume complete decontrol.

IV.4. THE MANDATORY THERMAL EFFICIENCY STANDARDS SCENARIO

The use of energy efficiency standards, whether in the form of thermal efficiency standards for new housing, minimum gasoline mileage standards for new automobiles or efficiency design standards for household appliances such as furnaces and water heaters, represents a fundamentally different approach to energy policy, an approach in which the desired impact acts initially through quantities rather than prices. Thus, the mandatory thermal efficiency standards scenario assumed in our analysis represents a non-price energy policy offering a distinct contrast to the energy price impacts of the base case and accelerated natural gas deregulation scenarios.

Energy efficiency standards, whether for appliances, automobiles, or homes, relate generally to new items, and thus their primary impact is through investment decisions in new appliances or new housing. That is, existing stocks of old capital are not affected. Of course, over time the standards involve an increasing portion of existing capital stocks since the new capital added each year must conform to the mandatory standards. In the case of residential housing stocks, however, it generally takes a relatively long period of time before significant aggregate energy consumption effects show up since annual new housing typically represents a small fraction of the total existing stock of housing. Thus, energy efficiency standards may show rather small effects at first, but we would expect these effects to slowly increase over time.

A second characteristic of energy efficiency standards which is relevant for our analysis is that they are likely to have sizable redistributional effects. This is because such standards apply only to the purchase of new capital, and the purchase of new energy-using appliances, especially new housing, is likely to be highly sensitive to income. Furthermore, the impacts of such standards have two dimensions: first, increased prices of capital goods due to the mandated increased energy efficiency; and second, reduced energy consumption from using the new appliance or home. Clearly, these effects are in opposite directions but they are not likely to be completely offsetting. This is because in the absence of such standards, assuming competitive markets and perfect information, new appliances which are more energy-efficient will be purchased voluntarily as long as the present value of the net benefits from purchasing and using the more efficient appliance are positive. Thus, if the mandatory energy standards are constraining when applied, this would imply higher purchase costs for new appliances which are less than offset by the savings from reduced energy consumption from using the new appliances, after suitable discounting. Furthermore, this net impact is not likely to be income-neutral since higher-income households are more likely to purchase new appliances and hence be affected by such standards.

The trade-off between design efficiency and energy consumption for new appliances is shown in Fig. IV.4. The trade-off curve or frontier, *TT'*,

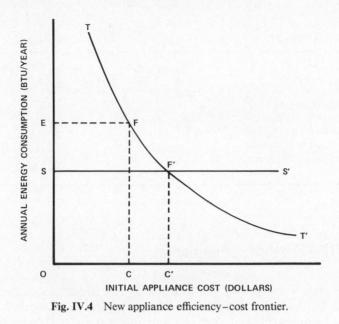

Fig. IV.4   New appliance efficiency–cost frontier.

indicates that designs which are more energy efficient, and hence have a higher initial cost but use less energy per unit of time, are represented by points which are further down the curve and to the right.   In the absence of mandated energy efficiency standards, assume that the cost – efficiency combination represented by point F is selected as the result of optimization assuming some given set of expected energy prices and a given discount rate.   Such a design has an initial cost of OC dollars and an annual energy usage rate of OE Btu/yr.   Now, assume that mandated energy efficiency standards represented by line SS' are implemented.   If these standards require a higher level of energy efficiency than indicated by point F, the result will be an increase in initial appliance cost of CC' and a reduction in annual energy consumption, given by ES.   Under the standards, the effective efficiency – cost trade-off frontier is reduced to segment $F'T'$, and the general result is increased appliance investment costs and induced savings in annual energy costs.   Assuming no change in either the discount rate or expected energy prices, point F' will clearly imply lower net benefits to the individual than point F, the point selected in the absence of standards.

132   IV. Alternative Residential Energy Policy Scenarios

TABLE IV.10

ASHRAE 90-75 Thermal Standards for New Housing by Region

	Region 1 Northeast	Region 2 North Central	Region 3 South	Region 4 West
R-value ceiling insulation	17.1	17.1	19.5	19.5
R-value wall insulation	15.4	15.4	9.5	9.5
Reduction in heating design temperature differential	12	14	12	14
Reduction in cooling design temperature differential	7	6	6	5

A. ASHRAE Building Standards

The residential energy efficiency standards used in our analysis were based on the 90-75 American Association of Heating, Refrigeration, and Air Conditioning Engineers (ASHRAE) voluntary thermal design standards for new housing. These ASHRAE standards were given serious consideration under the Carter Administration as a part of its energy conservation policies. Under these standards, all windows are stormed or double-glazed, walls and ceilings are insulated, heating and cooling system capacities are reduced, and tight construction is used to reduce infiltration. These standards vary by region due to differences in climate and are shown in Table IV.10.

B. Converting the ASHRAE Standards to Model Inputs

To model the impact of mandatory thermal efficiency standards for new housing, the ORNL model requires an estimate of the ratio of energy requirements under the standard to energy requirements in the absence of the standard, i.e., the base case scenario. This ratio was estimated for typical heating loads using a residential thermal model of heating and air conditioning developed by McFadden and Dubin (1982). The McFadden–Dubin thermal model was designed to be used with data from the EIA–DOE National Interim Energy Consumption Survey (NIECS) and can be used to estimate heating and cooling capacity requirements, energy usage, and various other heating, ventilating, and air conditioning (HVAC) characteristics for any given type and location of residential structure. In this model, cost data from engineering sources (R. S. Means, 1981) are used to estimate the capital and operating costs for 19 alternative HVAC systems, e.g., gas forced air, oil hydronic, electric resistance, for the given structure.

The McFadden–Dubin thermal model takes detailed account of basic heat transfer–engineering design principles and generally follows accepted engineering design practice. Basically, the heating and cooling system design capacities of a residential dwelling are determined by analyzing the rates of heat transfer between the interior and exterior under given weather conditions. Since this model was designed for use with the NIECS data and since the NIECS data set did not contain a complete physical description of each dwelling, it was necessary to base the required thermal estimates upon the available NIECS information. This necessitated a two-step approach in which thermal design capacity and usage were first related to a number of basic house characteristics in the first stage, followed by a second stage in which this full set of house characteristics was then related to the smaller subset of NIECS variables. Engineering design relationships were used in the first stage and required such information as wall, window and ceiling areas, house volume, geographic location, and feet of ducting for central heating systems. In the second stage, detailed information on 7 specific housing designs (ranging from a single-story, 4-room house with 576 ft^2 of area to a two-story, 9-room house with over 3000 ft^2 of area) was used to relate the full set of design characteristics to the NIECS variables. The latter included incomplete information on square footage, as well as the number of floors, rooms, and windows.

The HVAC capacity and energy consumption estimated by the McFadden–Dubin thermal model for each of three different thermal design efficiencies—observed NIECS houses, uninsulated design and the ASHRAE 90-75 standards—are shown in Table IV.11. It is interesting to note that observed or actual thermal performance achieves a substantial proportion of that achieved under the ASHRAE 90-75 standards. For example, for electric resistance heating, 81% of the energy conservation attainable under the ASHRAE standard, compared to the uninsulated case, is achieved under observed thermal design conditions. Nevertheless, substantial amounts of additional conservation are still attainable using the ASHRAE standards. For example, in the case of electric resistance heating, electricity consumption could have been reduced an additional 29% relative to actual designs, with comparable reductions for other heating systems.

Based on the estimates shown in Table IV.11, the ratio of observed to ASHRAE-standards energy consumption for electric resistance heat, 0.709, was assumed for purposes of modeling the standards impact using the ORNL model. Since the ratios for the other heating systems shown are all

TABLE IV.11

Estimated Thermal Characteristics of Alternative HVAC Systems

	Observed dwelling (A)	Uninsulated dwelling (B)	90-75 standards (C)	Energy consumption ratios	
				A/B	C/A
Air conditioning					
capacity[a]	26.9	42.4	19.7		
energy consumption[c]	4618	6856	3924	.674	.850
Electrical resistance heat					
capacity[b]	45.2	82.6	26.4		
energy consumption[c]	67560	154000	47910	.439	.709
Gas forced air					
capacity[a]	49.5	86.9	30.6		
energy consumption[c]	109970	236700	81180	.465	.738
Oil forced air					
capacity[a]	49.5	86.9	30.6		
energy consumption[c]	124630	268360	92020	.464	.738
Heat pump					
capacity[a]	49.5	86.9	30.6		
energy consumption[c]	39348	86290	29410	.456	.747

[a] Capacity for forced air central system in 10^6 Btu/hr.

[b] Capacity for noncentral baseboard system in 10^6 Btu/hr.

[c] Annual energy consumption in 10^3 Btu, including distribution losses.

slightly higher, the standard used in this analysis represents a *tight* standard in that it achieves maximum energy conservation across the alternative HVAC systems shown.

IV.5. POLICY RELEVANCE

As we stated earlier, the three alternative residential energy policy scenarios used in this study were selected in part because they provide a range of possible policy options, including both price and nonprice policies, and in part because they are representative of the kinds of programs given active consideration by Federal policy makers in recent years. In addition, these three scenarios provide a basis for comparing the two existing econometric-engineering microeconomic models of residential energy demand, REEPS and ORNL, both because each of these models was originally designed to handle such analyses and because the necessary input data are generally available on a consistent basis, either directly or by construction as outlined earlier in this chapter. Finally, the combination of the two models and the three policy scenarios provides an interesting and highly relevant matrix for analyzing a number of important modeling issues within the specific context of energy policy analysis.

The results of the comparative analyses to be presented in the remainder of this study, therefore, have a dual dimension: they provide a useful analysis both of model performance and of policy efficacy. Furthermore, such judgments can be made at several different levels of aggregation. That is, both models and policies can be compared at an aggregative level, e.g., using national level forecasts, or they can be compared along a variety of different disaggregate dimensions. Regional, income group, housing type, and fuel type are perhaps the more important disaggregate dimensions that are especially relevant for energy policy and model analysis. In general, however, both models are flexible enough to facilitate additional distributive analyses as well, although with varying accuracy. Such comparisons, especially in terms of the distributive impacts, are essential if better energy policies and improved energy models are to be forthcoming in the future.

CHAPTER **V**

Simulation Results from the REEPS Model

In this chapter we report the results obtained by using the REEPS model to simulate the three alternative policy scenarios—base case, deregulation, and standards—discussed in Chapter IV. The initialization of the REEPS model in terms of required input data for the policy scenario variables is discussed in the first section of this chapter. Following this introductory section, the next four sections analyze the simulation results in terms of national or aggregate results, income distribution results, end-use results, and regional results, respectively. These sections describe the various results obtained in considerable detail and allow us to compare results across the three policy scenarios in a variety of different dimensions. A parallel comparison is also available in terms of a similar presentation of the ORNL simulation results, presented in Chapter VI. A few concluding remarks are offered in the last section of this chapter.

The REEPS model, as outlined in detail in Chapter III, is a flexible model for forecasting residential energy demand in which household decisions pertaining to appliance ownership, energy efficiency, and energy usage are related to such exogenous variables as household characteristics, weather conditions, and energy prices within an economically consistent framework. The basic analysis takes place at the level of an individual household, using a representative sample of households created in the first step of the analysis. The energy choice models, which were estimated econometrically from household survey data, are then applied to the representative household sample to forecast appliance choice and energy-use decisions over time. Thus, the model predicts behavior for each case in the household sample under the assumption of intertemporal optimization. Finally, aggregation to any desired level can be carried out explicitly by summing the individual household simulation results over the appropriate households, which are first weighted to accurately reflect the total population.

The REEPS model reports residential energy usage and appliance stocks by seven end-use categories: space heating, water heating, central air conditioning, room air conditioning, cooking, dishwashing, and other (or residual). Three fuel types are used: natural gas, electricity, and fuel oil/other. Simulation results are reported in annual terms for two-year simulation periods beginning in 1977 and ending in 1991 — the period of analysis used in this study for REEPS.

V.1. MODEL – SCENARIO
IMPLEMENTATION

This section describes the initialization of the REEPS model to implement each of the three alternative policy scenarios used in our analysis. The working version of the REEPS model that we received prior to beginning this study already contained a full set of input data. This initial data set included housing projections, weather information, household frequency tables and energy price projections, as described in Chapter III. The basic strategy used in this study was to modify only those parameters and variables which were necessary to run the three scenarios and to ensure intermodel consistency, i.e., with the ORNL model. This policy was derived from the basic focus of our study, which was to evaluate the models in their existing form as received from their proprietors.

The REEPS base case scenario was implemented by adjusting the original REEPS baseline prices to match the EIA fuel price projections assumed for the base case scenario (see Chapter IV, Table IV.7). This was necessary since the original REEPS fuel price data contained information on price variations across either regions or states which the EIA projections did not

include. To use this interregional price variation information, the original
REEPS price projections were adjusted so that the weighted average of the
individual REEPS prices matched the more aggregate EIA price projections. Specifically, we calculated a factor α_t for each time period t such that

$$(1) \qquad \overline{P}_t = \alpha_t \sum_i w_i P_{it},$$

where $\overline{P}_t$ is the EIA price projection for period t, P_{it} the original REEPS price
for region i for period t, and w_i the consumption-based weight (proportion)
of fuel in 1977 for region i. The α_t factor so computed was then used to
adjust the original REEPS price projections, the P_{it}'s, using the formula

$$(2) \qquad P_{it}^* = \alpha_t P_{it}$$

yielding a final set of REEPS price projections, the P_{it}^*'s. This adjustment
process was used for each of three residential fuels: natural gas, oil, and
electricity. The result was a set of disaggregated fuel price projections which
were consistent with the EIA aggregate projections but which still preserved
the regional price variation available in the original REEPS model. The
preservation of this variation to the extent possible was important since one
of our goals was to analyze the distributional impacts of alternative energy
prices and policies with respect to both location and income.

The remainder of the original REEPS input data were left unchanged,
including behavioral and technological parameter values, initial-year variables other than fuel price, and various nonprice exogenous variable projections. The same set of values for these variables at the aggregate level was
also used in the ORNL model simulations to preserve intermodel comparability. In addition, the REEPS input data were used to create many of the
ORNL model inputs required to run the ORNL model at the income group
level, since this type of disaggregate data was not generally available from
other sources. In particular, information concerning the income distribution of energy-using appliances, energy usage, and housing stocks was
needed to carry out distributional analyses with the ORNL model.

The implementation of the accelerated natural gas deregulation scenario
in REEPS only required changing the base case natural gas price projections
for the years 1981–1984, since the base case scenario already assumed
complete decontrol beginning in 1985. This scenario was implemented in
REEPS by using an adjustment process similar to the one described above
for the natural gas price projections for the period 1981–1984. Minor
modification of this adjustment process was necessary to accommodate the
fact that the original REEPS price data for natural gas occurred at the
division, rather than the state, level.

As outlined in Chapter IV, the mandatory thermal efficiency standards scenario assumed that all post-1981 new housing complied with the existing 90–75 ASHRAE voluntary building standards. The following discussion outlines the procedures used to implement the ASHRAE standards in the REEPS model.

The energy efficiency of a heating system in REEPS is described by a single number which combines the thermal integrity of the building shell and the operating efficiency of the equipment. Similarly, cooling system efficiency in REEPS is a combination of equipment and shell efficiency. Thus, implementation of the standards scenario in REEPS requires setting lower bounds on the heating and cooling efficiencies permitted by the model. The resulting simulation impacts of the ASHRAE building standards are indistinguishable from equivalent standards for heating and cooling system operating efficiencies.

REEPS measures heating and cooling system efficiencies *relative* to average efficiencies of existing systems in the base year; i.e., the efficiency variables average to one for existing base-year housing. In the REEPS base case scenario, these variables are permitted to range between 0.5 and 2.0 in new construction, with the bounds reflecting technological limits. For the standards scenario, new larger lower bounds were established in each state, for both heating and cooling, so as to match the average energy-use improvements expected from the standards described in Chapter IV. Since the standards were defined and analyzed at the census region level and must be applied in REEPS at the household level, additional calculations are required to ensure consistent standards scenario specifications in REEPS and ORNL. We next describe these calculations.

Let x denote household heating efficiency in the absence of standards, and let $F(x)$ denote its cumulative distribution function in a specified population, with mean μ. Now suppose standards are imposed in the form of a lower bound m on efficiency. Households previously above this bound are unaffected, while those previously below the bound now increase their efficiency to m. Average efficiency with standards then satisfies

$$(3) \qquad x^*(m) = mF(m) + \int_m^\infty xF'(x)\,dx.$$

Integrating by parts, this formula becomes

$$(4) \qquad x^*(m) = m + \int_m^\infty [1 - F(x)]\,dx.$$

Let θ be the ratio of average heating energy consumption under the standards to average consumption without the standards; then θ is approximately equal to the ratio $\mu/x^*(m)$.[1] Hence, m satisfies

(5) $$\mu/\theta = m + \int_m^\infty [1 - F(x)]\,dx.$$

We assume that the distribution function F can be approximated in the relevant range by a logistic function,

(6) $$F(x) = 1/(1 + e^{-b(x-\mu)}),$$

which has mean μ and standard deviation $\pi/\sqrt{3}b$. The parameters μ and b were estimated using REEPS base case simulation results for 1981. Substituted in (5), this distribution yielded the condition

(7) $$\mu/\theta = m - (1/b)\log(1 + e^{-b(m-\mu)}).$$

Using data from the NIECS for households in a census region, the ratio of heating energy consumption with standards to that without, measured as described in Chapter IV, was regressed on a constant and the number of heating and cooling degree days. The fitted equation was scaled to be representative of post-1970 dwellings, and was then used to estimate a value of θ in each state. Equation (7) was then solved numerically to yield a lower bound on heating efficiency for each state. The entire calculation was repeated for cooling efficiency. These values were applied only to new housing decisions since the mandated standards policy scenario was assumed to apply only to new housing.

V.2. NATIONAL IMPLICATIONS

The results of the three REEPS simulations, one for each of the three alternative policy scenarios, at the national or aggregate level are presented and analyzed in this section. Parallel results for income group, end use, and regional levels of disaggregation are presented in the following three sections. It should be pointed out that all four sets of these results are based on various aggregations of the three basic REEPS simulations since the detail specified within the representative sample of households used by REEPS permits the basic simulation results to be consistently aggregated in a variety of dimensions, depending upon the specific issues to be analyzed.

TABLE V.1

Total Energy Consumption[a]

Year	Natural gas			Fuel oil			Electricity			Total consumption		
	B[b]	D[c]	S[d]	B	D	S	B	D	S	B	D	S
1979	5.88	5.88	5.88	1.88	1.88	1.88	2.30	2.30	2.30	10.06	10.06	10.06
1981	5.84	5.46	5.74	1.84	1.84	1.82	2.35	2.35	2.34	10.03	9.65	9.90
1983	5.77	5.52	5.61	1.71	1.71	1.71	2.37	2.38	2.36	9.85	9.61	9.68
1985	5.74	5.65	5.57	1.60	1.60	1.58	2.42	2.43	2.40	9.76	9.68	9.55
1987	5.84	5.78	5.62	1.54	1.54	1.52	2.56	2.56	2.54	9.94	9.88	9.68
1989	5.94	5.89	5.69	1.48	1.50	1.48	2.69	2.68	2.66	10.11	10.07	9.83
1991	5.98	5.92	5.72	1.46	1.46	1.44	2.82	2.83	2.80	10.26	10.21	9.96

[a] Quads = 10^{15} Btu. Source, REEPS model.
[b] B = base case scenario.
[c] D = deregulation scenario.
[d] S = standards scenario.

A. Base Case Scenario: National

Tables V.1 – V.2 show the basic national level results of the REEPS simulation model for the three alternative policies used in this study.   The base case results are in the columns labeled B, while the columns marked D and S contain the deregulation and standards results, respectively.   The base case results are interesting both for the general trends of energy use they exhibit and for establishing a basis of comparison for the other two policy analyses.

TABLE V.2

Total Energy Expenditure[a]

Year	Base case	Deregulation	Standards
1979	45.2	45.2	45.2
1981	51.0	54.8	50.6
1983	56.7	58.6	56.0
1985	63.8	63.6	62.9
1987	66.3	66.1	65.2
1989	68.7	68.6	67.5
1991	71.4	71.3	70.0

[a] Billions of 1975 dollars. Source, REEPS model.

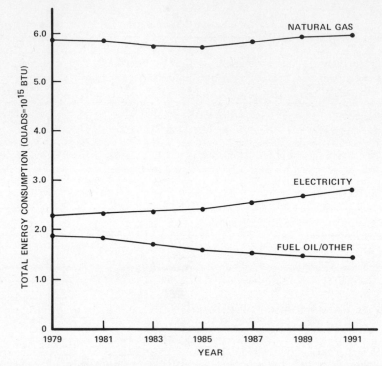

Fig. V.1   Annual residential energy consumption by fuel type — base case, 1979 – 1991.

From Table V.1 and Fig. V.1, we see that the base case simulation shows total energy use declining through 1985 and then rising until the end of the analysis period.   In 1985, the year of lowest energy use, total projected energy consumption is about 3% lower than in 1979; while 1991 energy consumption has increased by about 2% from the 1979 level.   The fuel-specific totals show that while fuel oil use is projected to decline steadily over this period and electricity consumption shows a steady increase, natural gas usage follows the total trend, falling slightly until 1985 after which it again increases out to 1991.   In general, consumption of natural gas remains relatively stable over the period shown, 1979 – 1991, with changes of only slightly over 4% in consumption between the highest and lowest years, while electricity and fuel oil show changes of 22.6 and 28.8%, respectively.

It is interesting to note that REEPS predicts substantial declines in per capita energy consumption over time.   As shown in Table V.3 and Fig. V.2, the energy usage of the average household falls from 128.0 million Btu/yr in 1979 to 106.8 million Btu/yr in 1991, a decline of over 16%.   This drop in

TABLE V.3

Base Case Average Annual Household Energy
Consumption and Expenditure 1979–1991[a]

Year	10^6 Btu/hh	1975 $/hh
1979	128.0	575.1
1981	122.6	623.5
1983	116.2	668.6
1985	111.3	727.5
1987	109.7	732.0
1989	108.1	734.9
1991	106.8	742.6

[a] Source, REEPS model.

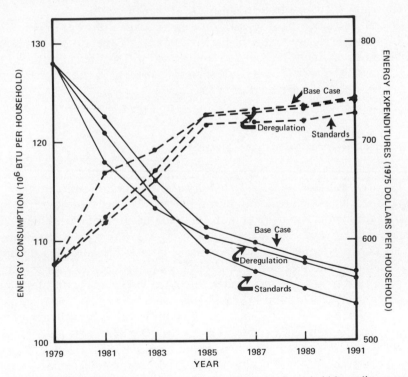

Fig. V.2 Annual energy consumption and expenditures per household by policy scenario, 1979–1991. Consumption (———), expenditure (– – –).

energy consumption is at least partly a response to real price increases for all fuels during the simulation period. The resulting long-run shift of appliance stocks and the retirement of old energy-intensive equipment is probably the major factor, though changing household composition and decreasing housing unit size may also play a role.

Energy expenditures, on the other hand, rise steadily over the period due to projected increases in the real prices of all three fuels and shifts towards the increased use of relatively expensive electricity. Although energy consumption declines slightly over the first 6 yr of the analysis, 1979–1985, expenditures increase substantially over the same period, with real expenditures being over 40% higher in 1985 than 1979 under the base case scenario. After 1985, expenditures on residential energy increase more slowly, with an increase of a little less than 12% over the period 1985–1991. The less rapid increase in expenditures after 1985 corresponds to a projected slowdown in price increases. As was described in Chapter IV, electricity prices are assumed to be stable in real terms after 1985, while natural gas prices rise only slightly; fuel oil prices are assumed to continue rising rapidly, however, encouraging further substitution towards other fuels.

Overall, fuel price increases raise total energy expenditure in 1991 to 158% of the 1979 levels, under the base case scenario. Expenditures per household correspondingly increase at a smaller but still significant rate over this period, with the typical household spending about 29% more on energy in real terms in 1991 compared to 1979.

B. Deregulation Scenario: National

The columns labeled D in Table V.1 show the REEPS simulation results for the second policy scenario, deregulation. Compared to the base case results, residential energy consumption under natural gas deregulation falls more rapidly out to 1983 and then begins to rise until by 1991 total energy consumption is almost identical in both scenarios. The effect of accelerated deregulation is almost entirely in natural gas consumption, with only a few minor changes in the consumption of other fuels. Gas consumption is approximately 5% lower in 1981 and 1983 under deregulation as compared to the base case. After 1985, natural gas consumption is still slightly lower under deregulation, due to changes in the mix and efficiencies of appliances induced by the higher natural gas prices between 1981 and 1985. After 1985, however, the consumption of natural gas in the deregulation scenario converges slowly back to base case consumption levels, reflecting the identical prices assumed under both scenarios after 1985.

Energy expenditures show results consistent with the induced changes in consumption levels, as seen in Table V.2. During 1981 and 1983, total energy expenditures increase by 7.5 and 3.4%, respectively, relative to the base case, reflecting significantly higher natural gas prices in those years. After 1985, however, expenditures are slightly lower due to reduced consumption of natural gas from the more efficient mix of appliances induced by the higher prices during the 1981–1985 period. Overall, the simulation results indicate that early deregulation would result in household energy bills that are higher by $3.8 billion in 1981 but would reduce energy expenditures by approximately $0.2 billion/yr by 1985 due to increased conservation and more efficient appliances.

Estimates for average annual household energy consumption and expenditures under the natural gas deregulation scenario are shown in Table V.4 and Fig. V.2 and indicate similar patterns relative to the base case results. Thus, annual energy consumption per household falls sharply between 1979 and 1985, while expenditures per household increase strongly due to the higher prices for natural gas. After 1985, average annual household energy consumption continues to decline, although at a reduced rate, until in 1991 the figure is about 17% lower than the 1979 consumption level. Compared to the base case result for 1991, accelerated natural gas deregulation results in a further reduction in annual energy consumption per household of about 0.6 million Btu by 1991. Annual household expenditures on energy are also lower under the deregulation scenario starting in 1985, resulting in a savings of $2.30 in 1985 and about $0.70 in 1991 per household.

TABLE V.4

Average Annual Household Energy Consumption
and Expenditure—Deregulation and Standards
Scenarios 1979–1991[a]

	Deregulation		Standards	
Year	10^6 Btu/hh	1975 $/hh	10^6 Btu/hh	1975 $/hh
1979	128.0	575.1	128.0	575.1
1981	118.0	669.9	121.0	618.6
1983	113.3	691.0	114.2	660.4
1985	110.4	725.2	108.9	717.2
1987	109.1	729.6	106.8	719.6
1989	107.7	733.7	105.1	721.9
1991	106.2	741.9	103.6	728.4

[a] Source, REEPS model.

C. Standards Scenario: National

Tables V.1, V.2, and V.4 and Fig. V.2 also show the simulation results for the mandatory thermal efficiency standards scenario, which imposes thermal efficiency standards on new housing. These results indicate that energy consumption under this scenario can be expected to follow the same basic patterns as under the base case scenario, but with a reduced level of consumption in every year of from 1 – 3%. In addition, as we would expect, the differential between energy consumption under the two scenarios grows over time as the share of the total housing stock affected by the efficiency standards steadily increases. By 1991, this reduction in total consumption brought about by the standards amounts to 0.3 quads, for a total savings in energy expenditures of approximately $1.4 billion.

Since the mandatory standards affect only the thermal efficiency of new housing, they tend to exert their primary impact through reduced energy usage for space heating and air conditioning. This is revealed in Table V.1 in terms of sizable reductions in the demand for natural gas, amounting to 0.26 quads by 1991 relative to the base case, and in smaller reductions in electricity consumption. Although some of these differentials look rather small in the aggregate, further analysis of the end-use simulation results (in a later section in this chapter) reveals rather sizable impacts on space heating demands for both of these fuels.

From Tables V.2 and V.4 we see that imposing the mandatory standards results in large reductions in energy expenditures. This is not surprising since the standards essentially induce nonvoluntary investment in capital, e.g., insulation, to increase energy efficiency. The direct expenditure savings from the standards grows over time and by 1991 amounts to an annual $1.4 billion reduction in energy expenditures.

This reduction in residential energy expenditures is not without cost, however. As shown in Table V.5, the imposition of mandatory standards requires substantial additional investment in heating system and thermal shell improvements. The additional capital requirement is estimated by the REEPS simulation to be well over $1 billion/yr nationwide in every forecast year from 1981 – 1991. On a housing unit basis, the standards policy results in increases in the capital requirements for space heating in new housing of over $1000/unit. However, this additional investment in the heating system effectively *buys* a stream of reduced energy bills over the lifetime of the heating system.

Net present value calculations for the additional energy-saving investments induced by the standards are presented in Table V.6. The net present value (NPV) of the standards varies substantially depending on the assump-

TABLE V.5
Effect of Mandatory Standards Policy[a]

Year	Annual additional capital investment	Annual decreased energy expenditure
1981	1.63	0.46
1983	1.45	0.67
1985	1.31	0.95
1987	1.32	1.26
1989	1.33	1.44
1991	1.22	1.37

[a] Billions of 1975 dollars. Source, REEPS model.

tions used in the calculations, as we might imagine. The calculations presented here were carried out assuming the following:

(i) There are no future additional investments made after 1991 and
(ii) the benefits received in 1991 continue at the same level for N years.

This last assumption implies that energy prices are flat after 1991 and that no retirement of the new housing stock affected by the standards occurs prior to N years after 1991, at which point all benefits due to the standards scenario

TABLE V.6
Net Present Value Calculations—
Mandatory Standards[a]

R^b (%)	N^c				
	5	10	15	20	25
0	2.68	9.53	16.38	23.23	30.08
1	1.75	7.42	12.82	17.95	22.84
2	0.96	5.66	9.92	13.78	17.27
5	−0.81	1.90	4.03	5.70	7.01
10	−2.44	−1.30	−0.61	−0.17	0.10

[a] Billions of 1975 dollars as of 1981. Source, REEPS model.
[b] R is the real interest rate.
[c] N is the number of years that the benefit stream continues past 1991.

are truncated. In Table V.6, NPV calculations are provided for a range of real interest rates (R), from $0-10\%$ and various values of N from $5-25$ yr. As seen in the table, the value of the standards increases monotonically with N and decreases monotonically with R. Reasonable choices for these parameters might be $R = 5$ and $N = 20$, implying that heating systems have an average life of about 20 yr and household cash outlays are discounted at a 5% real interest rate. At these values, the standards have a positive value of $5.70 billion nationwide. It is interesting to note that the standards have positive NPV even if the real interest rate is raised over 5%, assuming N is at least 10 yr. Thus, the standards appear to induce favorable gains in net benefits for most plausible values of the parameters.

It should be noted here that the estimate of an additional required investment of over $1000/new housing unit is substantially higher than a similar estimate from the thermal model of McFadden and Dubin (1982). Their estimate of $487/new housing unit in 1981 is less than half that of the REEPS estimate presented above. This discrepancy can be traced largely to differing assumptions about the downsizing of heating system capacity used in the two calculations. In McFadden and Dubin, the imposition of the standards results in smaller systems, as well as increased efficiency, while no such reduction in HVAC capacity is allowed by the REEPS model. This effect would cause REEPS to overestimate the capital costs associated with the standards, so that the estimates presented in Table V.6 may well underestimate the true NPV of mandatory thermal efficiency standards for new housing.

In summary, the REEPS simulation results at a national level of aggregation appear to be both reasonable and useful. The base case results indicate total residential energy consumption first falling and then rising over time, the result largely of partially offsetting trends in electricity and fuel oil usage reflecting changes in relative fuel prices and household incomes. However, the result of substantially higher real prices for residential energy by 1991 is an increase in total energy expenditures of over 50% compared to 1979. For the average household, annual energy consumption falls steadily between 1979 and 1991 while annual expenditures on energy increase significantly under the base case scenario. In contrast, the accelerated natural gas deregulation scenario indicates slightly lower levels of total energy consumption, especially for the 1981-1985 period, largely as a result of reduced natural gas usage. Total expenditures on energy are sharply higher during the 1981-1985 period, and are more or less comparable to the base case results for the remaining period. The imposition of mandatory thermal efficiency standards on new housing, on the other hand, produces rather different patterns in both energy consumption and expenditures. The standards scenario results in reduced energy consumption relative to the base case starting in

1981 and a consumption differential which increases steadily over time. Total energy expenditures reveal a similar pattern, although these reduced annual outlays for energy must be offset against the higher investment expenditures required initially to meet the mandatory standards. However, when the two expenditure streams are appropriately discounted, the resulting NPV estimates indicate substantial potential savings amounting to at least $5 billion, and perhaps $10 billion or higher.

V.3. INCOME DISTRIBUTION IMPLICATIONS

The REEPS simulation results detailing the economic impacts of the three alternative energy policy scenarios by income group are summarized in

TABLE V.7

Number of Households by Income Class[a]

Year	Income class[b]						Total
	1	2	3	4	5	6	
(a) Number of households[c]							
1979	16.1	15.9	15.5	18.7	10.1	2.4	78.6
1981	15.8	16.5	16.1	19.2	11.0	3.1	81.8
1983	16.1	17.2	16.8	19.8	11.5	3.4	84.8
1985	15.9	17.7	17.4	20.3	12.3	4.1	87.7
1987	15.3	18.2	18.0	20.8	13.3	5.0	90.6
1989	14.9	18.6	18.6	21.3	14.1	6.0	93.5
1991	14.5	18.9	19.1	21.7	14.9	6.9	96.1
(b) Proportion of households							
1979	.200	.201	.197	.238	.129	.031	1.00
1981	.190	.202	.197	.235	.135	.038	1.00
1983	.190	.203	.197	.234	.136	.040	1.00
1985	.181	.202	.198	.232	.140	.047	1.00
1987	.169	.201	.198	.230	.147	.055	1.00
1989	.159	.199	.199	.228	.151	.064	1.00
1991	.151	.197	.199	.226	.155	.072	1.00

[a] From REEPS model, 1977 base year.

[b] Income classes are defined by real family income in thousands of 1975 dollars, where 1 = 0–5000, 2 = 5000–10,000, 3 = 10,000–15,000, 4 = 15,000–25,000, 5 = 25,000–45,000, and 6 = over 45,000.

[c] Millions of units.

TABLE V.8

New Occupied Dwelling Units by Income Class[a]

Year	1	2	3	4	5	6	Total
Base[b]	15.7	15.4	14.8	17.6	9.3	2.3	75.1
1979–1980	0.40	0.45	0.69	1.04	0.72	0.17	3.47
1981–1982	0.35	0.41	0.63	0.94	0.69	0.19	3.20
1983–1984	0.33	0.41	0.62	0.91	0.69	0.20	3.16
1985–1986	0.31	0.40	0.62	0.89	0.71	0.23	3.16
1987–1988	0.28	0.39	0.60	0.87	0.74	0.28	3.15
1989–1990	0.27	0.39	0.87	0.76	0.76	0.32	3.20
1991–1992	0.23	0.36	0.56	0.79	0.72	0.33	3.00

[a] From REEPS model, 1977 base year. Millions of units.
[b] Total existing dwellings, 1977.

Tables V.9–V.11. These numbers are the result of aggregating households across the basic simulation results by income group, where the six income groups used were previously discussed in Chapter IV. Using these six income groups — 0–5000, 5000–10,000, 10,000–15,000, 15,000–25,000, 25,000–45,000, and over $45,000 — with household income measured in terms of 1975 dollars, the distribution of household income used in this analysis is shown in V.7. As can be seen in this table, real income is assumed to grow over the simulation period shown, with the relative proportions of households in the lower income groups declining while higher income groups show a corresponding increase. There is also a steady increase in the absolute number of households, with 22% more households assumed in 1991 than in 1979.

The numbers of new dwelling units in each 2-yr period, measured in millions of units, are shown in Table V.8. These numbers also reflect the general increase in real household income assumed in this analysis for all income groups. In addition, this table indicates that the proportion of new dwellings increases with income as might be expected, and that the total number of new dwellings per period tends to decline over the period of the analysis 1979–1991.

A. Base Case Scenario: Income Distribution

The base case simulation results, by income group and fuel type, are presented in Tables V.9–V.11. Table V.9 shows only one set of figures, i.e., base case, since the other two policy scenarios have no effect until 1981,

TABLE V.9

Average Annual Household Energy Consumption and Expenditures
by Income Class 1979 — Base Case[a]

Income class	Energy consumption per household[b]				Energy expenditures per household[c]			
	Gas	Oil	Electricity	Total	Gas	Oil	Electricity	Total
1	49.21	19.97	12.82	82.00	115.3	70.3	134.3	319.8
2	60.34	21.91	20.77	103.02	143.8	67.4	218.1	429.3
3	69.68	23.25	26.59	119.52	168.3	79.3	278.6	526.1
4	81.24	25.62	35.33	142.19	197.3	85.1	378.7	661.1
5	113.17	24.00	52.05	189.22	227.2	104.3	571.0	952.5
6	158.32	29.07	69.28	256.67	396.7	104.4	808.7	1309.7
Total	74.66	23.24	29.25	127.15	180.4	80.4	314.3	575.1

[a] Source, REEPS model.
[b] 10^6 Btu/hh.
[c] 1975 $/hh.

while Tables V.10 and V.11 present results for each of the three alternative policies.

Looking first at average annual energy consumption per household for 1979, in Table V.9, it is evident that consumption increases strongly with increases in family income. Comparing income groups 1 and 6, energy consumption per household increases by a factor of 4.1 while mean group income increases more than tenfold. On the other hand, average annual energy expenditures per household increases by a factor of 3.1 from the lowest to the highest income group, implying that the proportion of household income devoted to energy declines with income. Thus, energy consumption per household increases across the income groups shown while the energy budget share declines.

Looking at the fuel specific expenditures in Table V.9, we see that the mix of household fuels also changes with income, as higher income households use substantially more electricity relative to natural gas and fuel oil than do lower income households. Between the lowest and highest income groups, natural gas usage increases by over 200%, fuel oil usage by less than 50%, and electricity by over 500%. It is not surprising that electricity consumption is more income elastic than other fuels, since gas and oil are primarily used for basic needs such as heat and hot water while electricity is used for a larger variety of less *essential* needs.

The time trends for residential energy consumption and expenditures are apparent by comparing Tables V.9–V.11 — 1979, 1983, and 1991, respectively — for the base case. As these tables show, for every income class, energy consumption per household falls between both 1979–1983 and

TABLE V.10

Energy Consumption and Expenditure by Income Class 1983[a]

Income class	Case	Energy consumption per household[b]					Energy expenditures per household[c]				
		Gas	Oil	Elec.	Total	Pct. Dev.	Gas	Oil	Elec.	Total	Pct. Dev.
1	B	45.07	17.90	11.26	74.23		144.39	88.96	135.12	368.47	
	D	43.20	17.86	11.24	72.36	−2.5	158.71	88.89	135.07	382.67	+3.9
	S	43.26	17.83	11.22	72.22	−2.7	138.66	88.72	133.82	361.21	−1.5
2	B	53.06	16.29	18.90	88.25		172.87	82.10	228.91	483.88	
	D	50.62	16.33	18.90	85.85	−2.7	179.66	82.40	228.43	490.49	+1.4
	S	51.62	16.25	18.69	86.56	−1.9	168.48	82.07	226.23	476.78	−1.5
3	B	60.78	20.12	24.75	105.56		200.40	99.46	297.76	597.62	
	D	57.63	20.17	24.80	102.60	−2.8	216.93	100.29	298.12	615.34	+3.0
	S	59.04	20.01	24.55	103.60	−1.9	195.04	99.43	295.55	590.02	−1.3
4	B	72.42	22.06	32.95	127.43		238.25	109.32	405.58	753.15	
	D	69.00	22.14	33.11	124.42	−2.4	259.24	109.97	407.57	777.28	+3.2
	S	70.72	21.96	32.78	125.16	−1.8	232.72	109.43	403.86	746.01	−1.0
5	B	107.36	24.08	49.34	180.78		357.35	120.03	618.14	1095.52	
	D	103.29	24.29	49.32	176.90	−2.1	343.50	131.43	618.15	1133.14	+3.4
	S	105.08	23.86	49.18	178.12	−1.5	350.45	119.15	616.96	1085.89	−0.9
6	B	129.62	26.55	68.27	224.44		433.96	131.18	873.49	1438.63	
	D	126.69	26.59	68.74	222.02	−1.1	487.41	131.67	880.31	1499.39	+4.1
	S	127.44	26.43	68.11	221.98	−1.1	427.25	130.84	871.76	1429.65	−0.6
Total	B	68.01	20.17	28.04	116.19		223.63	100.31	344.57	668.51	
	D	65.09	20.23	28.05	113.37	−2.4	244.94	100.82	345.24	691.00	+3.4
	S	66.23	20.06	27.81	114.10	−1.8	218.10	100.00	342.58	660.68	−1.2

[a] Source, REEPS model.
[b] 10^6 Btu/hh.
[c] 1975 $/hh.

TABLE V.11

Energy Consumption and Expenditure by Income Class 1991[a]

Income class	Case	Energy consumption per household[b]					Energy expenditures per household[c]				
		Gas	Oil	Elec.	Total	Pct. Dev.	Gas	Oil	Elec.	Total	Pct. Dev.
1	B	38.20	13.38	9.93	61.64		152.61	92.73	128.02	373.36	
	D	37.86	13.36	9.93	61.29	−0.6	151.16	92.78	127.95	371.89	−0.4
	S	35.61	13.26	9.71	58.71	−4.8	142.50	91.98	124.42	359.90	−3.0
2	B	43.35	13.26	17.78	74.33		172.64	93.02	229.30	494.96	
	D	42.89	13.31	17.78	73.98	−0.5	170.74	93.39	229.30	493.23	−0.1
	S	40.95	13.18	17.47	71.52	−3.8	163.43	92.68	225.74	481.85	−2.7
3	B	54.49	14.53	22.98	92.15		215.58	100.83	296.42	612.83	
	D	54.16	14.20	23.22	91.59	−0.6	214.31	98.73	299.45	612.49	−0.1
	S	51.84	14.52	22.60	88.97	−3.5	205.62	100.98	292.43	599.03	−2.3
4	B	62.48	16.30	31.87	110.46		249.44	112.29	420.20	781.93	
	D	61.79	16.39	31.86	109.86	−0.5	246.82	113.04	420.16	780.02	−0.2
	S	59.62	16.19	31.56	107.18	−3.0	238.45	111.74	416.79	766.98	−1.9
5	B	94.01	18.14	49.07	160.98		380.75	126.35	657.45	1164.55	
	D	92.90	18.63	49.19	160.53	−0.3	375.85	129.70	658.88	1164.43	0
	S	90.86	18.00	48.70	157.53	−2.3	368.63	125.56	653.49	1147.78	−1.4
6	B	116.67	16.42	70.46	202.27		458.63	114.85	941.09	1514.57	
	D	116.45	16.51	70.60	202.27	0	458.39	116.15	942.40	1516.94	+0.2
	S	114.29	16.40	70.21	199.67	−1.3	449.43	115.24	938.52	1503.19	−0.8
Total	B	62.18	15.20	29.43	106.77		248.52	105.64	388.55	742.71	
	D	61.64	15.25	29.50	106.44	−0.4	246.32	106.09	389.58	741.99	−0.1
	S	59.48	15.04	29.11	103.73	−2.9	238.19	105.25	385.10	728.54	−1.9

[a] Source, REEPS model.
[b] 10^6 Btu/hh.
[c] 1975 $/hh.

153

1983–1991. However, expenditures show a consistent increase for all income groups as rising prices more than offset decreased consumption. This
trend of rising energy expenditures can also be seen in the energy budget
shares shown in Table V.15.

The amount of electricity used, relative to other household fuels, also
increases for all households over the period 1979–1991 under the base case.
This increase is more dramatic, though, for higher income households; in the
highest income group, 27% of the energy used in 1979 is electricity while in
1991 the corresponding figure is 35%. For the lowest income group, the
corresponding increase is from 15.6 to 16.1%, essentially no change. Thus,
electricity consumption reveals a strong income-sensitive trend across time
as well.

In contrast, per household fuel oil usage shows a decline for all income
classes. Households in the lowest income group used fuel oil for 24% of their
energy needs in 1979 and for only 22% in 1991. By contrast, oil consumption is relatively lower for the highest income households in all periods, but
still falls from 11% in 1979 to only 8% in 1991.

The change across income groups in the relative mix of natural gas in
household energy consumption does not have as consistent a pattern as
either fuel oil or electricity, although in general, low income households
show increasing relative natural gas usage while higher income groups show
slight declines across time. Natural gas consistently accounts for 60% of
household fuel usage, varying only from 62% of fuel used (lowest income
group in 1991) to 57% of fuel used (income group 4 in 1991). The share of
natural gas thus appears to be less responsive to income changes and to be
more stable over time.

Another way of analyzing the distributive impacts of energy policy across
income groups is to compute the cumulative proportions of both households
and residential energy consumption from the lowest to the highest income
group. An equiproportional or income-neutral impact would display the
same cumulative percentages between the two variables across income
groups, while an income-biased impact would show the cumulative percentage from the number of households rising faster than that for energy consumption, starting from the lowest income group. Such a bias would imply
that lower income households use less than a proportional share of residential energy, while higher income households consume more than their proportional share. Using the data in Tables V.9–V.11, these calculations have
been carried out and are shown in Tables V.12–V.14 for the years 1979,
1983, and 1991, respectively.

Tables V.12–V.14 show both the amount and cumulative percentage
from the lowest to the highest income groups for three variables: number of
households, energy consumption, and energy expenditures. The figures for

TABLE V.12

Residential Energy Demand — Base Case 1979 — Cumulative Proportions[a]

Income class	Households		Energy consumption		Energy expenditures		Energy budget share[e]
	Number[b]	Cum. %	Quads[c]	Cum. %	10^9 \$[d]	Cum. %	
1	16.1	20.5	1.32 (82.0)	13.1	5.15 (319.8)	11.4	9.1
2	15.9	40.7	1.65 (103.0)	29.6	6.83 (429.3)	26.5	5.4
3	15.5	60.4	1.86 (119.5)	48.1	8.15 (526.1)	44.5	4.1
4	18.7	84.2	2.68 (142.2)	74.7	12.33 (661.1)	71.8	3.5
5	10.1	97.0	1.92 (189.2)	93.8	9.62 (952.5)	93.1	2.7
6	2.4	100.0	0.62 (256.7)	100.0	3.14 (1309.7)	100.0	2.5
Total	78.6		10.06 (127.2)		45.22 (575.1)		3.8

[a] Source, REEPS model.
[b] Millions of households.
[c] Figures in parentheses are annual per household energy consumption, in 10^6 Btu/hh.
[d] Figures in parentheses are annual per household energy expenditures, in 1975 \$/hh.
[e] Energy expenditure as a percentage of before-tax family income, assuming mean income levels of \$3500, 8000, 13,000, 19,000, 36,000, and 51,000, respectively, for the six income groups.

number of households by income group are taken from Table V.7. Also shown are the estimated energy budget shares for each income group for each of the three years, where the energy budget share is defined as the proportion of household energy expenditure relative to total pretax household income. For the purposes of these calculations, we assumed mean pretax family income levels of \$3500, \$8000, \$13,000, \$19,000, \$36,000, and \$51,000 (1975 dollars) for the six income groups, respectively.

Looking first at the results for 1979, we see that the number of households, expressed in cumulative percentage terms, rises at a faster rate from the lowest to the highest income group than does energy consumption, which in turn rises slightly faster than energy expenditures. This implies that lower income households use more than their proportional share of residential energy. However, the lower income groups appear to pay a slightly lower average energy price, due primarily to the relatively larger use of cheaper fuel

TABLE V.13

Residential Energy Demand—Cumulative Proportions 1983[a]

Income class	Case	Households		Energy consumption		Energy expenditures		Energy budget share[e]
		Number[b]	Cum. %	Quads[c]	Cum. %	10^9 \$[d]	Cum. %	
1	B			1.20	12.2	5.93	10.5	10.6
	D	16.1	20.0	1.16	12.1	6.16	10.5	10.9
	S			1.16	12.0	5.82	10.4	10.3
2	B			1.52	27.6	8.32	25.1	6.1
	D	17.2	39.3	1.48	27.5	8.44	24.9	6.1
	S			1.49	27.4	8.20	25.0	6.0
3	B			1.77	45.6	10.04	42.8	4.6
	D	16.8	50.1	1.72	45.4	10.34	42.6	4.7
	S			1.74	45.4	9.91	42.7	4.5
4	B			2.52	71.2	14.91	69.1	4.0
	D	19.8	82.4	2.47	71.1	15.49	69.0	4.1
	S			2.49	71.1	14.77	69.1	3.9
5	B			2.08	92.3	12.60	91.4	3.0
	D	11.5	96.0	2.03	92.2	13.03	91.3	3.1
	S			2.05	92.3	12.48	91.3	3.0
6	B			0.76	100.0	4.89	100.0	2.8
	D	3.4	100.0	0.75	100.0	5.10	100.0	2.9
	S			0.75	100.0	4.86	100.0	2.8
Total	B			9.85		56.69		
	D	84.8		9.61		58.56		
	S			9.68		56.04		

[a] Source, REEPS model. See notes for Table V.12.

by these groups. Over time, as can be seen by comparing Table V.12 to Tables V.13 and V.14, this distributive impact across income groups seems to change only slightly. It is difficult to be very precise here since all three sets of cumulative percentage figures vary with time, indicating in part a general rise in real incomes across income groups and hence a decline in the relative size of the lower income groups. Surprisingly enough, the alternative policy scenarios appear to have little impact on these relationships, as can be seen in tables V.13 and V.14.

From the energy budget share estimates, which are summarized in Table V.15, it is clear that low income households spend a significantly larger proportion of their budget on energy compared to higher income households. In all three years, the energy budget share for the lowest income group, 1, is more than 3.5 times higher than that for the highest income

TABLE V.14

Residential Energy Demand—Cumulative Proportions 1991[a]

Income class	Case	Households Number[b]	Households Cum. %	Energy consumption Quads[c]	Energy consumption Cum. %	Energy expenditures 10^9 \$[d]	Energy expenditures Cum. %	Energy budget share[e]
1	B			0.89	8.7	5.41	7.6	10.7
	D	14.5	15.1	0.89	8.7	5.39	7.6	10.6
	S			0.85	8.5	5.22	7.5	10.3
2	B			1.40	22.3	9.35	20.7	6.2
	D	18.9	34.8	1.40	22.4	9.32	20.6	6.2
	S			1.35	22.1	9.11	20.5	6.0
3	B			1.76	39.5	11.71	37.1	4.7
	D	19.1	54.7	1.75	39.6	11.70	37.1	4.7
	S			1.70	39.2	11.46	36.8	4.6
4	B			2.41	63.0	17.03	61.0	4.1
	D	21.7	77.3	2.38	62.9	16.98	60.9	4.1
	S			2.34	62.7	16.70	60.7	4.0
5	B			2.40	86.4	17.41	85.4	3.2
	D	14.9	92.8	2.39	86.3	17.39	85.3	3.2
	S			2.34	86.1	17.17	85.2	3.2
6	B			1.40	100.0	10.45	100.0	3.0
	D	6.9	100.0	1.40	100.0	10.47	100.0	3.0
	S			1.38	100.0	10.37	100.0	2.9
Total								
	B			10.26		71.36		
	D	96.1		10.21		71.25		
	S			9.96		70.03		

[a] Source, REEPS model. See notes for Table V.12.

group, 6. All income groups experience higher relative energy expenditures over time due to the general rise in real residential energy prices. However, poorer households show larger relative increases in their energy budget shares, especially between 1979 and 1983, because of their smaller income base.

The base case simulation results, thus, show several interesting trends in terms of the pattern of residential energy consumption across income groups. First, there is a moderate income elasticity for residential energy in general, with fuel oil showing little income elasticity and electricity demand being considerably more income elastic. As might be expected, lower income groups spend a significantly larger percentage of their budget on energy. For all income groups, energy consumption per household falls over

TABLE V.15
Estimated Residential Energy Budget Shares[a]

Income class	Policy scenario	%		
		1979	1983	1991
1	B		10.6	10.7
	D	9.1	10.9	10.6
	S		10.3	10.3
2	B		6.1	6.2
	D	5.4	6.1	6.2
	S		6.0	6.0
3	B		4.6	4.7
	D	4.1	4.7	4.7
	S		4.5	4.6
4	B		4.0	4.1
	D	3.5	4.1	4.1
	S		3.9	4.0
5	B		3.0	3.2
	D	2.7	3.1	3.2
	S		3.0	3.2
6	B		2.8	3.0
	D	2.5	2.9	3.0
	S		2.8	2.9

[a] Energy expenditures as a percentage of before-tax family income assuming mean income levels of $3500, 8000, 13,000, 19,000, 36,000, and 51,000 (1975 $), respectively, for the six income groups. Source, REEPS model.

time while real expenditures per household tend to rise. Electricity use as a percentage of total energy consumption grows steadily over time, while fuel oil use decreases sharply. These trends in fuel usage and fuel mix are generally in the same direction across all income groups, but are of different magnitudes with relative dependence on electricity being higher and growing faster for higher income groups while the energy share of oil is higher but falling faster for low income groups. Natural gas remains the most important fuel for all income groups, with low income groups having a slight increase in their reliance on gas while high income groups show a slight decrease over time. Due to the differing mix of energy used by high income groups, they pay more for their energy. Expensive electricity accounts for a higher share of their energy consumption so that the expenditures of higher income groups are higher relative to consumption than for lower income groups.

B. Deregulation Scenario: Income Distribution

The income distribution effects of the two alternative policy scenarios, deregulation and standards, are also shown in Tables V.10, V.11, and V.13–V.15. These tables show only the two years, 1983 and 1991, which reflect the year of maximum impact of natural gas deregulation, 1983, and the end of the analysis period for REEPS, 1991, when the mandated efficiency standards policy should have its maximum impact. Looking first at 1983, we see that both policies have the expected effect of reducing consumption for all income levels. Energy consumption in 1983 is reduced more by deregulation than by standards, and the lower income groups tend to conserve slightly more proportionally than higher income groups. Both the deregulation and the standards policies have almost their entire effect on natural gas consumption, with usage of other fuel showing only minor changes. Although total energy consumption per household is reduced by only 1.1–3.1%, natural gas consumption per household is reduced by as much as 5% for most income groups.

The effects of natural gas deregulation on residential energy expenditures are generally larger than those on energy consumption, but show no consistent pattern by income group. There is some indication that deregulation may cause higher than proportional increases in energy expenditures for higher income households, presumably due to the larger relative use of natural gas. However, predicted expenditure increases are relatively small for all income groups since the price differential assumed to follow from accelerated natural gas decontrol is not very large even in 1983.

By 1991 deregulation shows almost no impact since the assumed price paths under the base case and deregulation scenarios are identical after 1985. There is still a small effect on usage due to the increased appliance efficiency resulting from new appliances purchased between 1981 and 1985. The small residential fuel savings that do remain by 1991 are spread rather evenly across income groups, although the highest income group shows almost no induced conservation effect while lower income households indicate slightly stronger impacts.

Energy expenditures also show very minor impacts in 1991 from accelerated natural gas deregulation. Most income groups show very small decreases in total energy expenditures, relative to the base case scenario, although expenditures for the highest income group are actually higher in 1991. This increase in energy expenditure is caused by higher consumption of alternative fuels which in turn are related to changes in the mix of appliance stocks. Since in 1991, both electricity and fuel oil are assumed to have higher Btu prices compared to natural gas, this fuel switching from the higher natural gas prices in the 1981 – 1985 period results in higher expenditures on residential energy.

C. Standards Scenario: Income Distribution

These same tables also present results showing the effects of mandatory thermal efficiency standards across income groups. As noted previously, the standards scenario results in reduced energy consumption for all income groups, although the impacts are somewhat stronger (in proportional terms) for the lower income groups and generally in 1991, as compared to 1983. Most of these effects show up under natural gas consumption, with the usage of other fuels exhibiting rather small changes.

The standards policy results in savings in direct energy expenditures of about 1% or so in 1983. The largest relative impacts are on the lower income groups, presumably because these households spend a larger proportion of their energy budget on space heating needs. However, the total impacts of the standards are not very large in absolute magnitude so that, in general, there are no strong distributional effects. Even though lower income households on a relative basis save approximately twice as much as higher income households, the 1983 effects of the standards generally result in less than a 1.5% savings on average annual residential energy expenditures relative to the base case scenario.

Mandatory standards show larger impacts by 1991 than does accelerated natural gas deregulation. Although the impact on average household consumption is still less than 3%, lower income groups experience a larger reduction in energy use. One reason for this could be that lower income groups occupy housing that is more likely to be affected by the imposition of the standards. In addition, space heating fuel is a larger percentage of the energy budget for lower income groups. Electricity and fuel oil usage decrease slightly under the standards policy but the majority of the effect is still on natural gas consumption. This is due both to the extensive use of gas in space heating and to the tendency for electrically heated homes to be more heavily insulated even without mandatory standards.

Expenditures show smaller declines than consumption because natural gas is the lowest priced residential fuel. There are still strong income group effects on direct energy expenditures, however, since the lowest income group saves over 3% due to imposition of mandatory standards while the highest income group saves less than 1% on a relative basis. The mandatory standards policy thus creates larger relative benefits for low income groups, at least with respect to direct energy expenditure.

TABLE V.16

Income Group Effects of Mandatory Standards Policy[a]

	Income group						
	1	2	3	4	5	6	Total
1981							
Δ Capital (+)	7.88	10.73	18.75	26.02	36.32	34.96	19.87
Δ Expend. (−)	3.19	4.91	4.35	4.93	6.90	7.27	5.63
1983							
Δ Capital (+)	6.70	8.80	16.10	22.67	31.50	31.07	17.06
Δ Expend. (−)	7.26	7.10	7.60	7.14	9.63	8.98	7.83
1985							
Δ Capital (+)	5.70	9.82	13.33	19.05	28.54	24.08	14.86
Δ Expend. (−)	9.12	9.55	10.25	10.84	10.86	12.70	10.88
1987							
Δ Capital (+)	4.96	7.15	13.06	17.97	27.28	25.07	14.54
Δ Expend. (−)	11.36	11.96	12.72	13.11	12.69	11.79	12.37
1989							
Δ Capital (+)	5.46	7.27	12.27	18.28	25.54	22.83	14.24
Δ Expend. (−)	13.11	13.49	13.18	14.22	15.11	13.33	13.39
1991							
Δ Capital (+)	4.30	6.30	11.64	15.52	22.47	20.02	12.65
Δ Expend. (−)	13.46	13.11	13.80	14.95	16.77	11.36	14.25
NPV by income group[b]							
R = 2%	133.74	108.63	52.33	3.10	−66.68	−92.12	51.68
R = 5%	87.17	65.85	14.22	−32.13	−97.35	−108.73	12.71

[a] Source, REEPS model. 1975 $/hh/yr.

[b] 1975 $/hh in 1981 ($N = 10$).

The new housing-related capital investments required under the mandatory standards, in contrast, increase substantially with income. Table V.16 shows the annual energy expenditure reduction and capital investment increase per household for each group due to imposition of the mandatory standards. It can be seen here that energy costs change very little with income, but capital investment requirements increase by a factor of about 5 between the lowest and highest income groups. When this is translated into NPV terms, we see that the average household gains about $52 from the standards, assuming a real interest rate of 2%. Low income households value the standards at about double that, however, while high income households lose about $92 due to imposition of the standards.

These results are consistent with the existence of discount rates which vary inversely with income. Under these assumptions, low income households would forego investments which would be undertaken by higher income individuals. Thus, the standards require additional investment in heating efficiency which appear to be economically inefficient investments for all groups. The investments by lower income groups may be socially beneficial, however, if the social discount rate is lower than the private rate used by these individuals. Differential discount rates could be caused by the existence of a credit constraint for low income households. To the extent that low income households are credit constrained and would voluntarily make the necessary investments to meet the standards if provided with credit, the majority of the benefits of the standards could be captured by a voluntary loan program.

There is at least one reason, however, why REEPS may tend to exaggerate the income effect of the standards. The standards are only binding on new housing so that the necessary investment falls on the original owner of a new housing unit. Presumably this increased cost results in higher future housing values and hence higher prices for future buyers. If the actual new housing market is dominated by higher income groups who then resell to lower income groups in the future, REEPS may overstate the amount of the associated cost burden born by the higher income groups.

In general, these results appear to indicate that at least some investments required by the standards would seem to be economically justified, i.e., on a private basis. However, for the mandatory standards to have value, they must induce socially worthwhile investments which are not currently being undertaken. A significant question, then, is why these investments are not made without the standards. As discussed above, this could be due to capital constraints or differential discount rates for certain individuals, in which case the mandatory standards will cause them to make investments which these individuals either do not want or cannot make. In turn, this will cause some loss in individual utility unless low-cost loans are made available.

Another possible cause for the effects of the standards is some sort of market failure leading to less than optimal investments in energy efficiency. One potential source of market failure is the lack of adequate information available to consumers. Since consumers may not be able to evaluate the degree of energy efficiency before purchase, they may undervalue investments in energy efficiency, leading builders to offer less than optimal levels of housing-related energy efficiency.

In summary, the REEPS simulation results on the income distribution effects of alternative residential energy policies indicate the general presence of substantial income effects. Energy consumption per household increases with increased family income, although the magnitude of the associated income elasticity varies widely across fuel type. In general, electricity shows a very strong association with changes in income, while fuel oil usage reveals little income effect. Presumably, this reflects the fact that electricity is used for less *essential* and, hence, more income sensitive demands, such as air conditioning, cooking, and dishwashing. Over time, the results generally indicate reduced levels of energy consumption per household, but these reductions do not offset the assumed increases in real energy prices so that annual household energy expenditures tend to rise rather dramatically. The fuel mix trends indicate a favored position for electricity, which is income sensitive as well, and a general decline in the relative role of fuel oil as a residential fuel. Natural gas, however, remains the dominant source of household energy for all income groups. As might be expected, energy budget shares tend to fall rapidly with increases in household income and to rise slowly over time due to changes in real energy prices.

The predicted results of accelerated natural gas decontrol and mandatory thermal efficiency standards for new housing also tend to be consistent with a priori expectations, although the magnitudes involved are generally small. Natural gas deregulation has its major impact in 1983, resulting in reduced levels of total energy consumption per household of 2–3% and somewhat larger decreases in natural gas consumption. The higher prices for natural gas tend to increase expenditures by 3–4%. There are only minor differential effects across income groups and by 1991 the impacts on both energy consumption and expenditures have largely disappeared. The standards scenario indicates somewhat reduced levels of energy consumption and expenditures per household in 1983, relative to the base case, but by 1991 these differences are in the 2–5% range as the proportion of post-1981 housing in the total housing stock increases. There are some interesting, although rather small, income effects with lower income households experiencing slightly higher savings in the form of reduced energy consumption. When the offsetting increases in capital investments required by the mandated standards are taken into account, they indicate substantial levels of positive net benefits for lower income households. Higher income households, however, experience negative benefits on a net basis as the result of significantly higher levels of required efficiency-related investments.

V.4. END-USE IMPLICATIONS

The basic REEPS simulation projections can also be aggregated by major residential energy end-use categories, such as space heating, air conditioning, and water heating, to analyze the end-use implications of energy policies. In this section, we report on the end-use simulations for four residential end-use categories: space heating, water heating, cooking, and central air conditioning. The two major end uses, space heating and water heating, account for over 60% of the total residential energy demand. All three residential fuels — electricity, natural gas, and fuel oil — are shown in the case of space

TABLE V.17

Residential Space Heating Fuel Consumption 1979–1991[a]

Year	Natural gas[b]			Electricity[c]			Fuel oil[d]		
	Base	Deregulation	Standard	Base	Deregulation	Standard	Base	Deregulation	Standard
1979	29.12	29.12	29.12	49.98	49.98	49.98	11.46	11.46	11.46
1981	28.46	26.42	27.45	49.19	49.69	46.34	11.10	11.18	11.03
1983	28.09	26.63	26.57	51.83	52.56	47.23	10.38	10.38	10.31
1985	27.12	26.54	25.42	55.49	56.23	49.46	9.59	9.66	9.52
1987	27.01	26.63	24.81	58.02	58.72	51.23	9.23	9.30	9.16
1989	27.15	26.71	24.66	60.50	61.02	52.48	8.87	8.94	8.80
1991	26.86	26.52	24.27	64.06	64.10	55.40	8.65	8.72	8.58

[a] Source, REEPS model.
[b] Natural gas consumption measured in 10^9 therms, where 1 therm = 1.0×10^5 Btu.
[c] Electricity consumption measured in 10^{10} kWh, where 1 kWh = 3412 Btu.
[d] Fuel oil consumption measured in 10^9 gal, where 1 gal = 138,700 Btu.

heating, since fuel oil generally accounts for over 30% of the total energy consumption in this category.   However, in the other three end uses analyzed, fuel oil plays a very minor role and has been left out.   The market shares for space heating are shown separately for new and existing housing, where saturation rate refers to the proportion of existing housing using a given fuel type and penetration rate refers to a similar proportion for the case of new housing.   Finally, consumption figures are shown in terms of physical units — therms of natural gas, kilowatt hours of electricity, and gallons of fuel oil — with conversion factors listed in the footnote section of Table V.17.

A. Base Case Scenario: End-Use Distribution

Tables V.17 – V.20 and Figs. V.3 – V.9 show the results of the end-use simulation runs in detail.   These tables give the end-use specific consumption and appliance saturations by major fuel types for the base case and alternative scenarios.

The base case predictions indicate electric space heating usage and saturation steadily increasing over the simulation period.   Although natural gas remains the most popular space heating fuel, with over 50% of both old and new households having gas space heating, the saturation of electric space heating increases by a factor of one-third from a little over 15% in 1979 to over 20% by 1991.   This effect is even stronger if we look at estimated appliance penetrations in new housing, where electricity accounts for 41% of new space heating installations by 1991.   On the other hand, the use of fuel oil for heating shows a steady decline so that by 1991 only 27% of existing households have oil heating, as opposed to 32% in 1979.   Furthermore, installations of new oil space heating equipment account for only 3.5% of the market by 1991.   Similar effects can be seen for space heating fuel consumption in Table V.17 as electric heating use increases by 28% while gas consumption for space heating decreases by 8%, from 1979 to 1991.

For water heating, electricity saturation rates are also projected to grow in the base case although at a very slow rate.   Natural gas water heating saturations also increase over the simulation period, but gas consumption remains relatively flat.   Thus, the trend in water heating, similar to that of space heating, shows a slow but steady decline in the use of fuel oil and correspondingly small increases for the other two fuels.

Cooking energy consumption shows strong increases in the use of both natural gas and electricity.   The use of electricity in cooking is projected to increase 88% during the simulation period, while natural gas use shows a corresponding increase of 32% in cooking fuel usage, despite a decline in the saturation rate of gas stoves from 44 to 40%.   The dominant effect here is a

TABLE V.18

Market Shares for Electric and Natural Gas Space Heating 1979–1991[a]

Year	Natural gas						Electricity					
	Existing (%)			New (%)			Existing (%)			New (%)		
	Base	Deregulation	Standard	Base	Deregulation	Standard	Base	Deregulation	Standard	Base	Deregulation	Standard
1979	52.4	52.4	52.4	57.2	57.2	57.2	15.6	15.6	15.6	29.9	29.9	29.9
1981	52.1	52.1	52.1	56.8	51.4	56.8	15.5	15.5	15.5	33.4	37.8	33.4
1983	51.6	52.3	52.6	57.0	54.4	57.0	16.4	16.6	16.4	34.6	36.6	34.6
1985	52.6	52.1	52.6	55.0	55.0	55.0	17.4	17.7	17.4	38.3	38.3	38.3
1987	52.5	52.2	52.5	57.5	57.5	57.5	18.3	18.6	18.3	38.0	38.0	38.0
1989	52.5	52.3	52.5	55.2	55.2	55.2	19.5	19.8	19.5	40.0	40.0	40.0
1991	52.1	51.9	52.1	55.5	55.5	55.5	20.6	20.8	20.6	41.0	41.0	41.0

[a] Source, REEPS model.

TABLE V.19

Water Heating Fuel Saturation Rates and Energy Consumption 1979–1991[a]

| | Natural gas | | | | | | Electricity | | | | | |
| | Saturation rate (%) | | | Consumption[b] | | | Saturation rate (%) | | | Consumption[c] | | |
Year	Base	Deregulation	Standard	Base	Deregulation	Standard	Base	Deregulation	Standard	Base	Deregulation	Standard
1979	50.8	50.8	50.8	10.51	10.51	10.51	34.0	34.0	34.0	70.07	70.07	70.07
1981	50.8	50.8	50.8	10.39	9.93	10.39	34.3	34.3	34.3	71.65	71.98	71.65
1983	51.3	51.2	51.3	10.44	10.08	10.44	34.6	34.6	34.6	71.52	71.38	71.52
1985	51.8	51.5	51.8	10.32	10.15	10.32	34.2	34.7	34.2	71.16	71.22	71.16
1987	51.6	51.4	51.6	10.33	10.18	10.33	34.6	34.8	34.6	72.56	71.98	72.56
1989	51.7	51.4	51.7	10.38	10.28	10.38	34.8	35.1	34.8	73.47	73.17	73.47
1991	51.7	51.3	51.7	10.50	10.39	10.50	34.9	35.2	34.9	73.92	74.39	73.92

[a] Source, REEPS model.
[b] Natural gas consumption measured in 10^9 therms, where 1 therm = 1.0×10^5 Btu.
[c] Electricity consumption measured in 10^{10} kWh, where 1 kWh = 3412 Btu.

TABLE V.20

Cooking Fuel Saturation Rates and Energy Consumption 1979–1991[a]

	Natural gas				Electricity			
	Saturation rate (%)		Consumption[b]		Saturation rate (%)		Consumption[c]	
Year	Base	Deregulation	Base	Deregulation	Base	Deregulation	Base	Deregulation
1979	44.0	44.0	9.71	9.71	47.5	47.5	61.95	61.95
1981	44.3	44.3	10.41	10.09	47.5	47.5	69.36	69.80
1983	42.9	42.6	10.29	10.11	49.1	49.4	74.89	75.37
1985	42.7	42.3	11.36	11.24	49.8	50.0	81.93	82.70
1987	42.3	42.0	11.10	12.09	50.1	50.5	93.04	92.88
1989	41.4	40.9	12.61	12.70	51.3	51.6	102.69	101.78
1991	40.1	39.7	12.85	12.79	52.5	53.2	116.61	116.92

[a] Source, REEPS model.
[b] Natural gas consumption measured in 10^9 therms, where 1 therm = 1.0×10^5 Btu.
[c] Electricity consumption measured in 10^{10} kWh, 1 kWh = 3412 Btu.

steady increase in the overall demand for cooking energy due to a large income elasticity for cooking fuel in the REEPS model. However, this large elasticity may be due to the basic problem of inferring change over time from cross-section estimates.

Table V.21 and Fig. V.10 show the projected patterns of air conditioning ownership for the base case scenario. Saturations of central air conditioning are expected to increase substantially over the period shown; housing units with central air conditioning increase from 34% of the total in 1979 to 53% by 1991. With respect to new housing, the installation rate of heat pumps more than doubles over the simulation period, with over 17% of new housing having heat pumps by 1991.

In general, the base case scenario exhibits a number of interesting characteristics. The residential use of fuel oil for space heating declines gradually over time as oil heating equipment is replaced by other fuels in new housing. Electricity consumption and saturation generally grow across end uses, displacing both oil and to a smaller extent natural gas. The use of natural gas decreases in space heating and increases in cooking but remains relatively stable overall. Cooking fuel use in general increases dramatically, perhaps as a side effect of new household formation. The saturation of central air conditioning also increases substantially over the simulation period as new housing increasingly comes equipped with central air conditioning. Thus, the overall effects of these changes under the base case scenario are decreasing usage of fuel oil, increasing electricity consumption, and relatively minor changes in natural gas usage.

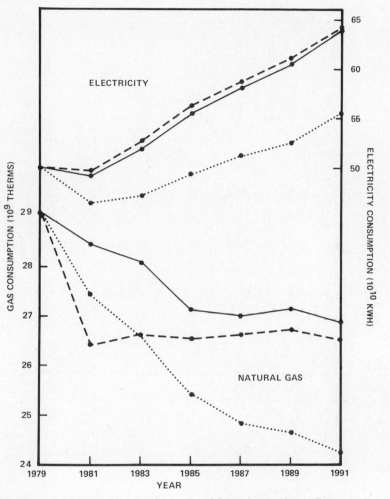

Fig. V.3 Space heat energy consumption—electricity and natural gas. Base case (———), deregulation (– – –), standards (· · ·).

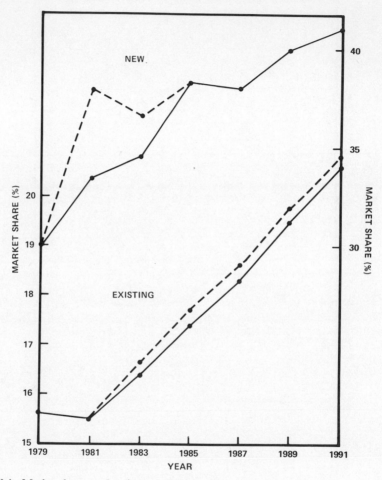

Fig. V.4 Market shares—electric space heating. Base case and standard (———), deregulation (----).

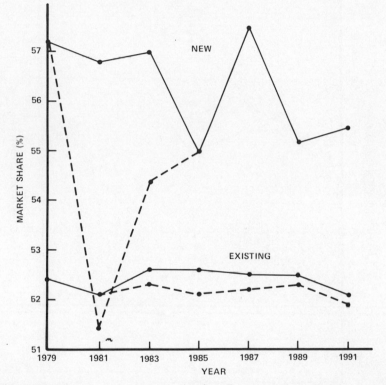

Fig. V.5 Market shares — natural gas space heating. Base case and standards (————), deregulation (‑‑‑).

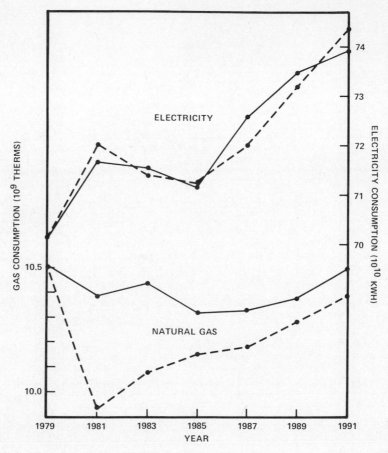

Fig. V.6 Water heat energy consumption—electricity and natural gas. Base case and standards (———), deregulation (---).

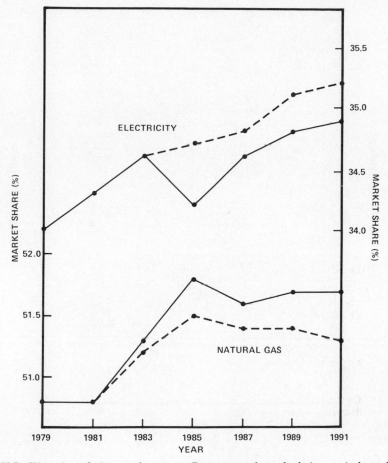

Fig. V.7 Water heat fuel saturation rates. Base case and standards (————), deregulation (————).

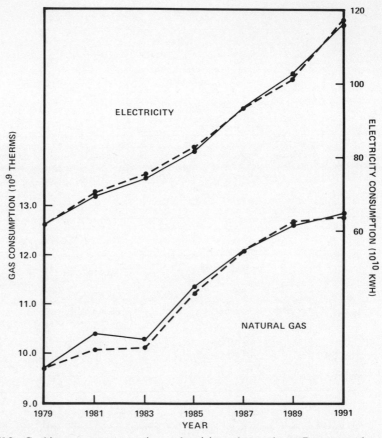

Fig. V.8 Cooking energy consumption — electricity and natural gas. Base case and standards (————), deregulation (----).

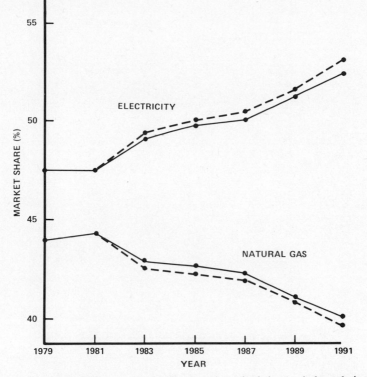

Fig. V.9   Cooking fuel saturation rates.   Base case and standards (———), deregulation (---).

TABLE V.21

Market Shares of Central Air Conditioning — Base Case[a]

Year	Saturation in existing dwellings (%)	Penetration in new dwellings (%)		
		Conventional	Heat pump	Total
1979	33.9	48.1	8.5	56.6
1981	37.5	47.4	10.3	57.7
1983	42.3	44.1	12.6	56.7
1985	45.0	44.0	14.7	58.8
1987	47.4	44.5	14.7	59.2
1989	50.2	45.3	15.3	60.6
1991	53.4	43.6	17.2	60.8

[a] Source, REEPS model.

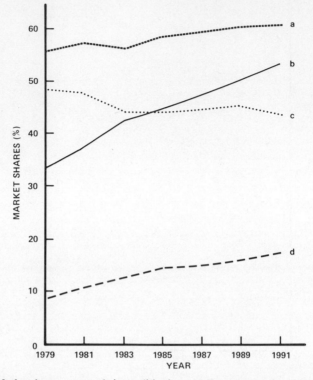

Fig. V.10 Market shares — central air conditioning. (a) Total penetration, new dwellings, (b) saturation in existing dwellings, (c) penetration in new conventional dwellings, (d) penetration in new heat pump dwellings.

B. Deregulation and Standards Scenarios: End-Use Distribution

The accelerated decontrol of natural gas has varying effects across the various energy end uses shown. For example, in Table V.17, space heating consumption of natural gas declines by approximately 7% in 1981 as a result of deregulation. Some increase in electric space heating consumption is shown, but the majority of the decreased gas usage appears to be conservation effects rather than the substitution of alternative residential fuels. The space heating saturation rates indicate rather small effects from deregulation, with only 0.5% of the existing housing units switching from natural gas to another space heating fuel by 1985. The effects of this switch can still be seen in 1991, although by this time only 0.2% of the households still use a nongas space heating fuel relative to the base case.

The effects on the penetration rates of new equipment are larger, as we would expect. In 1981, the year of the largest price difference due to natural gas deregulation, 5.4% of new housing units shift from gas heating systems to other fuels, primarily electricity. It should be pointed out that in REEPS the effects of deregulation on new housing occur only in 1981 and 1983, as prices are assumed to be the same in all other years. Thus, the amount of fuel shifting projected for this period is probably exaggerated by the model since expectations are assumed to be myopic; that is, households assume that any observed price differences in the year of construction will remain permanently. This expectational structure conflicts with the definition of the base case and deregulation scenarios which assume price parity after 1985, so that a consumer with *rational expectations* would look only at the price differences in 1981 and 1983. This results in a smaller incentive to switch away from natural gas heating.

The deregulation scenario also has the expected effects on saturations of water heating and cooking appliances and their corresponding fuel use. Consumption of natural gas is lower under deregulation for both cooking and water heating, although these changes are small. Small effects on saturations are also evident as some shifting away from gas appliances is observed.

The standards policy, on the other hand, has no impact on nonspace heating or cooling energy use. As noted before, however, there are substantial impacts on the amounts of energy used for space heating purposes. Space heating fuel usage is reduced more from standards than from deregulation in all years except 1981. The standards, however, have no significant impact on appliance penetrations.

Both the standards and decontrol policies have the bulk of their impact on the domestic use of natural gas. This focus on natural gas is not surprising since natural gas is the primary fuel for space heating. In addition, the standards primarily affect space heating requirements and deregulation affects natural gas prices directly. Some substitution of other fuels for natural gas is observed primarily in the deregulation case, but the majority of the effects of the two policies appears to be conservation rather than fuel switching in behavior. Neither policy appears to have dramatic effects on energy consumption, but this is not unexpected since both policies result in essentially rather minor changes; decontrol results in higher natural gas prices only for a 4-yr period while the mandatory standards impose constraints which may already be in widespread use. These policies do result in large absolute changes in direct energy purchases. Natural gas decontrol can be projected to cause consumers to pay approximately $10 billion extra in higher energy bills from 1981 to 1990, while the standards case results in energy bills approximately $11 billion lower than otherwise. These large amounts are due primarily to the size of total consumer energy expenditures, estimated to be approximately $70 billion in 1991, so that even small relative changes result in large absolute effects. Even when the associated increases in capital costs are considered, the standards policy appears to result in large savings in NPV terms.

V.5. REGIONAL DISTRIBUTION IMPLICATIONS

To understand the geographic or regional impacts of alternative energy policies as predicted by the REEPS model, four states were tabulated separately. The results for each of these states—New York, the Carolinas (North and South combined), Illinois, and California—for 1983 are shown in Tables V.22–V.25. These particular states were chosen for two reasons: they represent significant geographic variation and their relatively large populations ensured adequate representation in the REEPS sample. The year selected for this analysis, 1983, was used because it was the year of maximum impact under deregulation, and hence should provide reasonable representation of the regional impacts of alternative energy policies.

A. Base Case Scenario: Regional Distribution

First, it is interesting to note the forecasted regional differences in energy use for the base case scenario. From the four tables shown, it can be seen that per capita energy use is significantly higher in the cold weather states of New York and Illinois than in the warm weather states of California and the Carolinas. For example, average total energy use is 65% higher in Illinois than in the Carolinas. Most of this difference is due to the large differential in heating needs between these two areas since there are approximately twice as many heating degree days in Illinois than in either of the Carolinas. Average total energy consumption is displayed graphically in Fig. V.11, which also reflects the fact that substantial differences in energy-use patterns exist at the state level. As we would expect, New York and Illinois have higher than average per capita energy use while households in California and the Carolinas use less than the national average.

TABLE V.22

Annual Household Energy Consumption and Expenditure by Income Class 1983—New York[a]

Income Class	Case	Energy consumption per household[b]					Energy expenditures per household[c]				
		Gas	Oil	Elec.	Total	Pct. dev.	Gas	Oil	Elec.	Total	Pct. dev.
1	B	27.8	47.8	7.1	82.7		69.4	250.3	135.1	454.9	
	D	26.8	47.8	7.1	81.7	−1.21	76.8	250.3	135.1	462.2	1.62
	S	26.8	47.7	7.1	81.6	−1.33	67.0	250.0	135.1	452.1	−.62
2	B	46.3	44.3	11.0	101.6		115.9	232.4	208.0	556.3	
	D	44.6	44.3	11.0	99.9	−1.67	127.9	232.4	208.0	568.3	2.16
	S	45.0	44.3	11.0	100.3	−1.28	112.7	232.4	207.8	552.9	−.61
3	B	67.6	36.3	14.6	118.5		169.4	190.3	275.3	635.1	
	D	65.2	36.2	14.6	116.0	−2.21	186.8	190.3	275.3	652.4	2.72
	S	66.0	36.3	14.5	116.8	−1.43	165.3	190.3	275.3	630.9	−.66
4	B	58.9	53.0	22.3	134.2		147.4	277.7	421.9	847.0	
	D	56.5	52.9	22.3	131.7	−1.86	162.0	237.4	421.9	861.3	1.69
	S	57.4	53.0	22.3	132.7	−1.12	143.8	277.7	421.9	843.43	−.43
5	B	128.4	41.9	39.7	210.0		321.6	219.7	750.7	1291.9	
	D	124.4	41.9	39.7	206.0	−1.90	356.7	219.7	750.7	1327.1	2.72
	S	124.6	41.9	39.6	206.1	−1.86	311.9	219.6	750.7	1282.1	−.70
6	B	171.9	41.9	53.4	267.2		430.2	220.0	1009.9	1660.2	
	D	167.9	42.1	53.4	263.4	−1.42	481.6	220.6	1010.3	1712.4	3.14
	S	169.0	41.6	53.4	264.0	−1.12	423.1	218.0	1009.9	1651.0	−.55
Total	B	70.8	45.0	20.8	136.6		177.3	235.7	374.7	787.7	
	D	68.4	45.1	20.8	134.3	−1.68	196.2	235.7	374.7	806.6	2.40
	S	68.9	44.9	20.8	134.6	−1.46	172.7	235.6	374.7	783.0	−.60

[a] Source, REEPS model. Heating degree days = 6369, cooling degree days = 473.
[b] 10⁶ Btu/hh.
[c] 1975 $/hh.

TABLE V.23

Annual Household Energy Consumption and Expenditure by Income Class 1983—Carolinas[a]

Income class	Case	Energy consumption per household[b]					Energy expenditures per household[c]				
		Gas	Oil	Elec.	Total	Pct. dev.	Gas	Oil	Elec.	Total	Pct. dev.
1	B	24.5	25.1	15.7	65.3		94.9	116.9	183.6	395.4	
	D	22.5	26.1	15.7	64.3	−1.56	101.9	119.1	183.8	404.7	2.35
	S	22.5	26.0	15.4	63.9	−2.14	88.6	118.9	179.7	387.2	−2.07
2	B	31.8	4.2	23.3	59.3		127.6	18.8	267.3	413.6	
	D	30.0	4.3	23.2	57.5	−3.04	137.7	19.6	266.0	423.3	2.34
	S	30.9	3.7	23.1	57.7	−2.70	123.7	17.0	265.1	405.8	−1.89
3	B	34.6	20.4	28.8	83.8		136.9	92.8	334.7	564.5	
	D	32.6	20.4	28.9	81.9	−2.27	147.6	92.6	336.6	576.8	2.18
	S	34.1	20.6	28.2	82.9	−1.07	134.8	93.6	328.4	556.8	−1.36
4	B	22.6	28.1	44.1	94.8		89.0	127.1	507.5	723.6	
	D	21.8	29.5	44.9	96.2	1.48	98.3	133.6	516.6	748.5	3.44
	S	22.3	27.7	43.9	93.9	−.95	87.5	125.2	505.8	718.5	−.70
5	B	61.6	.8	67.1	129.5		242.4	3.8	791.1	1037.3	
	D	58.1	1.2	66.7	126.0	−2.70	262.2	5.4	785.6	1053.0	1.51
	S	61.5	.8	66.4	128.7	−.62	242.1	3.5	783.4	1029.0	−.80
6	B	38.6	41.0	90.1	169.7		144.8	181.2	1031.6	1365.6	
	D	40.8	40.6	94.1	175.5	3.42	181.4	181.8	1070.2	1433.4	4.97
	S	33.7	41.0	89.7	164.4	−3.12	131.3	183.8	1026.8	1341.9	−1.74
Total	B	31.8	18.9	34.1	84.8		125.9	85.3	395.4	606.6	
	D	30.2	19.3	34.4	83.9	−1.06	137.2	87.3	398.8	623.2	2.74
	S	30.9	18.7	33.8	83.4	−1.65	122.1	85.1	391.5	598.7	−1.30

[a] Source, REEPS model. Heating degree days = 3267, 2447, cooling degree days = 1410, 1855.
[b] 10^6 Btu/hh.
[c] 1975 $/hh.

TABLE V.24

Annual Household Energy Consumption and Expenditure by Income Class 1983 — Illinois[a]

Income class	Case	Energy consumption per household[b]					Energy expenditures per household[c]				
		Gas	Oil	Elec.	Total	Pct. dev.	Gas	Oil	Elec.	Total	Pct. dev.
1	B	66.0	16.7	7.7	90.4		180.5	73.7	116.1	370.3	
	D	63.5	16.1	7.7	87.3	−3.43	199.2	70.9	115.6	385.7	3.99
	S	64.1	16.6	7.7	88.4	−2.21	175.4	73.6	116.0	365.0	−1.43
2	B	95.3	4.2	16.6	116.1		260.1	18.2	248.6	527.5	
	D	89.8	5.5	16.8	112.1	−3.45	281.2	24.4	251.7	557.3	5.65
	S	94.1	4.1	16.6	114.8	−1.12	257.4	18.2	248.6	524.2	−.63
3	B	83.8	20.9	17.9	122.6		229.1	92.6	267.4	589.1	
	D	80.4	20.9	17.9	119.2	−2.77	252.0	92.6	267.2	611.7	3.84
	S	82.2	20.9	17.9	121.0	−1.30	224.9	92.5	267.4	584.8	−.73
4	B	106.6	17.8	26.6	151.0		291.4	78.8	397.9	768.1	
	D	102.5	18.7	26.6	147.8	−2.12	321.1	78.8	397.1	747.0	3.76
	S	105.1	17.8	26.6	149.5	−1.13	287.6	78.8	397.9	764.3	−.49
5	B	160.1	19.9	39.1	219.1		437.7	88.5	583.8	1110.0	
	D	153.8	19.6	39.1	213.5	−2.56	482.1	86.6	584.9	1153.5	3.91
	S	157.6	19.9	39.1	216.6	−1.14	431.0	88.4	583.8	1103.2	−.61
6	B	96.7	36.6	78.8	212.1		264.5	162.1	1178.4	1604.9	
	D	91.3	36.6	79.1	207.0	−2.40	286.0	162.1	1181.9	1630.1	1.57
	S	94.0	36.5	78.8	209.3	−1.30	257.2	161.4	1178.4	1597.0	−.49
Total	B	99.5	16.7	23.3	139.5		272.0	73.9	348.9	694.8	
	D	98.2	16.9	23.3	135.4	−2.94	298.5	74.2	349.4	722.2	3.94
	S	97.8	16.7	23.3	137.8	−1.22	267.6	73.8	348.8	690.3	−.65

[a] Source, REEPS Model. Heating degree days = 5952, cooling degree days = 1073.
[b] 10^6 Btu/hh.
[c] 1975 $/hh.

TABLE V.25

Annual Household Energy Consumption and Expenditure by Income Class 1983—California[a]

Income class	Case	Energy consumption per household[b]					Energy expenditures per household[c]				
		Gas	Oil	Elec.	Total	Pct. dev.	Gas	Oil	Elec.	Total	Pct. dev.
1	B	51.0	1.3	8.7	61.0		170.3	7.2	84.8	262.5	
	D	48.6	1.4	8.6	58.6	−3.93	186.1	7.2	84.4	277.7	5.79
	S	46.8	1.3	8.4	56.5	−7.38	156.5	6.7	82.0	245.2	−6.59
2	B	50.9	3.8	19.3	74.0		170.1	19.8	189.1	378.9	
	D	48.8	3.9	19.3	72.0	−2.70	187.2	19.8	189.6	396.5	4.65
	S	48.4	3.8	18.6	70.8	−4.32	162.0	19.8	181.8	363.6	−4.04
3	B	65.5	2.0	24.5	92.0		219.1	10.7	239.7	469.6	
	D	61.8	2.3	24.5	88.6	−3.70	236.8	11.6	240.0	488.4	4.00
	S	61.6	2.0	24.0	87.6	−4.78	206.1	10.3	236.3	452.7	−3.60
4	B	79.9	3.2	33.9	117.0		267.0	16.8	332.1	616.0	
	D	74.8	2.9	34.4	112.1	−4.18	286.5	15.1	337.1	638.7	3.68
	S	74.8	3.0	33.5	111.3	−4.87	250.1	15.4	328.1	593.6	−3.64
5	B	96.3	8.8	54.9	160.0		322.1	45.2	537.9	905.3	
	D	92.8	8.8	54.8	156.4	−2.25	356.1	44.9	537.0	938.0	3.61
	S	91.5	8.4	54.3	154.2	−3.62	305.8	43.4	532.3	881.5	−2.63
6	B	134.1	0	75.0	209.2		448.6	0	735.6	1184.2	
	D	129.6	0	75.1	204.7	−2.15	496.5	0	735.6	1232.5	4.08
	S	128.5	0	74.5	203.0	−2.96	429.7	0	730.4	1160.0	−2.04
Total	B	71.4	3.9	30.0	105.3		241.1	18.6	297.2	556.9	
	D	68.0	3.4	30.2	101.6	−3.51	262.9	18.3	298.4	579.6	4.06
	S	67.9	3.45	29.8	101.2	−3.89	227.1	17.8	292.5	537.5	−3.49

[a] Source, REEPS model. Heating degree days = 2490, cooling degree days = 1105.
[b] 10^6 Btu/hh.
[c] 1975 $/hh.

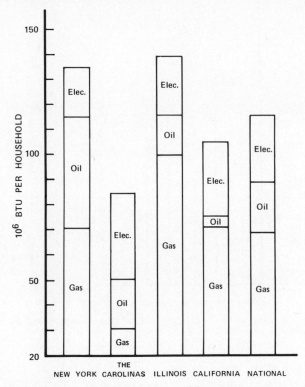

Fig. V.11   Average annual household energy consumption in selected states — REEPS projections 1983.

Differences between states are also evident in the mix of residential fuels used in each.   The amount of natural gas consumed per household varies from 31.8 million Btu in the Carolinas to 99.5 million Btu in Illinois, more than a threefold increase.   Natural gas accounts for approximately 70% of household energy use in Illinois but only 40% in the Carolinas.   On the other hand, electricity use is higher than the national average in both of the warm weather states, probably due to the higher relative share of residential electric heat used in these areas.   The low usage of electricity in Illinois and New York reflects the relatively low shares of electric heating in areas of severe winters.   The fuel oil usage share reflects the fact that this fuel is used widely in New York and the Carolinas, while accounting for relatively less usage in Illinois and practically none in California.

The graphs in Figs. V.12 and V.13 display some of the income group patterns of energy use by state for the base case scenario.   These figures show

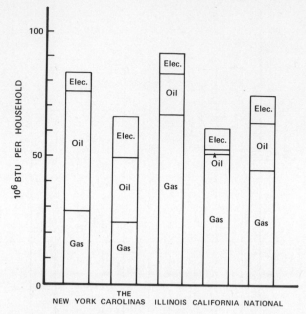

Fig. V.12   Average annual household energy consumption in selected states — REEPS projections 1983, lowest income group.

the average total energy consumption of households in the lowest and highest income groups in each state.   It is clear from these tables that energy use rises significantly with income in each state.   Some variation in the income elasticity of energy use between states is evident, however, with New York and California showing increases of 240% or so and Illinois and the Carolinas showing increases of roughly 150% in energy consumption from lowest to highest income groups.

As in the national results, electricity consumption is the most income elastic.   Average fuel oil usage actually declines with income in New York and California, although there were no sampled high income households with oil usage in California.   Average natural gas usage increases with income in all states but increases proportionally more in New York and less in Illinois.

Energy expenditures by income class are also shown in Tables V.22 – V.25.   The general trend in all four states is nearly identical, with a strong upward trend in energy consumption with increasing income.   In all income groups, average energy expenditure per household is higher in New York and

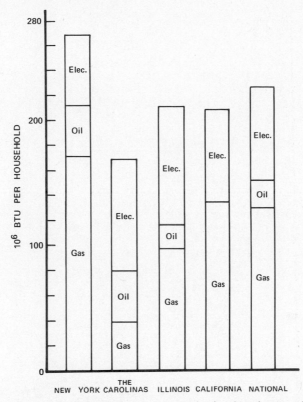

Fig. V.13 Average annual household energy consumption in selected states — REEPS projections 1983, highest income group.

lower in California. For example, the average California household spends $230 less on energy in 1983 than does its New York counterpart under the base case scenario. Since average prices for electricity are higher in New York while natural gas prices are higher in California, the average household spends more on electricity in New York while using less, as well as spending less on natural gas and using slightly less. The biggest difference between New York and California is the expenditure on fuel oil, which is 30% of New York energy expenses but less than 3% in California.

Estimated energy budget shares by income group for New York and California in 1983 under the base case scenario are shown in Fig. V.14. As these energy budget shares indicate, low income groups in New York spend considerably more of their income on fuel than do similar low income groups in California. This is especially evident in the lowest income group, which in New York spends 13% of its income on energy and in California only 7.5%.

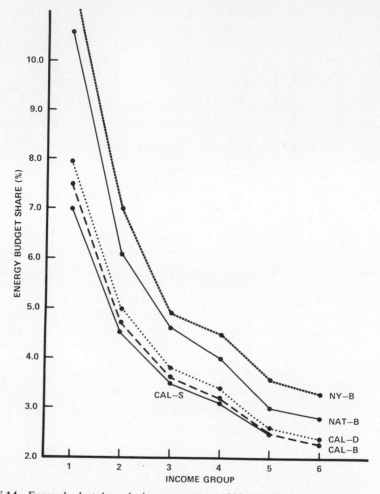

Fig. V.14 Energy budget shares by income group — 1983, New York and California. NY-B, New York – base case; NAT-B, National – base case; CAL-D, California – deregulation; CAL-B, California – base case; CAL-S, California – standards.

B. Deregulation and Standards Scenario: Regional Distribution

The two alternative energy policies, accelerated natural gas deregulation and mandatory standards, also have much stronger impacts in some regions than in others. Looking first at the natural gas decontrol results, it can be seen from Tables V.22 – V.25 that California and Illinois show more response in terms of both energy consumption and expenditure. For example, total energy usage per household drops 3.5% in California but only 1% in the Carolinas relative to the base case. The relative importance of natural gas in a region's energy mix is, of course, the primary factor determining the strength of the impact of natural gas decontrol. Thus, natural gas accounts for a higher proportion of energy consumption in California and Illinois than in New York or the Carolinas. This is also apparent in terms of household energy expenditures which increase 4% in California and Illinois and only about 2.5% in the Carolinas and New York due to decontrol. However, it should be pointed out that the pricing pattern used in REEPS for this analysis assumed that the 1977 price variation by state does not change under natural gas deregulation. To the extent that decontrol also results in different regional price patterns relative to the base case, the forecasted regional differentials in energy demand may change.

The standards policy also has its strongest impact on California. The mandatory standards, of course, affect new housing only, so that their impact on energy consumption is felt most strongly in areas where larger amounts of new construction occur. This may explain why California is the only one of the four states shown to record a drop in energy consumption greater than the national average as a result of the standards. Energy consumption in California is predicted to fall more as a result of the standards than from decontrol, even in 1983. The Carolinas also show stronger conservation effects from the standards than from decontrol. Expenditures per household on energy fall from the standards in all states, though in percentage terms expenditures in California fall 6 times the amount for either New York or Illinois. In general, the average family in California saves $20 on annual energy bills due to the mandatory efficiency standards while a household in either New York or Illinois saves less than $5/yr.

These savings in terms of energy expenditures come with corresponding increases in required efficiency-related investment, however. Table V.26 shows the estimated capital and operating expenditure changes for 1983. We can see from this table that although the average California family saves 4 times as much per year on energy compared to the average New York family, the required investment differs by a factor of over 10. In general, these figures show that in the states where the standards have little impact, New York and Illinois, the standards also cost very little. The average new house in Illinois requires only an additional $295 to meet the thermal standards whereas a new house in California costs an additional $1360. Since these figures are shown only for 1983, they are of course somewhat suggestive but the implication is that mandatory standards on new housing will benefit the New York–Illinois types of states more than the California–Carolinas states. This appears to be because the standards are less binding and hence

TABLE V.26

Regional Implications of Mandatory Standards Policy 1983[a]

	New York	Carolina	Illinois	California	National
Mean change in annual energy expenditure (1975 $/Yr)	−4.70	−7.90	−4.55	−19.46	−7.83
Mean change in annual capital investment (1975 $/Yr)	3.34	24.91	4.25	36.61	17.06
Additional capital investment per new housing unit (1975 $)	631	996	295	1360	1087
Total energy expenditure change (Millions of 1975 $)	−29.9	−27.8	−19.0	−188	−664
Total capital expenditure change (Millions of 1975 $)	21.2	87.6	17.8	354	1450

[a] Source, REEPS model.

cost less in terms of additional investments in New York and Illinois, while in states like California and the Carolinas the imposition of the standards may cause considerable overinvestment in residential thermal efficiency.

Interestingly enough, all states except the Carolinas are better off than the national average if we compare the ratio of energy saving to capital investment in 1983. Since on a national aggregate basis the standards appear to have a net positive value, we can infer that New York, Illinois, and California all benefit more from the standards than the national average.

Decontrol appears to have little effect on income distribution within these states, though there is some indication that energy bills will increase more in percentage terms for poorer households, at least in Illinois and California. The standards policy does, however, reduce energy expenditures more proportionately for lower income groups in all four states, and particularly in California. Thus, the energy budget shares of low income groups are affected more than those of high income groups: decontrol raises energy budget shares and has regressive effects on energy expenditures, while the standards lower energy budget shares in a more progressive fashion. The effects in California are, of course, stronger than in any of the other states studied but are still qualitatively similar to the national trends.

V.6. CONCLUSIONS

One of the major strengths of the REEPS model in terms of policy analysis is its ability to forecast distributional impacts along a variety of alternative dimensions. In this chapter we have presented analyses of several energy policies in terms of such dimensions as fuel type, income group, end use, and region, as well as in terms of aggregate impacts.

Beginning with the aggregate forecasts, our results indicate steadily declining energy consumption per household and a significant upward trend in energy expenditures per houshold over the next decade under the base case scenario. In contrast, accelerated natural gas decontrol results in slightly lower levels of energy consumption and sharply higher energy expenditures for the 1981–1985 period. After 1985, the deregulation scenario predictions tend to converge towards the base case results. The standards scenario results in reduced energy consumption beginning in 1981, relative to the base case, and a total consumption differential which increases steadily over time as an increasing proportion of the housing stock becomes subject to the mandatory thermal standards. The resulting present value estimates indicate potential savings from such standards amounting to at least $5 billion, and perhaps double that figure, per year.

Turning to the distributional impacts of these effects across income groups, the REEPS forecasts generally indicate substantial differential effects. These effects are perhaps best summarized in terms of the estimated energy budget shares, shown in Table V.15, which tend to fall rapidly with increasing household income and to rise slowly over time due to changes in real energy prices under the base case scenario. The results for the two alternative policy scenarios, accelerated natural gas decontrol and mandatory thermal efficiency standards, also indicate differential effects across income groups although they are generally relatively small in magnitude. In the case of the standards scenario, however, the present value estimates indicate substantial levels of positive net benefits for lower income households and negative net benefits for higher income households as the result of increased levels of efficiency-related investments.

The end-use implications are less dramatic but are nevertheless interesting, especially when considered jointly with the fuel-type forecasts. For example, the REEPS results for the base case scenario indicate a gradual decline over time in the residential use of fuel oil for space heating as oil-heating equipment is replaced by other fuels in new housing. On the other hand, electricity consumption tends to increase consistently across end uses, displacing both fuel oil and to a lesser extent natural gas. The use of natural gas declines in space heating and increases in cooking but tends to remain relatively stable overall.   Both the deregulation and standards policies result in sizable decreases in the demand for natural gas, primarily as a result of reduced space heating needs.   While some degree of interfuel substitution is evident, the dominant impact appears to be from conservation effects.

Perhaps the most striking distributional effects concern the regional impacts using the four representative states—New York, the Carolinas, Illinois, and California.   While these results are primarily due to weather differences, they are still interesting in terms of both policy and modeling implications.   For example, the REEPS results indicate higher levels of per capita energy consumption in the cold weather states, New York and Illinois, and lower levels in California and the Carolinas.   The mix of residential energy use also varies dramatically, as might be expected, with relatively high natural gas consumption and relatively low electricity usage in both Illinois and New York.   Fuel oil, on the other hand, is used widely in New York and the Carolinas but accounts for a negligible portion of residential energy consumption in California.   There are also substantial differences in impacts across income groups among the four states.   The alternative policy scenarios also reveal differential impacts across regions with California showing the largest impacts.   In the case of natural gas decontrol, this is the result of the relative dominance of natural gas as a residential fuel in California, while the mandatory standards effects are clearly due to the higher rate of new housing construction in that state.   Finally, there are also sizable differences across the four states in terms of both increased thermal-efficiency investment and reduced energy consumption as the result of the standards scenario, with New York and Illinois having smaller impacts and both California and the Carolinas having rather large impacts.

This general ability to model distributional impacts in a variety of dimensions represents an important addition to the current inventory of state-of-the-art energy models since energy policies are especially likely to have significant redistributional impacts which will go unnoticed if the policy analysis is restricted to a more aggregate dimension.   Furthermore, these distributional effects are likely to be multidimensional (e.g., income, housing tenure, location, type of housing, size and composition of household, age and sex of head) so that policy analyses along a variety of dimensions may be necessary to fully assess the complete impact of any given policy.

As we discussed in Chapter II, one of the fundamental principles for judging models is realism or accuracy in performance.   An implication of this criterion is that model performance must ultimately be judged in terms of a direct comparison of the forecasts of alternative models, where the models are first standardized in terms of both initialization and calibration. This point is, of course, the primary thesis of this study.   Thus, having presented a detailed analysis of the REEPS model projections for each of three alternative residential energy policies, we must now consider the parallel set of forecasts resulting from similar runs made with the ORNL model of residential energy consumption.   Following this discussion in Chapter VI, we then turn to a comprehensive comparison of the two sets of forecasts at both aggregate and disaggregate levels of analysis.

[1] This approximation is not exact because average consumption is proportional to the expectation of the reciprocal of efficiency, which does not in general equal the reciprocal of the expectation of efficiency.   A more accurate procedure would have been to carry out the entire analysis in terms of the energy service ratio, the reciprocal of efficiency.

CHAPTER **VI**

Simulation Results from the ORNL Model

This chapter reports the results from using the Oak Ridge National Laboratory – Hirst Residential Energy Consumption (ORNL) model to simulate the economic impacts of the same three alternative energy policy scenarios: base case, deregulation, and standards. The first section discusses the initialization of the ORNL model in terms of implementing each of the three policy scenarios for the purposes of our analysis. Following this introductory discussion, the next three sections present the national, income distribution, and end-use simulation results, respectively, along with related analyses. The ORNL model was not used to analyze state impacts, as was the REEPS model, since the ORNL model is basically designed to simulate economic impacts at a more aggregate level. The final section of this chapter contains a concluding discussion of the ORNL simulation results.

The ORNL model is a large scale engineering – econometric model of the residential sector which forecasts residential energy use at either the national or regional level. Essentially, the model predicts changes relative to base- or initial-year energy consumption, based on related changes in demographic characteristics, economic conditions, and the technological possibilities for energy conservation. Although the basic level of economic analysis is aggregate, i.e., all consumers in the nation or in a given region, energy consumption is disaggregated in terms of several dimensions — fuel type, end use, and dwelling type. Five residential fuel categories are included: electricity, natural gas, fuel oil, other, and none; while the eight end-use categories include space heating, air conditioning (room, central, none), water heating, refrigeration, food freezing, cooking, lighting, and other. Three basic dwelling types are modeled: single-family, multi-family, and mobile home, and dwellings are also distinguished by tenure, i.e., new or existing. The ORNL model can be run for as many as 31 yr, e.g., 1970 – 2000, although for the purposes of our analysis it was run from 1977 – 2000.

VI.1. MODEL – SCENARIO IMPLEMENTATION

For the purposes of this study, the ORNL model was run at both the national and the income group level for each of the three alternative policy scenarios. The resulting income distribution analysis was then compared to that predicted by the REEPS model. It was also possible to analyze the results by end use and fuel type, both at the national level and by income group, since ORNL includes these dimensions as part of its output stream. Regional analysis at the state level was not carried out using ORNL, as was done with REEPS, since the ORNL structure and initialization requirements are not well suited to this level of disaggregation. Thus, the ORNL results to be discussed in this chapter include national, income group, and end-use forecasts.

The same six income groups used in the REEPS model, and shown in Table IV.6, were also defined for use with the ORNL model. The use of the REEPS income groups in the ORNL analysis made it possible to compare the results of the two models with respect to the predicted income distribution effects. Furthermore, since little of the required information for initializing the ORNL model at the income group level of analysis was available from published sources, we used the REEPS model to generate a number of the simulation input values required by the ORNL model. In addition to making it possible to run the ORNL model at the income group level, this use of common input values for the two models also enhanced the validity of the comparison between the two sets of simulation results. As shown in Table IV.6, the required income group information was obtained from the

U.S. Population Census for 1977, and the per capita income group data were deflated from 1977 to 1975 dollars for use in the ORNL model.

The model inputs required to initialize the ORNL model by income group are shown in Table VI.1, along with the data source used for each variable. With the exception of the behavioral and technological parameters and the per capita income variable, the required data were generated from REEPS simulation results since the REEPS model includes household income as one of its dimensions. For example, the average fraction of new homes with room versus central air conditioning and average 1977 energy usage data per household were obtained for each income group by appropriate aggregation of the REEPS data. In the case of the energy consumption variables, it was also necessary to convert from the physical units used by REEPS—therms of natural gas, kWh of electricity, and gallons of fuel oil—to a Btu basis for use with the ORNL model.

The housing stock variables were generated using the data from version 7.1 of the ORNL model. These values were also used to initialize the REEPS model. The conditional probabilities by income group level were

TABLE VI.1

ORNL Model Inputs—Variables and Sources[a]

Input	Source of data
Average fraction of new homes with room – central air conditioning	REEPS simulation
Per capital income	U.S. Census[b]
Average 1977 energy usage per household for each fuel–dwelling type–end-use combination (Btu/unit)	REEPS simulations, with conversion from physical units to Btu
1977 market shares by fuel–dwelling type–end-use combination	REEPS simulation
Market shares for new equipment installations in 1977 by fuel and end use, for existing and new structures	REEPS simulation
Stocks of occupied housing units (in millions) by type by year	National data from ORNL model, version 7.1, broken into 6 income groups using conditional probabilities from SAMPLER program
New construction of occupied housing units (in millions) by type by year	
Number of retrofit units (in millions) by housing type by year	SAMPLER program, using conditional income probabilities given housing type

[a] For additional detail concerning the ORNL model and variables, see "RESENU—A Model of Residential Energy Use," CET-002/RESENU, Oak Ridge National Laboratory, Engineering Physics Information Centers.
[b] See Table IV.6.

generated by the SAMPLER subroutine in the REEPS model. As described in Chapter III, the function of SAMPLER is to produce synthetic microeconomic observations at the household level for further processing by REEPS, with these observations then being correctly weighted to reflect true population characteristics for various subgroups of the population, e.g., by region, income group, dwelling type, and end use.

The model inputs required to simulate the three alternative energy policy scenarios — base case, deregulation, and standards — consisted of fuel price projections for three residential fuels — electricity, natural gas, and fuel oil/other — and minimum efficiency standards for new housing. The fuel price projections assumed for the base case and natural gas deregulation scenarios were discussed in Chapter IV, and are given in Table IV.7. Although the ORNL model has room for five categories of residential fuels — electricity, natural gas, fuel oil, other, and none — the fuel oil and other categories were combined while the none category was deleted for the purposes of this analysis. The result was three residential fuel types — electricity, natural gas, and fuel oil/other — an equivalent specification to that used in the REEPS model analysis.

In the case of the mandated thermal efficiency standards scenario, a value of 0.70 for the relative thermal shell conductivity variable, starting in 1980 and continuing to the year 2000, was used based on the housing thermal efficiency analysis presented in Table IV.11. This value assumed that the new housing thermal efficiency standards mandated a maximum average level of energy consumption equivalent to 70% of that prevailing in 1977 in the absence of any such standards.

All other input variables, primarily behavioral and technological parameters, were left unchanged in our analysis, that is, the original ORNL values were used.

VI.2 NATIONAL IMPLICATIONS

A. Base Case Scenario: National

Simulation results from the ORNL model using the base case scenario run at the national level are shown in Tables VI.2 – VI.4 and the accompanying figures. Although the base case results are interesting in their own right, the basic purpose of this scenario is to establish a basis for comparative analysis of the other two alternative policy scenarios: accelerated natural gas deregulation and mandated thermal efficiency standards for new housing.

A total of 21 simulation runs using the ORNL model were carried out, six income groups and an aggregate or national run for each of the three policy scenarios.   In the following discussion, we first analyze the national or aggregate runs for the three policy scenarios, followed by similar discussions of the income group and end-use results.   Finally, a brief discussion of possible aggregation error from running the ORNL model at the income group (rather than the national) level is presented.

From Table VI.2, we see that the base case model, starting from a total residential energy consumption of just under 10 quads in 1977, predicts that energy consumption will fall steadily through 1985 and then rise again to the year 2000.   Total energy consumption in 2000 is forecasted to be only slightly above the 1977 level.   This trend of an initial decline followed by steadily rising demand is also reflected to some extent in electricity consumption, although the low point is reached rather early, i.e., in 1979.   Both fuel oil and natural gas consumption show fairly steady declines, with the 2000 forecasts being approximately 10% lower in both cases than the corresponding consumptions in 1977.   The overall result is that the forecasted increase in electricity demand of about 1 quad between 1977 and 2000 is almost exactly offset by declines in natural gas and fuel oil consumption.

TABLE VI.2

Total Energy Consumption[a]

Year	Natural gas			Fuel oil[e]			Electricity			Total consumption		
	B[b]	D[c]	S[d]	B	D	S	B	D	S	B	D	S
1977	5.72	5.72	5.72	1.88	1.88	1.88	2.35	2.35	2.35	9.95	9.95	9.9
1979	5.74	5.74	5.74	2.00	2.00	2.00	2.18	2.18	2.18	9.92	9.92	9.9
1981	5.53	5.21	5.51	1.93	1.95	1.92	2.20	2.21	2.20	9.66	9.36	9.6
1983	5.32	5.03	5.29	1.84	1.87	1.82	2.26	2.27	2.25	9.41	9.16	9.3
1985	5.15	5.01	5.12	1.77	1.79	1.75	2.33	2.34	2.32	9.25	9.13	9.1
1987	5.13	5.03	5.10	1.77	1.79	1.74	2.42	2.43	2.40	9.32	9.25	9.2
1989	5.15	5.07	5.11	1.79	1.80	1.75	2.51	2.52	2.50	9.44	9.38	9.3
1991[f]	5.13	5.06	5.09	1.78	1.79	1.74	2.60	2.59	2.59	9.51	9.45	9.4
1995	5.09	5.03	5.05	1.76	1.77	1.72	2.79	2.80	2.77	9.64	9.60	9.5
2000	5.12	5.07	5.07	1.68	1.69	1.64	3.35	3.35	3.32	10.15	10.11	10.0

[a] Source, ORNL model. Quadrillion (10^{15}) Btu.

[b] B = base case scenario.

[c] D = deregulation scenario.

[d] S = standards scenario.

[e] Fuel oil = oil plus *other fuel* consumption.

[f] 1991 estimate based on linear interpolation between 1989 and 1995 forecasts.

TABLE VI.3
Total Energy Expenditure[a]

Year	Natural gas			Fuel oil[b]			Electricity			Total expenditures		
	B	D	S	B	D	S	B	D	S	B	D	S
1977	11.1	11.1	11.1	5.2	5.2	5.2	22.4	22.4	22.4	38.7	38.7	38.7
1979	14.1	14.1	14.1	6.7	6.7	6.7	23.2	23.2	23.2	43.9	43.9	43.9
1981	16.2	20.1	16.2	7.9	7.9	7.8	24.8	24.9	24.8	48.9	52.8	48.7
1983	18.3	19.8	18.2	9.1	9.3	9.1	27.5	27.6	27.3	54.9	56.7	54.6
1985	20.8	20.2	20.7	10.7	10.9	10.6	30.4	30.6	30.3	61.9	61.6	61.5
1987	21.2	20.8	21.1	11.2	11.3	11.0	31.6	31.7	31.4	64.0	63.8	63.5
1989	21.8	21.4	21.6	11.7	11.8	11.5	32.9	33.0	32.7	66.4	66.3	65.9
1991[c]	22.7	22.3	22.5	12.5	12.6	12.3	34.1	34.2	33.9	69.3	69.2	68.7
1995	24.5	24.2	24.3	14.1	14.2	13.8	36.5	36.5	36.2	75.1	74.9	74.3
2000	24.6	24.4	24.3	15.8	15.9	15.5	43.9	44.0	43.6	84.3	84.2	83.4

[a] Source, ORNL model. Billions of 1975 $.
[b] Fuel oil = oil plus *other fuel* consumption.
[c] 1991 estimate based on linear interpolation between 1989 and 1995 forecasts.

Projected expenditures for residential energy, measured in constant 1975 dollars, are shown in Table VI.3 and indicate a rising trend in expenditures both in total and for each of the three fuel components. These results are consistent with inelastic energy demand, at least for the early 1980s when rising prices tend to dominate the generally downward trend in consumption. Total energy expenditures in the year 2000 are projected to be 118% higher than in 1977, while the corresponding percentage increases for natural gas, fuel oil, and electricity expenditures are 122, 204, and 96, respectively. Thus, fuel oil shows the strongest increase in expenditures, a result which is primarily due to the projected tripling of real world oil prices by the year 2000 as discussed earlier in Chapter IV.

Present-value expenditure calculations, including fuel, new equipment, and thermal integrity expenditures, discounted over the period 1981–2000 are shown in Table VI.4. These estimates are based on an assumed real discount rate of 10%. National figures are shown at the bottom of the table, and indicate a combined energy consumption of over 240 quads for the 20-yr period, with present value expenditures of almost $760 billion for the base case. Of this estimated expenditure total, fuel accounts for about 80% while expenditures on thermal integrity (TI) improvements (or retrofits) account for only 1.2%. Expenditures for new equipment account for the remainder, about 20% of the discounted 20-yr total.

TABLE VI.4
Present Value Expenditures 1981–2000[a]

Income class	Case	Fuel consumption		Total expenditures[b]							
		10^{15} Btu	% dev.	Fuel	% dev.	Equip.	% dev.	TI[c]	% dev.	Total	% dev.
1	B	26.5		66.3		18.7		1.0		86.1	
	D	26.2	−1.1	67.1	+1.2	18.8	+0.5	1.0	0	86.9	+0.9
	S	26.3	−0.8	66.0	−0.5	18.7	0	1.3	+30.0	86.0	−0.1
2	B	39.7		97.8		23.5		1.4		122.7	
	D	39.4	−0.8	98.8	+1.0	23.5	0	1.4	0	123.7	+0.8
	S	39.4	−0.8	97.3	−0.5	23.4	−0.4	1.7	+21.0	122.5	−0.1
3	B	45.7		112.4		27.3		1.5		141.2	
	D	45.3	−0.9	113.4	+0.9	27.4	+0.4	1.6	+6.7	142.4	+0.8
	S	45.1	−1.3	109.9	−2.2	27.1	−0.7	2.2	+47.0	139.2	−0.4
4	B	62.6		160.3		35.4		2.6		198.2	
	D	62.1	−0.8	161.8	+0.9	35.4	0	2.7	+3.8	199.9	+0.9
	S	62.0	−1.0	158.8	−0.9	35.2	−0.6	3.6	+38.0	197.6	−0.3
5	B	48.7		122.8		27.0		1.8		151.6	
	D	48.3	−0.8	123.8	+0.8	27.1	+0.4	1.9	+5.6	152.7	+0.7
	S	48.1	−1.2	121.5	−1.1	26.9	−0.4	2.7	+50.0	151.0	−0.4
6	B	21.7		49.4		11.0		0.5		61.0	
	D	21.5	−0.9	49.7	+0.6	11.1	+0.9	0.6	+20.0	61.3	+0.5
	S	21.4	−1.4	48.9	−1.0	11.0	0	0.8	+60.0	60.7	−0.5
National											
	B	242.3		605.1		143.7		8.8		757.6	
	D	240.3	−0.8	610.7	+0.9	144.0	+0.2	9.0	+2.3	763.7	+0.8
	S	240.0	−0.9	600.2	−0.8	143.3	−0.3	12.1	+37.5	755.6	−0.3

[a] The real interest rate is assumed to be 10% for purposes of computing discounted present values. Source, ORNL model.

[b] 10^9 1975 $.

[c] TI refers to thermal integrity expenditures

In general, the base case scenario predicts declining energy consumption in the residential sector for most of the 1980s, followed by a slow rate of increase to the year 2000. Electricity, which accounted for less than one-fourth of total residential energy consumption in 1977, is forecasted to show a steadily increasing share and to account for about one-third of total consumption by 2000. The share of fuel oil remains fairly steady over this period, falling slightly from 19 to 17%, while the share of natural gas falls from almost 60% in 1977 to about 50% by the year 2000.

B. Deregulation Scenario: National

The simulation results for accelerated natural gas decontrol, starting in 1981 rather than 1985 as currently mandated by the NGPA, are also shown in Tables VI.2 – VI.4 in the columns and rows labeled D. Compared to the base case, the deregulation results indicate reduced levels of total residential energy consumption due to the increased relative price of natural gas and the corresponding rise in the aggregate price of residential energy, especially over the 1981 – 1985 period. The consumption of natural gas beginning in 1981 is reduced by over 0.3 quads, a gap relative to the base case which is maintained in 1983, after which it slowly starts closing. This latter result is due both to the fact that the post-1985 price of natural gas is assumed to be the same in both the base case and deregulation scenarios and to the fact that energy choice in the ORNL model depends only upon current relative fuel prices, i.e., a naive-expectations model is implicitly assumed. The forecasted consumption of fuel oil remains fairly steady at just under 2.0 quads, and is only slightly less than the base case forecasts in each year. Electricity consumption is slightly higher in most years, indicating a mild substitution relationship between natural gas and electricity, as well as fuel oil to some extent.

The energy expenditure results for the deregulation scenario in Table VI.3 indicate a significant increase in both total energy and natural gas expenditures over the period of accelerated natural gas decontrol. For example, in 1981 expenditures for natural gas are 24% higher than under the base case scenario, while total energy expenditures are about 8% higher. The expenditure results for both fuel oil and electricity indicate much smaller increases, the result presumably of interfuel substitution effects vis-a-vis natural gas.

The present value results in Table VI.4 indicate a rather small increase in total discounted expenditures over the 20-yr period shown. However, there are somewhat more varied changes, relative to the base case results, in the three components. For example, total fuel expenditures increase by 0.9%

even though total fuel consumption for the 20-yr period is about 1% lower. As expected, the higher natural gas prices result in a 2.3% increase in total discounted thermal integrity expenditures, as households replace older inefficient appliances with newer more efficient ones. Total expenditures for new equipment in new structures also show a small increase of about 0.2% compared to the corresponding base case estimate.

C. Standards Scenario: National

The ORNL model simulation results from assuming a set of mandated thermal efficiency standards for new housing, starting in 1981, are also shown in Tables VI.2 – VI.4 in the columns and rows labeled S. Again, relative to the base case, the standards scenario results indicate rather small changes, although they are all in the correct directions from a theoretical point of view. For example, in Table VI.2, total energy consumption, as well as consumption for each of the three fuel components, is slightly lower as a result of the mandated standards, although the extent of the reduction is not very large in any case. Relative to both the base case and deregulation results, the consumption of natural gas and fuel oil, as well as total energy consumption up to 1987, indicates an intermediate position, being lower than the base case results but higher than the deregulation results. Only in the case of electricity consumption are the forecasts under the standards scenario lower than those for the other two scenarios, essentially because electricity consumption under deregulation generally shows a slight increase.

In the case of energy expenditures, shown in Table VI.3, the results from imposing minimum efficiency standards appear to be rather small, essentially the result of small reductions in energy consumption at unchanged prices, although by the year 2000 the total savings amounts to $0.9 billion relative to the base case forecast. These minor reductions in both annual energy consumption and expenditures are also reflected in the estimated present value expenditures reported in Table VI.4. On the other hand, discounted total expenditures for improvements in thermal integrity indicate a 38% increase relative to the base case results, from $8.8 to 12.1 billion. This increase in thermal integrity expenditures of $3.3 billion over the 20-yr period, however, is more than offset by reductions in the other two components, especially fuel expenditures, so that total discounted expenditures under the standards policy indicate a slight decrease from the base case results as we might expect.

In general, the two alternative policy scenarios—accelerated natural gas decontrol beginning in 1981 and mandated thermal efficiency standards for new housing—do not result in very dramatic impacts on either energy consumption or expenditures at the aggregate national level, although the effects predicted by the ORNL model are all consistent with economic theory. Thus, the higher natural gas prices resulting from accelerated deregulation result in reduced residential consumption of natural gas and increased use of fuel oil and electricity, while the imposition of new housing standards reduces the annual consumption of all three residential fuels. The results for predicted energy expenditures are also consistent: higher expenditures for natural gas as the result of increased prices due to deregulation and reduced fuel expenditures under the standards scenario. In general, however, the magnitudes of these changes are all rather small. The only sizable impact is on total discounted expenditures for thermal integrity improvements over the period 1981–2000 under the standards policy, almost a 40% increase as shown in Table VI.4.

The generally small impacts due to the two alternative energy policies, deregulation and standards, as predicted by the ORNL model may not be too surprising, however. Although the natural gas prices assumed under accelerated decontrol show a substantial increase in 1981 from 3.81 to 5.00 $/million Btu, this price shock only lasts until 1985 and steadily decreases in magnitude for each of the years between 1981 and 1985. In the case of the mandated thermal standards for new housing, it is likely that the imposition of these standards, based on voluntary professional guidelines already in use, may not be very critical since much of the new housing stock may already conform substantially to these standards. If so, the additional impact from bringing the remaining new housing stock up to these standards may not be very large.

So far, this analysis of the ORNL model simulation results has only been based on aggregate or national forecasts. Since there is reason to suspect that the corresponding impacts across various income groups may be quite different, we now turn to an analysis of the income group results.

VI.3. INCOME DISTRIBUTION IMPLICATIONS

A. Base Case Scenario: Income Distribution

Summaries of the income group results using the ORNL model and the base case, or status quo, policy scenario are shown in Tables VI.4–VI.8. These numbers are the result of using the ORNL model to simulate each

income group separately by initializing the model with income group specific values for the various exogenous variables. Since the ORNL model was
not specifically designed to operate at the income group level, some aggregation error is surely involved.

Before discussing the base case scenario results, a description of how the
annual number of households in each of the six income groups was estimated
is in order. The numbers used in both the ORNL and the REEPS models,
with minor differences due to round-off error, are shown in Table VI.5.
These numbers were based upon actual data for the year 1977 and were
forecasted for the rest of the years using the ORNL housing submodel which
predicts new housing construction for each year. The income group housing stocks for both existing and new housing were then estimated using
conditional probabilities for type of housing by income group derived

TABLE VI.5

Number and Proportion of Households by Income Class

	Income class[a]						
Year	1	2	3	4	5	6	Total
(a) Number of households[b]							
1977	13.2	15.5	13.9	19.4	10.8	2.5	75.4
1979	16.4	15.8	15.4	18.6	10.1	2.5	78.7
1981	15.8	16.5	16.1	19.2	11.0	3.1	81.7
1983	16.1	17.2	16.8	19.8	11.5	3.5	84.8
1985	15.9	17.7	17.4	20.3	12.4	4.2	87.8
1987	15.3	18.2	18.0	20.8	13.2	5.1	90.6
1989	14.9	18.6	18.6	21.3	14.1	6.0	93.3
1990	14.7	18.8	18.8	21.5	14.4	6.5	94.5
1995	15.1	19.8	19.9	22.6	15.1	7.2	99.8
2000	15.9	20.8	20.9	23.6	15.7	7.5	104.3
(b) Proportion of households							
1977	.175	.206	.185	.258	.143	.033	1.00
1979	.208	.201	.196	.236	.128	.032	1.00
1981	.193	.202	.197	.235	.135	.038	1.00
1983	.190	.203	.198	.233	.136	.041	1.00
1985	.181	.202	.198	.231	.141	.048	1.00
1987	.169	.201	.199	.230	.146	.056	1.00
1989	.160	.199	.199	.228	.151	.064	1.00
1990	.156	.199	.199	.228	.152	.069	1.00
2000	.152	.199	.200	.226	.151	.072	1.00

[a] Income classes, as indicated, are defined by real family income in thousands of
1975 $.

[b] From REEPS model, 1977 base year, in millions.

from the REEPS SAMPLER program. Further adjustment was also required to account for the 2-yr time periods used by REEPS and the fact that REEPS assumes that new housing is built at the beginning of each period while ORNL assumes it is built at the end of each period. The use of an equivalent set of household forecasts for the two models, ORNL and REEPS, was necessary to permit a valid comparison of the simulation results for the two models under each of the three policy scenarios to be carried out.

As can be seen from the second half of Table VI.5, the first three and the fifth income groups have approximately the same proportion of households in 1977, between 14 and 20%, while the fourth group has slightly over 25% and the sixth or highest income group has about 3%. Over time, there is a steady shift of households from lower to higher income groups, due to real economic growth, so that by the year 2000, the lowest income group has about 15% of the households while the highest income group has over 7%, or more than double the 1977 proportion. In absolute terms, there is a steady growth in the total number of households, from 75 million in 1977 to 104 million by the year 2000, for a total increase of about 38% over the 24-yr period.

Total energy consumption and expenditure for each of the six income groups and for each of the three policy scenarios are shown in Table VI.6 for the years 1977, 1983, 1990, and 2000. By construction, there is no difference in these variables across policy scenarios for the year 1977, although these numbers are still relevant for comparing changes across time. Since the number of households in each income group changes over time, it is better to analyze these results in terms of changes in both energy consumption and energy expenditures *per household*. Table VI.7 illustrates the corresponding per-household estimates by income group, both for each of the three primary fuel types — natural gas, fuel oil, and electricity — and for total energy.

Looking at the base case scenario results in the rows marked B in Table VI.7, we see that total energy consumption per household increases with income and is about twice as high for the highest as for the lowest income group. This variable generally decreases over time, the only exception being the highest income group where the estimate for the year 2000 is slightly higher than that forecasted for 1990. The specific fuel components, however, show a somewhat more varied pattern. Electricity consumption per household, and to a lesser extent natural gas consumption per household, increases with income; the ratio of the highest income group figure to the lowest income group figure being about 3. Among other things, this implies that the demand for electricity is more income elastic than for all residential energy in total, a result which is certainly not surprising. The income elasticity of demand for fuel oil is both smaller and appears to decrease with

TABLE VI.6

Total Energy Consumption and Expenditure by Income Class—1977, 1983, 1990, 2000[a]

Income class	No. of households[b]	Energy consumption[c]			Energy expenditures[d]		
		B	D	S	B	D	S
(a) 1977							
1	13.2	1.17	1.17	1.17	4.22	4.22	4.22
2	15.5	1.70	1.70	1.70	6.43	6.43	6.43
3	13.9	1.77	1.77	1.77	6.82	6.82	6.82
4	19.4	2.86	2.86	2.86	11.13	11.13	11.13
5	10.8	1.93	1.93	1.93	7.78	7.78	7.78
6	2.5	0.52	0.52	0.52	2.21	2.21	2.21
National	75.4	9.95	9.95	9.95	38.7	38.7	38.7
(b) 1983							
1	16.1	1.21	1.18	1.21	6.66	6.86	6.63
2	17.2	1.58	1.54	1.57	9.01	9.30	8.98
3	16.8	1.77	1.72	1.76	10.18	10.51	10.13
4	19.8	2.50	2.44	2.49	14.76	15.24	14.67
5	11.5	1.75	1.70	1.74	10.58	10.92	10.50
6	3.5	0.56	0.55	0.56	3.43	3.54	3.41
National	84.8	9.42	9.16	9.36	54.9	56.7	54.6
(c) 1990							
1	14.7	1.02	1.02	1.02	7.02	7.01	6.98
2	18.8	1.56	1.55	1.55	10.90	10.88	10.83
3	18.8	1.80	1.79	1.78	12.65	12.62	12.54
4	21.5	2.45	2.44	2.43	17.72	17.68	17.54
5	14.4	1.92	1.90	1.89	14.07	14.02	13.89
6	6.5	0.84	0.84	0.83	6.19	6.17	6.11
National	94.5	9.52	9.46	9.43	67.9	67.7	67.2
(d) 2000							
1	15.9	1.04	1.04	1.04	8.38	8.37	8.31
2	20.8	1.65	1.65	1.64	13.57	13.56	13.47
3	20.9	1.93	1.92	1.91	15.89	15.87	15.73
4	23.6	2.57	2.56	2.54	21.73	21.70	21.46
5	15.7	2.08	2.07	2.05	17.72	17.69	17.49
6	7.5	1.05	1.05	1.04	9.04	9.02	8.93
National	104.3	10.15	10.11	10.03	84.3	84.2	83.4

[a] Source, ORNL model.
[b] In millions.
[c] In Quads.
[d] Billions of 1975 $.

TABLE VI.7

Energy Consumption and Expenditure per Household by Fuel by Income class[a]

Income class	Case	Energy consumption per household[b]					Energy expenditures per household[c]				
		Gas	Oil	Elec.	Total	% dev.	Gas	Oil	Elec.	Total	% dev.
a) 1977											
1		49.0	22.2	17.1	88.4		94.8	61.5	163.9	320.2	
2		62.5	22.9	24.1	109.5		121.1	63.1	230.0	414.3	
3		73.3	24.1	29.4	126.8		142.1	66.8	280.7	489.6	
4		85.4	27.1	35.0	147.5		165.5	74.8	333.7	574.0	
5		104.3	27.6	46.2	178.2		202.4	76.7	439.9	719.0	
6		118.9	27.2	59.1	205.1		232.3	74.8	563.0	870.1	
National		75.9	24.9	31.2	132.0		147.3	68.9	297.2	513.3	
b) 1983											
1	B	40.5	20.2	14.3	75.0		139.7	100.6	173.2	413.4	
	D	38.2	20.4	14.3	73.0	−2.7	150.8	101.8	173.8	425.8	+3.0
	S	40.4	20.1	14.2	74.8	−0.3	139.0	99.9	173.2	411.5	−0.5
2	B	51.0	20.6	20.4	92.0		175.5	102.0	247.8	525.4	
	D	48.3	20.8	20.5	89.6	−2.6	190.7	103.2	248.4	542.3	+3.2
	S	50.9	20.5	20.3	91.7	−0.3	174.9	101.5	246.6	523.6	−0.3
3	B	60.1	21.1	24.3	105.6		207.0	104.4	295.3	607.4	
	D	56.9	21.4	24.5	102.7	−2.7	224.3	106.2	297.1	627.1	+3.2
	S	59.8	20.9	24.2	105.0	−0.6	205.8	103.8	294.2	604.4	−0.5
4	B	70.7	24.3	31.4	126.5		243.2	120.8	382.2	746.2	
	D	66.9	24.7	31.6	123.2	−2.6	263.9	122.9	383.7	770.5	+3.3
	S	70.4	24.0	31.3	125.6	−0.7	242.2	118.8	380.2	741.7	−0.6
5	B	87.7	22.8	41.6	152.2		301.7	113.0	504.3	920.0	
	D	83.0	23.2	41.7	148.1	−2.7	327.8	115.7	507.0	949.6	+3.2
	S	87.1	22.4	41.3	151.0	−0.8	300.0	111.3	501.7	913.0	−0.8
6	B	93.3	22.9	46.1	162.3		321.7	113.0	559.4	994.2	
	D	88.4	23.2	46.4	158.0	−2.6	347.8	115.9	562.3	1026.0	+3.2
	S	92.8	22.3	45.8	160.9	−0.9	318.8	110.1	556.5	988.4	−0.6
National	B	62.7	21.7	26.7	111.0		215.9	107.8	323.9	647.7	
	D	59.3	22.0	26.8	108.1	−2.6	234.0	109.4	325.3	668.9	+3.3
	S	62.4	21.5	26.6	110.4	−0.5	214.8	106.8	322.4	644.2	−0.5
c) 1990											
1	B	36.2	17.9	15.6	69.7		154.8	120.1	204.0	478.9	
	D	35.7	18.1	15.6	69.4	−0.4	152.8	120.7	204.6	478.2	−0.1
	S	36.1	17.7	15.5	69.3	−0.6	154.2	118.7	203.3	476.1	−0.6
2	B	44.2	18.2	20.6	83.0		188.8	122.1	270.4	581.3	
	D	43.6	18.4	20.7	82.7	−0.4	186.7	122.7	270.9	580.3	−0.2
	S	44.0	18.0	20.5	82.6	−0.5	188.3	120.5	268.8	577.6	−0.6

TABLE VI.7—*Continued*

Income class	Case	Energy consumption per household[b]					Energy expenditures per household[c]				
		Gas	Oil	Elec.	Total	% dev.	Gas	Oil	Elec.	Total	% dev.
3	B	52.3	18.1	25.0	95.4		223.6	121.1	327.1	671.8	
	D	51.5	18.3	25.0	94.8	−0.6	220.4	122.1	328.2	670.2	−0.2
	S	51.9	17.8	24.8	94.5	−0.9	222.0	119.0	325.0	666.0	−0.9
4	B	60.3	21.6	32.2	114.1		258.3	144.3	422.5	824.6	
	D	59.4	21.7	32.3	113.5	−0.5	254.1	145.2	423.5	822.7	−0.2
	S	59.9	21.0	32.0	113.0	−1.0	256.4	140.5	419.3	816.2	−1.0
5	B	73.2	19.0	41.1	133.4		313.6	127.5	538.7	980.5	
	D	72.1	19.2	41.3	132.5	−0.7	308.7	128.2	540.1	977.0	−0.4
	S	72.5	18.5	40.8	131.8	−1.2	310.8	123.3	533.8	967.9	−1.3
6	B	71.3	19.2	39.9	130.4		304.5	128.3	524.0	956.7	
	D	70.2	19.3	40.0	129.5	−0.7	299.8	129.8	524.0	953.6	−0.3
	S	70.5	18.7	39.6	128.7	−1.3	301.4	125.2	517.8	944.4	−1.3
National											
	B	54.5	18.8	27.4	100.7		233.4	125.8	358.8	717.9	
	D	53.7	19.0	27.4	100.1	−0.6	230.0	126.7	359.6	716.2	−0.2
	S	54.1	18.4	27.2	99.8	−0.9	231.8	123.1	356.3	711.0	−1.0
(d) 2000											
1	B	33.1	15.7	16.7	65.6		159.0	147.7	220.0	526.7	
	D	32.9	15.8	16.7	65.4	−0.3	157.8	148.3	220.0	526.1	−0.1
	S	32.9	15.5	16.7	65.1	−0.8	158.4	145.8	218.7	522.3	−0.8
2	B	39.7	16.1	23.7	79.5		190.6	151.1	311.4	653.0	
	D	39.4	16.1	23.8	79.3	−0.3	189.1	151.6	311.8	652.6	−0.1
	S	39.5	15.8	23.6	78.9	−0.8	189.6	148.7	309.9	648.2	−0.7
3	B	47.2	15.5	29.6	92.3		226.9	146.0	388.2	760.7	
	D	46.8	15.6	29.6	92.0	−0.3	224.5	146.5	388.7	759.7	−0.1
	S	46.8	15.2	29.3	91.3	−1.1	224.5	142.7	385.4	753.0	−1.0
4	B	52.9	19.0	37.3	109.2		253.8	178.7	489.4	922.3	
	D	52.4	19.1	37.3	108.8	−0.4	251.7	179.5	489.8	921.1	−0.1
	S	52.4	18.5	37.0	107.9	−1.2	251.7	173.6	485.6	910.9	−1.2
5	B	66.2	16.0	50.2	132.4		318.1	150.1	659.0	1127.0	
	D	65.6	16.0	50.2	131.9	−0.4	315.5	150.8	659.0	1125.0	−0.2
	S	65.4	15.5	49.7	130.6	−1.4	314.2	145.7	653.3	1112.0	−1.3
6	B	69.2	16.5	54.9	140.6		332.0	155.3	721.6	1210.0	
	D	68.7	16.6	55.0	140.2	−0.3	329.3	155.3	721.6	1207.0	−0.2
	S	68.4	16.1	54.5	138.8	−1.3	328.0	151.3	716.2	1195.0	−1.2
National											
	B	49.1	16.1	32.1	97.3		235.7	151.9	421.1	808.6	
	D	48.6	16.2	32.1	96.9	−0.4	233.6	152.5	421.5	807.6	−0.1
	S	48.6	15.7	31.8	96.2	−1.1	233.4	148.1	418.0	799.4	−1.1

[a] Source, ORNL model.
[b] 10^6 Btu/hh.
[c] 1975 $/hh.

time, since the differential in household energy consumption between the highest and lowest income groups is positive but declines over time. Looking across the four individual years shown — 1977, 1983, 1990, and 2000 — energy consumption per household declines across time for both natural gas and fuel oil. Again, electricity consumption indicates a more complex trend. Generally, the consumption of electricity per household is lower in 1983 than in 1977, and then begins to increase slowly after that. However, for the highest two income groups, this increase in per-household consumption of electricity does not begin until sometime after 1990.

Energy expenditures per household, both in total and by fuel type, are also shown in Tables VI.7 and, of course, reflect the projected trends in both energy prices and household energy consumption. It is interesting to note that higher income groups appear to pay higher, rather than lower, energy prices on average since the ratio of expenditures per household between the highest and lowest income groups is larger than the corresponding ratio for consumption per household. Indeed, this general relationship is true for each of the four years shown.

This variation in average energy price across income group is clearly due to differences in household fuel mix since fuel prices for each of the three residential fuels were assumed to be the same for all households. By looking at the proportion of each fuel in total energy consumption per household across income groups and across time, using the estimates shown in Tables VI.7, a more definitive pattern emerges. In general, the proportion of natural gas used is fairly constant across income groups for any given year, while there is a significant substitution away from fuel oil and towards the use of electricity as income rises. For example, in 1977, the proportion of natural gas to total energy consumption per household is approximately 56–57% for all six income groups, while the proportion of oil consumption falls from 25% for the lowest income group to about 13% for the highest income group. The corresponding figures for electricity consumption per household are 19 and 29%. Across time, the proportion of natural gas per household used in the residential sector slowly falls, reaching approximately 50% by the year 2000. Interestingly enough, the corresponding numbers for oil consumption remain fairly constant across time, i.e., approximately 25% for the lowest income group and declining with income to a figure of about 12% or so for the highest income group. This clearly implies that the electricity proportions must rise over time for all income groups, from the 19–29% range in 1977 to a 22–31% range in 1990, and a 25–39% range by the year 2000. Thus, natural gas consumption indicates little income sensitivity and a steady decline over time, both due possibly to availability constraints since the real price of natural gas remains fairly constant, especially after 1985, while its relative price actually falls. On the other hand, electricity con-

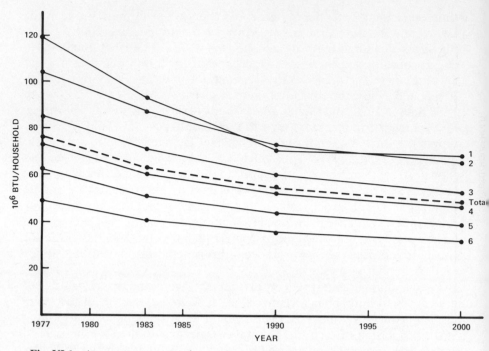

Fig. VI.1 Average gas consumption per household by income group; 1977–2000, base case scenario.

sumption appears to be rather income elastic in the residential sector and to slowly increase over time, due largely to a favorable relative price trend.

These patterns of energy consumption per household over time are summarized in Figs. VI.1–VI.4, which show plots over time of the average consumption data by income group from Table VI.7. Looking first at Fig. VI.4 which shows total energy consumption per household for the period 1977–2000, the general pattern of declining energy consumption over time, except for the highest income group is clearly evident. Figures VI.1–VI.3, natural gas, fuel oil, and electricity consumption per household, respectively, highlight the patterns of changes in residential fuel mix over time. The average gas consumption plots in Fig. VI.1 reveal the basic source of the general decline in total energy consumption over time since natural gas accounts for at least half of estimated residential consumption per household. A convergence of average gas consumption per household for the highest two income groups is also evident, with little difference between the two groups indicated after about 1985. Figures VI.2 and VI.3 reveal the substitution effect between oil and electricity and the relationship of this

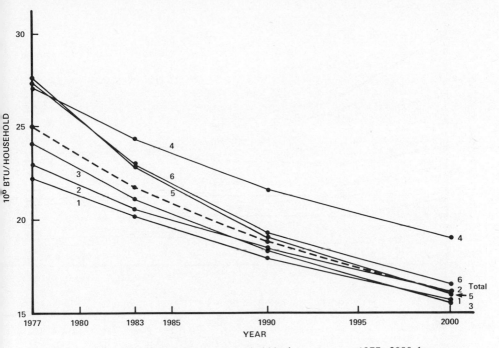

Fig. VI.2 Average oil consumption per household by income group; 1977–2000, base case scenario.

effect with household income. In general, substitution of electricity for fuel oil as a residential fuel is evident for all income groups, especially after 1983 and shows a decided tendency to increase with income. For example, by the year 2000, the average fuel oil consumption per household for the highest income group is approximately equal to that of the second lowest income group, while in terms of average gas consumption per household the highest income group has the highest average consumption level.

The income distributive effects of alternative energy policies are perhaps shown most clearly in Table VI.8, which contains cumulative percentage estimates by income group from lowest to highest for such variables as number of households, total energy consumption, energy expenditures, and family income. The estimated energy budget shares, i.e., energy expenditures as a percentage of total before-tax family income, for each group are shown in Table VI.9. These budget shares are based on estimated mean incomes for the six income groups of $3500, 8000, 13,000, 19,000, 36,000, and 51,000, respectively, derived from the 1977 U.S. Population Census.

The energy budget shares indicate a highly skewed relationship between

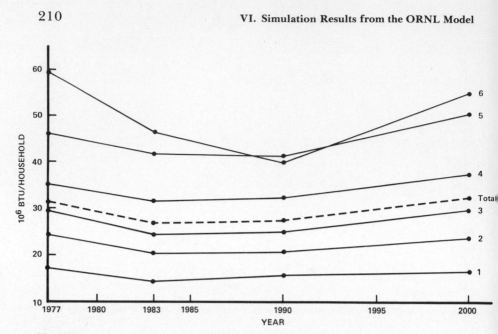

Fig. VI.3   Average electricity consumption per household by income group; 1977–2000, base case scenario.

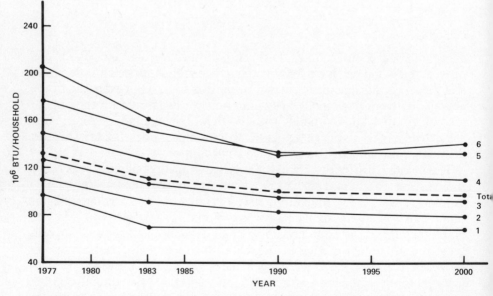

Fig. VI.4   Average energy consumption per household by income group; 1977–2000, base case scenario.

TABLE VI.8

U.S. Residential Energy Consumption—Cumulative Proportions[a]

Income class[b]	Case	Households		Energy consumption		Energy expenditures		Income	
		No.[c]	Cum. %	Quads[d]	Cum. %	1975 $[e]	Cum. %	1975 $	Cum %
(a) 1977									
1		13.2	17.5	1.17	11.8	4.22	10.9	46.2	3.7
2		15.5	38.1	1.70	28.8	6.43	27.6	124.0	13.7
3		13.9	56.6	1.77	46.6	6.82	45.3	181.0	28.4
4		19.4	82.3	2.86	75.4	11.13	74.1	369.0	58.2
5		10.8	96.7	1.93	94.8	7.78	94.3	389.0	89.7
6		2.5	100.0	0.52	100.0	2.21	100.0	128.0	100.0
Total		75.4		9.95		38.59		1237.0	
(b) 1983									
1	B			1.21	12.8	6.66	12.1		
	D	16.1	19.3	1.18	12.9	6.86	12.1	56.4	4.1
	S			1.21	12.9	6.63	12.1		
2	B			1.58	29.6	9.01	28.5		
	D	17.2	39.9	1.54	30.0	9.30	28.5	138.0	14.0
	S			1.57	29.7	8.98	28.9		
3	B			1.77	48.4	10.18	47.1		
	D	16.8	59.8	1.72	48.5	10.51	47.0	218.0	29.8
	S			1.76	48.5	10.13	47.1		
4	B			2.50	74.9	14.76	74.0		
	D	19.8	82.9	2.44	75.1	15.24	73.9	376.0	57.1
	S			2.49	75.1	14.67	74.0		
5	B			1.75	93.5	10.58	93.2		
	D	11.5	96.1	1.70	93.7	10.92	93.2	414.0	87.0
	S			1.74	93.7	10.50	93.2		
6	B			0.56	100.0	3.43	100.0		
	D	3.5	100.0	0.55	100.0	3.54	100.0	179.0	100.0
	S			0.56	100.0	3.41	100.0		
National	B			9.42		54.9			
	D	84.8		9.16		56.7		1381	
	S			9.36		54.6			
(c) 1990									
1	B			1.02	10.7	7.02	10.3		
	D	14.7	15.6	1.02	10.8	7.01	10.4	51.5	3.0
	S			1.02	10.8	6.98	10.4		
2	B			1.56	27.1	10.90	26.4		
	D	18.8	35.4	1.55	27.2	10.88	26.4	150.0	11.8
	S			1.55	27.3	10.83	26.5		
3	B			1.80	46.0	12.65	45.0		
	D	18.8	55.3	1.79	46.1	12.62	45.1	244.0	26.2
	S			1.78	46.1	12.54	45.2		

TABLE VI.8—*Continued*

Income class[b]	Case	Households No.[c]	Households Cum. %	Energy consumption Quads[d]	Energy consumption Cum. %	Energy expenditures 1975 $[e]	Energy expenditures Cum. %	Income 1975 $	Income Cum. %
4	B			2.45	71.7	17.72	71.1		
	D	21.5	78.1	2.44	71.9	17.68	71.2	409.0	50.1
	S			2.43	71.9	17.54	71.3		
5	B			1.92	91.9	14.07	91.8		
	D	14.4	93.3	1.90	92.0	14.02	91.9	518.0	80.5
	S			1.89	91.9	13.89	91.9		
6	B			0.84	100.0	6.19	100.0		
	D	6.5	100.0	0.84	100.0	6.17	100.0	332.0	100.0
	S			0.83	100.0	6.11	100.0		
National									
	B			9.52		67.9			
	D	94.5		9.46		67.7		1705	
	S			9.43		67.2			
(d) 2000									
1	B			1.04	10.2	8.38	9.9		
	D	15.9	15.2	1.04	10.3	8.37	9.8	55.7	3.0
	S			1.04	10.4	8.31	10.0		
2	B			1.65	26.5	13.57	26.0		
	D	20.8	35.2	1.65	26.6	13.56	26.0	166.0	11.7
	S			1.64	26.7	13.47	26.1		
3	B			1.93	45.5	15.89	44.9		
	D	20.9	55.2	1.92	45.6	15.87	44.9	272.0	26.1
	S			1.91	45.8	15.73	45.0		
4	B			2.57	70.8	21.73	70.7		
	D	23.6	77.9	2.56	70.9	21.70	70.7	448.0	49.8
	S			2.54	71.1	21.46	70.7		
5	B			2.08	91.3	17.72	91.7		
	D	15.7	92.9	2.07	91.4	17.69	91.7	565.0	79.7
	S			2.05	91.5	17.49	91.7		
6	B			1.05	100.0	9.04	100.0		
	D	7.5	100.0	1.05	100.0	9.02	100.0	383.0	100.0
	S			1.04	100.0	8.93	100.0		
National									
	B			10.15		84.3			
	D	104.3		10.11		84.2		1890	
	S			10.03		83.4			

[a] Source, ORNL model.

[b] Classified by total before-tax family income (in 1975 $).

[c] Millions of households.

[d] Quadrillion (10^{15}) Btu delivered energy.

[e] Billions of 1975 $.

TABLE VI.9
Estimated Household Energy Budget Shares[a]

Income class	Policy scenario	1977	1983	1990	2000
1	B		11.8	13.6	15.0
	D	9.1	12.2	13.6	15.0
	S		11.8	13.6	14.9
2	B		6.5	7.3	8.2
	D	5.2	6.7	7.3	8.2
	S		6.5	7.2	8.1
3	B		4.7	5.2	5.8
	D	3.8	4.8	5.2	5.8
	S		4.6	5.1	5.8
4	B		3.9	4.3	4.9
	D	3.0	4.1	4.3	4.8
	S		3.9	4.3	4.8
5	B		2.6	2.7	3.1
	D	2.0	2.6	2.7	3.1
	S		2.5	2.7	3.1
6	B		1.9	1.9	2.4
	D	1.7	2.0	1.9	2.4
	S		1.9	1.8	2.3
Total	B		4.0	4.0	4.5
	D	3.1	4.1	4.0	4.5
	S		4.0	3.9	4.4

[a] Energy expenditure as a percentage of before-tax family income. Source, ORNL model.

energy expenditures and household income, with the lowest income group spending over 9% of its income for energy while the highest income group spent less than 2% of its income in 1977. Another way of seeing this non-proportionality or regressiveness between energy expenditures and income is to note from Table VI.8 that the lowest income group has less than 4% of total household income but accounts for almost 11% of total residential energy expenditures. Combining the two lowest income groups, the corresponding figures become 13.7% for income and 27.6% for energy expenditures. Furthermore, this income–energy expenditure relationship worsens over time, as shown in Table VI.9, since the range of estimated energy budget shares, from lowest to highest income group, increases from a range of 9.1 to 1.7 for 1977 to a range of 15.0 to 2.4 for the year 2000. It is also clear that most of the impact of this steadily worsening income–energy relationship is borne by the lower income groups since the energy budget share of the highest two income groups remain fairly constant: approximately 2% over this period. It appears then that the burden of low economic growth and steady increases in the real price of energy in the residential sector are quite likely to be borne more than proportionately by the lower income groups, at least for the base case policy scenario.

B. Alternative Policy Scenarios: Income Distribution

The income distribution impacts for the two alternative energy policies, accelerated deregulation of natural gas and the imposition of mandatory thermal efficiency standards for new housing, are also shown in Tables VI.4 and VI.6 – VI.9. Looking at the energy consumption and energy expenditure per household estimates in Table VI.7, it is clear that these results are consistent with economic theory in terms of direction of change but are not very large in terms of magnitude. In addition, the redistributive effects across income groups from these two policies appear to be minimal. For example, accelerated natural gas deregulation results in a decrease in total energy consumption per household of about 2.7% in 1983, probably the year of maximum impact from this policy, and an increase in energy expenditures per household of approximately 3.0%, both effects due to the increased price of natural gas. Furthermore, these impacts show almost no variation with income. Even the substitution away from natural gas, a major component of total energy consumption, shows little income sensitivity. Across time, the impacts of reduced energy consumption and increased expenditure continue, although the magnitudes of these impacts are considerably reduced from the earlier years. By the year 2000, energy consumption per household under the deregulation scenario is only 0.3% less than that under the base case scenario, while energy expenditures are essentially equivalent for the two scenarios. Again, there appears to be little variation in this pattern across income groups.

The thermal standards scenario also indicates predictable effects, namely, reductions in both residential energy consumption and energy expenditures. However, in contrast with the deregulation effects, there does appear to be some variation in these effects across income groups. In general, the decreases shown in both consumption and expenditures per household for the highest income group are approximately double the size of the corresponding reductions for the lowest two income groups. Further, these reductions increase somewhat over time in percentage terms, again in contrast to the reductions over time under the deregulation scenario. These increased reductions over time for the standards scenario are presumably due to the increasing proportion of the total housing stock which meets the new thermal standards over time as new housing consistent with these standards is added to the existing stock. As the average thermal efficiency of the total housing stock increases over time, this results in increasing reductions in energy consumption, *ceteris paribus*.

The simulation results in terms of the cumulative percentage estimates shown in Table VI.8 reflect similar patterns, namely reduced consumption and increased expenditures (relative to the base case results) for the deregulation scenario, and reductions in both consumptions and expenditures in the case of the standards scenario. Again, however, none of these effects is very large in magnitude, indicating that neither of the two alternative policies appears to have significant redistribution impacts across income groups. This general conclusion is perhaps best demonstrated by the estimated budget shares presented in Table VI.9, which show little variation across the three policies, although the shares do consistently increase slightly under the deregulation policy for all income groups.

Finally, Table VI.4 indicates some interesting differential impacts across both income groups and alternative scenarios with respect to total (present value) discounted expenditures over the 24-year period, 1977–2000. Of particular interest are the results with respect to both equipment and thermal integrity (TI) expenditures. The natural gas deregulation scenario results in relatively small increases in both expenditure categories, relative to the base case, for several (though not all) of the income groups. These increased expenditures are presumably related to the higher cost of natural gas and the resulting substitution towards more efficient, but more expensive, residential appliances and housing. On the other hand, the standards scenario results in rather small reductions in equipment expenditures and substantial increases (in proportional terms) in thermal integrity expenditures. Furthermore, the rate of increase in TI expenditures is fairly income sensitive, the estimated differential effect in percentage terms for the highest income group being at least twice as large as that for the lowest two income groups. Apparently, this reflects both the fact that higher income households are more likely to be able to finance expenditures for increasing the thermal efficiency of their homes, and the fact that their homes are larger and hence require more insulation to achieve any given level of thermal efficiency. However, while the estimated increases in thermal integrity expenditures are significant in a proportional sense, in terms of absolute magnitude they amount to only a small fraction of the expenditures on either equipment or fuel.

VI.4. END-USE IMPLICATIONS

Since residential end use is one of the dimensions of the ORNL energy consumption forecasts, the ORNL model can be used to analyze the end use implications of alternative energy policies. In this section, we discuss the residential end-use forecasts for three end uses: space heating, water heating, and cooking. Taken together, these three end uses account for over 70% of total residential energy consumption. All three residential fuels — natural gas, electricity, and fuel oil — are included in the analysis of space heating energy usage since all three fuels play a significant role in residential space heating. However, for both water heating and cooking, only estimates for natural gas and electricity are presented since fuel oil is not a significant source of household energy for these end uses.

The ORNL space heating forecasts are summarized in Tables VI.10 and VI.11 for each of the three alternative policy scenarios, while the water heating results are presented in Table VI.12. Table VI.13 contains the results for cooking and includes only two scenarios — base case and deregulation — since the mandated thermal efficiency standards scenario impacts the thermal efficiency of new structures, resulting only in space heating effects.

A. Base Case Scenario: End-Use Distribution

The base case forecasts for space heating fuel consumption presented in Table VI.10 indicate a steady decline in total energy consumption after 1979, with the estimate for the year 2000 being slightly over 10% lower than that for 1979, in spite of a substantial increase in the number of households over that period. This reduction in total energy usage for space heating is the result of significant declines in both natural gas and fuel oil consumption, with a partially offsetting increase in electricity usage. The basic source of this change in fuel mix is evident in Table VI.11, which indicates generally falling market shares for natural gas for both existing and new housing, and a strong upward trend in the market share for electricity. In the case of natural gas, the saturation rate among existing households declines by about 7% between 1977 and 2000, from 54% to around 50%, while the penetration rate for new housing shows an even stronger downward trend, about 15% over the same period. By the year 2000, the market share of natural gas space heating among new structures is estimated to be around 40%, although

TABLE VI.10

Space Heating—Fuel Consumption by Fuel Type 1977–2000[a]

Year	Natural gas			Electricity			Fuel oil[b]			Total		
	B	D	S	B	D	S	B	D	S	B	D	S
1977	2.98	2.98	2.98	0.17	0.17	0.17	1.58	1.58	1.58	4.74	4.74	4.74
1979	2.97	2.97	2.97	0.18	0.18	0.18	1.68	1.68	1.68	4.83	4.83	4.83
1981	2.79	2.59	2.77	0.18	0.18	0.17	1.61	1.63	1.60	4.58	4.40	4.55
1983	2.63	2.47	2.61	0.18	0.18	0.17	1.53	1.55	1.51	4.35	4.20	4.29
1985	2.54	2.47	2.51	0.18	0.18	0.18	1.47	1.49	1.44	4.20	4.14	4.14
1987	2.55	2.50	2.52	0.19	0.19	0.18	1.48	1.49	1.45	4.22	4.19	4.15
1989	2.58	2.54	2.55	0.21	0.21	0.20	1.49	1.51	1.46	4.28	4.26	4.20
1990	2.57	2.54	2.54	0.21	0.21	0.20	1.48	1.50	1.45	4.28	4.26	4.19
1995	2.59	2.56	2.55	0.23	0.23	0.22	1.48	1.49	1.44	4.31	4.29	4.22
2000	2.63	2.61	2.58	0.26	0.26	0.25	1.43	1.43	1.38	4.32	4.30	4.21

[a] In quads. Source, ORNL model.
[b] Includes fuel oil plus other fuel consumption.

TABLE VI.11

Space Heating—Saturation–Penetration Rates, Natural Gas and Electricity 1977–2000[a]

Year	Natural gas						Electricity					
	Existing			New			Existing			New		
	B	D	S	B	D	S	B	D	S	B	D	S
1977	53.9	53.9	53.9	47.9	47.9	47.9	15.6	15.6	15.6	33.4	33.4	33.4
1979	53.5	53.5	53.5	45.8	45.8	45.8	16.3	16.3	16.3	34.0	34.0	34.0
1981	53.0	52.8	53.0	42.3	36.4	42.3	17.0	17.1	17.0	36.8	39.3	36.8
1983	52.5	51.9	52.6	39.3	34.4	43.0	17.7	17.9	17.6	39.7	41.8	38.8
1985	51.9	51.4	52.2	37.3	38.8	41.1	18.3	18.5	18.3	41.0	40.3	40.9
1987	51.5	51.1	51.8	37.9	40.0	39.9	18.9	19.0	18.9	39.6	38.7	41.2
1989	51.1	50.8	51.4	38.9	39.9	39.9	19.3	19.4	19.5	38.7	38.3	41.1
1990	50.8	50.6	51.1	39.0	39.9	39.8	19.7	19.8	19.9	38.6	38.3	41.2
1995	50.4	50.3	50.7	39.2	40.4	39.5	20.2	20.2	20.6	38.4	39.2	42.6
2000	50.1	50.0	50.2	40.8	40.9	39.2	21.0	21.1	21.7	40.2	40.2	44.0

[a] Saturation rates refer to market shares for existing structures, while penetration rates refer to market shares for new structures. Source, ORNL model. In percentages.

it falls even lower in 1985 before rebounding slightly. The estimates for electrical space heating consumption indicate even stronger trends in an upward direction. In the case of existing housing, the saturation rate for electricity increases steadily from slightly over 15% in 1977 to 21% by the year 2000. The penetration rate also increases generally over the same period, although the 1985 forecast of 41% is slightly higher than that shown for 2000. The explanation of this local peak for electricity in 1985 is not clear, although the general upward trend is due no doubt to the increasing substitution of natural gas towards electricity in residential space heating.

The water heating story displayed in Table VI.12 is similar to that for space heating, due no doubt to the strong interdependency between the two end uses. Over the period shown, 1977–2000, natural gas consumption for water heating purposes declines by almost 20%, while the saturation rate for existing housing falls from about 53% to slightly less than 45%. Electricity usage, however, exhibits a strong upward trend although total electrical consumption for water heating generally amounts to only one-fourth of that for natural gas. Nevertheless, electricity use increases by over 40% over the period shown under the base case scenario, while the saturation rate rises from 32 to 42%.

Cooking is nowhere nearly as important a residential energy end use as either space heating or water heating, yet the estimates shown in Table VI.13 for cooking are interesting since they also reflect significant substitution

TABLE VI.12

Water Heating — Fuel Consumption and Saturation Rates, Natural Gas and Electricity 1977–2000[a]

	Natural gas						Electricity					
	Consumption (quads)			Saturation (%)			Consumption (quads)			Saturation (%)		
Year	B	D	S	B	D	S	B	D	S	B	D	S
1977	1.13	1.13	1.13	53.4	53.4	53.4	0.22	0.22	0.22	32.1	32.1	32.1
1979	1.10	1.10	1.10	52.7	52.7	52.7	0.22	0.22	0.22	32.7	32.7	32.7
1981	1.07	1.00	1.07	51.9	51.5	51.9	0.23	0.23	0.23	33.6	33.9	33.6
1983	1.03	0.97	1.03	50.8	49.9	50.8	0.24	0.24	0.24	34.7	35.3	34.7
1985	0.98	0.95	0.98	49.7	48.8	49.7	0.24	0.24	0.24	35.9	36.6	35.9
1987	0.97	0.95	0.97	48.7	47.9	48.7	0.26	0.26	0.26	37.1	37.6	37.1
1989	0.96	0.95	0.96	47.8	47.1	47.8	0.26	0.27	0.26	38.1	38.6	38.1
1990	0.95	0.94	0.95	47.0	46.5	47.0	0.27	0.27	0.27	39.0	39.3	39.0
1995	0.92	0.92	0.92	45.8	45.4	45.8	0.29	0.29	0.29	40.6	40.8	40.6
2000	0.92	0.92	0.92	44.8	44.6	44.8	0.31	0.31	0.31	42.3	42.4	42.3

[a] In percentages. Source, ORNL model.

TABLE VI.13

Cooking—Fuel Consumption and Saturation Rates, Natural Gas
and Electricity 1977–2000[a]

	Natural gas				Electricity			
	Consumption (quads)		Saturation (%)		Consumption (quads)		Saturation (%)	
Year	B	D	B	D	B	D	B	D
1977	0.53	0.53	42.6	42.6	0.12	0.12	49.6	49.6
1979	0.53	0.53	41.6	41.6	0.12	0.12	50.5	50.5
1981	0.52	0.50	40.8	40.6	0.13	0.13	51.4	51.5
1983	0.50	0.48	40.1	39.8	0.13	0.13	52.2	52.6
1985	0.50	0.48	39.5	39.1	0.15	0.15	53.0	53.4
1987	0.49	0.48	38.9	38.6	0.15	0.15	53.8	54.0
1989	0.49	0.47	38.5	38.2	0.16	0.16	54.4	54.6
1990	0.49	0.48	38.2	38.0	0.16	0.16	54.9	55.1
1995	0.48	0.47	37.8	37.6	0.17	0.17	55.7	55.8
2000	0.47	0.47	37.3	37.2	0.19	0.20	56.7	56.9

[a] Source, ORNL model.

effects away from natural gas and towards the increased use of electricity.
Based on the forecasts shown in Table VI.13, natural gas consumption for
cooking declines by over 11% between 1977 and 2000, while electricity
cooking use increases by almost 60% over the same period.

B. Alternative Policy Scenarios: End-Use
Distribution

Turning to the results for the accelerated natural gas decontrol scenario,
the basic impact on space heating is a small decline in total energy use, largely
the result of reduced consumption of natural gas, as seen in Table VI.10.
This effect has its maximum impact in 1981 and slowly diminishes after that,
until by 2000 the differential impact has almost completely disappeared.
The usage of electricity and fuel oil for space heating are essentially unaffected by the deregulation scenario. The reasons for these trends are evident
in Table VI.11 where we see only minor changes in the estimated penetration
rates for both natural gas and electricity and essentially no changes in the
saturation rates. Although the market shares for electricity in new housing
do increase substantially as a result of accelerated natural gas deregulation,

the effect does not amount to much in the aggregate given the rather small amount of total electrical energy used for space heating in general. The water heating forecasts shown in Table VI.12 also tell the same general story: a small substitution effect away from natural gas use and towards electricity, with the major impact occurring during the 1981–1983 period. Again, this is not surprising given the deregulation scenario assumptions used in our analysis. With respect to cooking, the deregulation effects appear to be rather small and probably should not be considered significant.

The ORNL results for the mandated thermal efficiency standards scenario for new housing are also shown in Tables VI.10–VI.12, and generally indicate reduced consumption across all three fuels as the direct result of increased thermal efficiency in structures. The increasing impact through new housing is also evident since the magnitude of this induced energy savings slowly increases over time, reaching almost 3% of the total base case space heating fuel consumption by 2000. The market share forecasts shown in Table VI.11 indicate a moderate increase in the penetration rate for electricity under the standards scenario, with natural gas penetration rates also showing small increases relative to the base case results. Thus, it is clear that the market share of fuel oil in new housing declines considerably under the influence of mandated thermal efficiency standards. As discussed earlier, the standards scenario has no effect on either water heating or cooking usage since the standards by assumption only affect the thermal efficiency of new structures.

VI.5. CONCLUSIONS

As we have seen, the simulation results from the ORNL model of residential energy demand are generally consistent in sign or direction with the results predicted by economic theory. For example, an increase in the relative price of natural gas results in decreased use of this fuel and a general substitution towards electricity and fuel oil in response to their reduced relative prices. To the extent that these simulation results are consistent with economic theory, it provides at least partial evidence in support of the general validity of the ORNL model, at least at the aggregate level.

The general picture projected by the ORNL model, whether for the base case or existing scenario, the accelerated natural gas deregulation scenario or the mandated thermal efficiency standards scenario, is one of declining energy consumption in the residential sector for most of this decade, followed by slow but steady growth in energy consumption during the 1990s. In general, the share of electricity is forecasted to increase substantially over the next 20 yr or so, while the share of natural gas declines, even in the absence of natural gas decontrol. Interestingly enough, the two alternative energy policy scenarios, accelerated natural gas deregulation and thermal efficiency standards for new housing, appear to have only mild aggregative impacts. One possible explanation for this result is that the two policies are actually not very constraining on residential energy demand. For example, the accelerated natural gas deregulation policy induces a mild price shock only between 1981 and 1985, since after that period the price decontrol features of the existing NGPA take over, i.e., in 1985. Furthermore, the standards for new housing thermal efficiency assumed in this analysis may also not be very constraining since they are based on a set of voluntary ASHRAE standards which have already been accepted by professional engineers. To the extent that these standards are already being implemented in new construction, the effects of mandatory standards will be minimal and will be confined to the few cases of substandard efficiency choice under the existing policy of nonmandatory standards.

Turning to the income group effects discussed under the distributive analysis, these results indicate a positive income elasticity of demand for energy with the highest income group consuming about twice as much energy per household as the lowest income group. In contrast with the aggregate results which showed total energy consumption generally declining over the 1980s and then increasing slowly during the 1990s, the income group analysis indicates that the total energy consumption *per household* declines over both decades for all income groups except the highest. Thus, on a per household

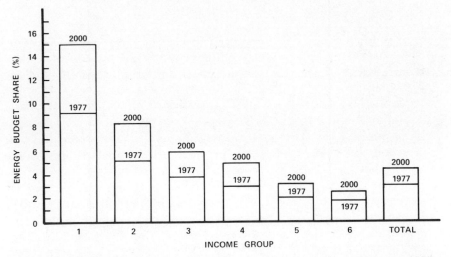

Fig. VI.5   Energy budget shares by income group, ORNL projections; 1977 versus 2000.

basis, there are clear signs of a perverse distributive effect, since the lower income groups appear to share disproportionately in the general reduction in real standards of living caused by higher energy prices. This general impression is reinforced by looking at the estimated energy budget shares, energy expenditures as a proportion of before-tax household income, across both income groups and time. As seen in both Table VI.9 and Fig. VI.5, these numbers indicate that the energy budget share for the lowest income group is over 5 times larger than that of the highest income group. Furthermore, this discrepancy between income groups widens over time so that by 2000 the ORNL model predicts that the energy budget share for the lowest income group is about 15% compared to only 2.4% for the highest income group. Thus, it appears that the burden of slow economic growth and steady increases in the real price of energy, which are likely to continue over the next two decades, will be borne more heavily by the lower income groups.

The distributive effects of accelerated natural gas decontrol appear to be minimal. In general, the aggregative effects are fairly small and there is little variation in these effects across income groups. In contrast, the thermal efficiency standards scenario does indicate some, though generally a rather small, distributive impact. For example, the reductions in both energy consumption and energy expenditures for the highest income group are roughly twice the size of the corresponding reductions for the lowest two income groups. It also appears that these reductions in energy use are

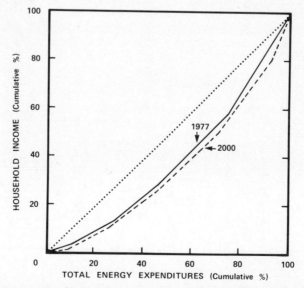

Fig. VI.6 Lorentz curves for household energy expenditures, ORNL projections; 1977 and 2000, base case scenario.

directly related to the pattern of expenditures on new equipment and thermal integrity, particularly the latter. For example, the rate of increase in thermal integrity expenditures under the standards scenario for the highest income group is about double that for the lowest income groups.

One method for summarizing income distributive effects is by use of a Lorentz curve, as shown in Fig. VI.6. The Lorentz curve for energy expenditures plots total energy expenditures by income group in cumulative percentage terms against total household income by income group, also in cumulative percentage terms. Only two curves are shown, 1977 and 2000, since the alternative policy impacts of the three policy scenarios on the distribution of income are not very large, as can be seen from the estimated Gini coefficients reported in Table VI.14. It is also clear from this table that the Lorentz curves for 1983 and 1990 would lie between the two curves shown in Fig. VI.6. All of the required data come from Table VI.8. These curves summarize the distributive impacts forecasted by the ORNL model, namely,

(i) a substantial disproportionate distribution of energy consumption and expenditures across income groups under existing policy, as evidenced by the deep curvature in the 1977 lines,

(ii) a steady worsening of this regressive distributive relationship over time due primarily to increases in the real price of energy, as indicated by the increased curvature of the year 2000 line, and

(iii) a minimal ability of alternative energy policies to change this energy consumption–income relationship, either for better or worse.

TABLE VI.14

Estimated Gini Coefficients for Household Energy
Expenditures[a]

Year	Base case	Deregulation	Standards
1977	.766	.766	.766
1983	.757	.757	.755
1990	.729	.728	.727
2000	.740	.739	.739

[a] The Gini coefficient is defined as the ratio of the area under the cumulative household energy expenditure versus cumulative household income curve to the area under the 45° or equal distribution effects curve, both shown in Fig. VI.6. The actual curve, shown for 1977 and 2000 only, is a piecewise linear curve based on the data in Table VI.8. Source, ORNL model.

Finally, we should point out that although the ORNL model has generally performed well in terms of the predicted sign or direction of movements, we do not have any verification of the predicted magnitudes of these impacts. This is particularly important with respect to the distributive analysis for at least two reasons:

1. the ORNL model was not designed for the purposes of analyzing distributive impacts of energy policy so that some degree of simulation error may be expected and

2. the forecasted differential impacts by income group of alternative energy policies appear in general to be rather small, and in some cases, zero.

Since this last result does not seem altogether intuitive, it may be a figment of the model's structure, rather than an accurate forecast. It would therefore be useful to have independent corroboration of these results if we are to have much faith in the ORNL policy conclusions. Fortunately, such a comparison is possible using a similar set of simulation results from the REEPS model of residential energy demand, a comparison to which we now turn in Chapter VII.

CHAPTER **VII**

A Comparative Analysis of Model Performance: REEPS versus ORNL

In chapters III – VI, we have presented in-depth outlines of the methodology and structure used in each of the two residential energy demand models analyzed in this study, the REEPS model and the ORNL model, as well as detailed analyses of the results of using each model to simulate three alternative energy policy scenarios over the next decade or so. With these discussions in mind, we now turn to a comparative analysis of the performances of the two models in terms of their policy simulation results.

VII.1. INTRODUCTION

This chapter contains a detailed comparative evaluation of the performance of each of the two residential energy demand models, REEPS and

225

ORNL, with respect to the projected aggregative and distributive impacts of alternative energy policies as they affect residential energy demand. At the aggregative level, we focus on total energy consumption and expenditures, consumption and expenditures per household, and the energy-saving investment implications of mandatory standards covering the thermal performance of new housing. The distributional comparisons include several different distributional dimensions: fuel type, end use, and income group. We did not attempt to run the ORNL model jointly by region by income group, since the model is not designed for this purpose, and hence did not make regional comparisons. However, the three distributional dimensions used in this study—fuel type, end use, and income group—should still permit a useful assessment of the comparative performance of the two models with respect to predicting distributional impacts in general.

A. Principles of Model Comparison

The performance of forecasting models in general can be evaluated in terms of at least four criteria:

(i) the theoretical consistency of the predictions of the model in terms of the direction of the projected impacts;
(ii) the reasonableness of the results predicted by the model, in terms of the size or magnitude of the estimated impacts;
(iii) the ability of the model to predict or forecast accurately when compared to known data; and
(iv) the flexibility and usefulness of the model in terms of the range of alternative scenarios or situations which can be analyzed and the number of different dimensions which can be evaluated.

The first criterion, theoretical consistency, can be judged by comparing the direction of an impact projected by a model, i.e., the qualitative impact, to the direction or sign of the effect predicted by economic theory. For example, according to the theory of consumer behavior, own-price effects will generally be negative so that we would expect a model of residential energy demand to predict an increase in electricity consumption given a decline in the real price of electricity, all other variables held constant. On the other hand, a model which predicted a reduction in electricity demand under these conditions would normally be judged to be inconsistent with economic theory. The second criterion, the reasonableness of estimated magnitudes, is considerably more difficult to use since on an a priori basis we typically have little information as to what constitutes a *reasonable* forecast in terms of magnitude. However, in some cases it may be possible to have a fairly precise a priori notion as to at least a reasonable range of possible magnitudes. In such cases, model projections can be judged to be either reasonable or unreasonable in a quantitative sense as well.

The predictive performance of a model, the third criterion, is usually judged by comparing model forecasts with actual data for a time period other than the one used to estimate the model in the first place. If the time period selected for comparison is prior to the time period used to calibrate the model, model forecasts, or *backcasts* as they are sometimes referred to in this situation, can be compared to the known data and the overall predictive performance can be summarized in terms of *goodness-of-fit* statistics. A similar procedure can also be used for predictive comparisons over a post-calibration time period. In our study, however, the models were not used to predict over a known period, so that model performance in our case cannot be judged using the third criterion.

The fourth criterion, flexibility in both applications and analysis, is especially important for the purposes of policy analysis. This is because policy designers and evaluators typically do not have the luxury of having access to a large number of different models, but instead must usually rely upon one, or perhaps several, models which are used to analyze a variety of policy scenarios. In addition, the relevant dimensions for analyzing any particular policy issue will vary widely with the issue at hand. In some cases, the most important issue may be aggregate in nature (e.g., the impact of an increase in world oil prices upon total U.S. imports) while in other cases, the primary focus of the analysis may be upon distributional concerns or upon a particular segment of the economy. The ideal model would, of course, be one which is flexible in terms of both application and analytic dimensions, although in practice there are likely to be trade-offs, with any individual model being more specialized in some sense and hence less flexible. Even so, models which are more flexible are likely to be more useful for policy evaluation purposes.

In this discussion of the performances of the REEPS and ORNL models of residential energy demand, we shall be concerned with the first, second, and fourth of these four criteria. In addition, we shall also be interested in comparing the quantitative projections of these two models in as many dimensions as possible to judge model performance on both an absolute and a relative basis. Before carrying out this comparative evaluation of the two models, however, it is first necessary to calibrate the models consistently, i.e., between each other, so that the results of the two models can be meaningfully compared. The calibration procedures used in this study are described in the following section.

B. Implementation of the REEPS–ORNL Comparisons

As has been pointed out earlier, although both the REEPS and ORNL models are sophisticated models of residential energy demand in which key model dimensions are similarly disaggregated (e.g., four fuel types, eight end uses, several different housing types), there still remain important differences in terms of both model structure and variable definitions which require consideration and adjustment to make valid comparison of the forecasts of the models possible. These differences include differences in model structure, so that adjustments to model inputs were required to make the two models act as similarly as possible, and differences in variable definitions, which require the adoption of a common set of data definitions.

One of the basic differences in model structure between the two models involves the way in which the exogenous housing stock variable is computed from input data on new housing units and the total housing stock of the last period. The REEPS model adds new housing units to the existing housing stock to get the total housing stock at the *beginning* of each period, while the ORNL model adds new housing units to the existing housing stock at the *end* of each period. Furthermore, the REEPS model uses 2-yr periods in its analysis, so that, for example, the period labeled 1981 in REEPS includes both 1981 and 1982, while the ORNL model assumes single-year periods. The result is that the ORNL model, for example, would not take into account the additional energy consumption due to new 1981 housing, i.e., housing constructed during 1981, until 1982, while the REEPS model would include this additional consumption under its 1981 period. Furthermore, since the REEPS model works in terms of 2-yr periods and thus adds two years of new housing each time, the 1981 total housing stock for REEPS would include both 1981 and 1982 new housing.

To account for these differences so as to permit valid comparisons between the two sets of projections, we adjusted the ORNL model as follows. First, we had the ORNL model build 2 yrs of new housing in each even year and none in the odd years. Second, the existing and new housing stock numbers in the ORNL model were moved back 1 yr, e.g., from 1981 to 1980. The overall result was that in each even year, 2 yrs of new housing for the 2 yrs following the even year were built so that, for example, the new housing data for 1980 was the sum of new housing units actually built in 1981 and 1982. Since the REEPS total housing stock in 1981 includes new housing for both 1981 and 1982 also, the result of these two adjustments was to make the odd-year forecasts of the two models comparable. Unfortunately, it was necessary as a result to ignore the even-year forecasts for the purposes of intermodel comparison.

A third and related adjustment was also necessary to produce consistency in terms of the annual fuel prices that each model used or assumed in making its new housing thermal efficiency decisions. This adjustment consisted of setting even-year fuel prices equal to the next (i.e., odd) year prices in ORNL so that the ORNL model would *see* the same set of exogenous fuel prices for the purposes of new housing investment decisions as the REEPS model assumes. Finally, a fourth adjustment in the case of the standards scenario involved imposing the thermal efficiency upper bound or constraint in ORNL starting in 1980, as compared to 1981 for the REEPS model. The result was that both models took into account the standards constraint on minimum thermal efficiency starting at the same point in time, i.e., with new 1981 housing.

Another important difference between the two models that required adjustment is that the REEPS model includes *other fuel* in its *fuel oil* category, since it has only three categories of residential fuels, whereas the ORNL model has separate categories for *fuel oil* and *other fuel*. Accordingly, we combined the original 1977 fuel oil and other fuel consumptions under the fuel oil category when initializing the ORNL model. The original *other fuel* input data were left unchanged since the ORNL model will not run with zero values for initial-year fuel consumption. For the forecast years (i.e., all years following 1977) we report total fuel consumption across fuel type which is net of the ORNL forecast for *other fuels* to avoid double counting.

In all other cases, similar values for both the base-year or initial-year input data and the exogenous variable input data for all other years were used. For example, the same set of (pre-adjusted) exogenous housing stock data for both total and new housing was used in both models. In the case of the income group analyses using the ORNL model, the necessary input data were generally not available from published sources. In this case, projections from the REEPS model at the income group level were used, both to provide the required input data for running the ORNL model and to ensure comparability between the two models. Finally, the same set of exogenous fuel price forecasts for all years modeled was used for both models.

The only set of variable values which was not changed to produce a comparable starting point for the two models were the behavioral and technological parameters. In each case, the values which came with the original model were used and no attempt was made to either change or standardize these input values. The underlying rationale for this approach, briefly discussed earlier, was to produce a set of model projections based on running each model on its own terms, that is, as the policy analyst would presumably use the model. Thus, the set of behavioral and technological parameter values which came with version 7.1 of the ORNL model was used to produce the ORNL projections, while the REEPS forecasts were based on the set of parameter values supplied with the version of the REEPS model made available to us by the Electric Power Research Institute.

VII.2. COMPARISON OF MODEL PROJECTIONS

The two microeconomic models of residential energy demand used in our analysis of energy policy impacts, ORNL and REEPS, differ fundamentally in terms of both concept and architecture, as pointed out in Chapter III. It is not surprising then that the projections of the two models with respect to a number of energy demand variables should also differ. In this section, we compare the two sets of model projections in terms of a variety of dimensions: aggregate energy consumption and expenditures, type of residential fuel, end use, new versus existing housing, alternative policy scenario, and income group. The purpose of this discussion is not necessarily to pass judgment upon either of the two models, but rather to compare the two alternative sets of model projections and to examine the potential for explaining significant differences between the two sets of forecasts.

A. Aggregate Energy Consumption and Expenditures

The ORNL and REEPS projections for total energy consumption and expenditures are shown side by side in Tables VII.1 and VII.2 for each of the three policy scenarios and for the odd years between 1979 and 1991. Since the two models were calibrated using a common set of input data for 1977 and since the two alternative policy scenarios—accelerated natural gas deregulation and mandatory thermal efficiency standards—do not have impacts until 1981, we date the beginning of all tables at 1979. It should also be pointed out that the ORNL results for 1991 are based on linear interpolation between its 1989 and 1995 projections, since the ORNL model did not produce 1991 projections directly. Furthermore, the REEPS forecasts end with 1991.

Table VII.1 shows the total residential energy consumption projections for the two models for each of the three policy scenarios, measured in 10^{15}

TABLE VII.1

Total Energy Consumption: REEPS versus ORNL Projections[a]

Year	Base case			Deregulation		Standards	
	REEPS	ORNL	% diff.	REEPS[b]	ORNL[b]	REEPS[b]	ORNL[b]
1979	10.06	9.92	−1.4	—	—	—	—
1981	10.03	9.66	−3.7	−3.8	−3.1	−1.3	−0.4
1983	9.85	9.41	−4.5	−2.4	−2.7	−1.7	−0.5
1985	9.76	9.25	−5.2	−0.8	−1.3	−2.2	−0.6
1987	9.94	9.32	−6.2	−0.6	−0.8	−2.6	−0.8
1989	10.11	9.44	−6.6	−0.4	−0.6	−2.8	−0.8
1991[c]	10.26	9.51	−7.3	−0.5	−0.5	−2.9	−0.9

[a] In quads. Source, REEPS, ORNL models.

[b] Percent difference from own base case estimate.

[c] 1991 ORNL estimates based on linear interpolation between 1989 and 1995 projections.

Btu or quads. For the base case forecasts, differences between the two projections are shown in the fourth column as a percentage of the REEPS estimate. For the two alternative policy scenarios, deregulation and standards, the percentage figures shown in the fifth through eighth (last) columns represent the percentage difference between the alternative policy scenario projection and the base case projection for the same model. Thus, an ORNL figure for the deregulation case of −3.1%, at the top of the sixth

TABLE VII.2

Total Energy Expenditures: REEPS versus ORNL Projections[a]

Year	Base case			Deregulation		Standards	
	REEPS	ORNL	% diff.	REEPS[b]	ORNL[b]	REEPS[b]	ORNL[b]
1979	45.2	43.9	−2.9	—	—	—	—
1981	51.0	48.9	−4.1	+7.5	+8.0	−0.8	−0.4
1983	56.7	54.9	−3.2	+3.4	+3.3	−1.2	−0.5
1985	63.8	61.9	−3.0	−0.3	−0.5	−1.4	−0.6
1987	66.3	64.0	−3.5	−0.3	−0.3	−1.7	−0.8
1989	68.7	66.4	−3.3	−0.1	−0.2	−1.8	−0.8
1991[c]	71.4	69.3	−2.9	−0.1	−0.1	−2.0	−0.9

[a] In billions of 1975 $. Source, REEPS, ORNL models.

[b] Percent difference from own base case estimate.

[c] 1991 ORNL estimates based on linear interpolation between 1989 and 1995 projections.

column, indicates that the ORNL deregulation projection was 3.1% lower than the corresponding ORNL base case projection. A similar format is also used in Table VII.2.

For the base case scenario, both models indicate total residential energy demand falling through 1985, followed by an increasing trend throughout the remainder of the decade. A major difference between the two projections, however, is that the REEPS model predicts that energy demand will reach the 1979 level again by 1989, while ORNL projects a level of total energy consumption in 1989 that is still 5% lower than its 1979 estimate. This difference is further reflected in the fact that the two sets of base case projections tend to diverge over time, as shown by the numbers in the fourth column, so that by 1991 the ORNL estimate of total residential energy consumption is 7.3% less than the corresponding REEPS estimate. Since the absolute difference between these two forecasts is about three-fourths of a quad, this difference should not be considered insignificant.

The projections of both models for the two alternative policy scenarios seem reasonable from a qualitative point of view, indicating reduced energy demand under both natural gas deregulation and thermal efficiency standards. There are some interesting quantitative differences, however. In the case of natural gas deregulation, the REEPS model indicates a larger reduction for 1981 and somewhat smaller reductions for 1985 and later years. Moreover, in the case of the standards policy, the REEPs model projects significantly larger reductions for each of the years shown. For example, the REEPS forecast for 1991 under the standards scenario is a full two percentage points lower, relative to its own base case forecast, than the corresponding ORNL projection difference. Thus, the REEPS model appears to project a significantly larger impact on energy consumption from mandatory thermal efficiency standards than does the ORNL model. Turning back to the two sets of forecasts under the deregulation scenario, it should be pointed out that the general pattern of a large reduction in energy demand in 1981 and 1983, followed by a steadily closing gap relative to the base case projection, is quite reasonable. This is because the accelerated natural gas decontrol scenario assumes an immediate *fly up* of natural gas prices in 1981, lasting until 1984, followed by an assumed price path (after 1984) which is equivalent to that assumed for the base case scenario. The generally declining gap between the two scenarios after 1984 is the result of the declining relative influence of new housing constructed during the 1981 – 1984 period.

The total residential energy expenditure forecasts in Table VII.2 for both models also seem consistent with a priori judgment, although there are some quantitative differences between the two sets of projections which primarily reflect the differences in forecasted energy consumption discussed above. For the base case scenario, both models predict a steady increase in real expenditures between 1979 and 1991, with the 1991 estimates being almost 60% higher than those for 1979. For the REEPS forecasts, this increase occurs somewhat more rapidly, so that by 1987 its projected real energy expenditures are $2.3 billion higher than the corresponding ORNL projection. Furthermore, this gap remains about the same for 1989 and 1991. Both deregulation projections are similar and indicate substantially higher energy expenditures for 1981 and 1983 as a result of the higher natural gas prices, with the 1981 expenditure impact estimated to be over $7 billion in magnitude. Finally, the projections for the mandatory thermal efficiency standards scenario indicate small reductions in total energy expenditures for both models, although the REEPS reductions are consistently higher than the ORNL reductions.

B. Household-level Projections

Tables VII.3 – VII.10 contain a summary of the REEPS and ORNL residential energy projections on a per household basis for each of the three policy scenarios for the period 1979 – 1991. Total (across fuel type) energy consumption forecasts per household are shown in Table VII.3, while similar projections for energy expenditures per household are shown in Table VII.4. Tables VII.5, VII.7, and VII.9 contain energy consumption forecasts per household broken down into the three major residential fuels — electricity, natural gas, and fuel oil — so that the impacts on individual fuel demands can be analyzed. Tables VII.6, VII.8, and VII.10 show the household fuel consumption data in the previous tables in fuel-share form.

In Table VII.3, both models predict a substantial decline in per-household consumption of energy for the base case scenario over the next decade, due to the increasing real cost of residential fuels in general. Starting from an assumed common value of 134.0×10^6 Btu/hh for 1977 (not shown), both models indicate a steady decline over the period although there are differences in the predicted extent of this decline. The REEPS model predicts that average household energy consumption will decline by about 20% between 1977 and 1991, while the ORNL model predicts a 25% decline over the same period. Clearly, this difference corresponds to the forecast differences between the two models with respect to total residential energy consumption, shown in Table VII.1, since both models used the same set of exogenous annual housing stock estimates. However, the per-household projections are more fundamental since the total consumption estimates are the result of multiplying predicted annual average energy consumption per household by the given number of households for each year in the analysis.

TABLE VII.3

Total Energy Consumption per Household: REEPS versus ORNL Projections[a]

Year	Base case			Deregulation		Standards	
	REEPS	ORNL	% diff.	REEPS	ORNL	REEPS	ORNL
1979	128.0	126.0	−1.6	128.0	126.0	128.0	126.0
1981	122.6	118.2	−3.6	118.0	114.6	121.1	117.7
1983	116.2	111.0	−4.5	113.3	108.1	114.0	110.4
1985	111.3	105.4	−5.3	110.4	104.0	109.0	104.7
1987	109.7	102.9	−6.2	109.1	102.2	106.4	102.2
1989	108.1	101.1	−6.5	107.6	100.5	105.1	100.3
1991[b]	106.8	99.6	−6.7	106.3	99.1	103.7	98.7

[a] 10^6 Btu/hh. Source, REEPS, ORNL models.
[b] 1991 ORNL estimates based on linear interpolation between 1989 and 1995 projections.

With respect to the two alternative policy scenarios, the projections from both models are consistent with a priori expectations, namely, a reduction in total energy consumption per household in each case. However, the differences between the two sets of projections, across both time and policy scenarios, are now more transparent. For example, although the REEPS model projects a substantially larger impact under the standards scenario than does the ORNL model, this impact does not appear to show up in columns 7 and 8 of Table VII.3 which shows a REEPS estimate of 103.7 versus an ORNL estimate of 98.7 million Btu/hh for 1991. The explanation of this apparent inconsistency is evident by noting that the ORNL model projects a more rapid decline in average household energy consumption under the base case scenario than does the REEPS model, and that this is the primary reason for the lower ORNL estimates shown in column 8. The projected impacts of mandatory thermal efficiency standards can be seen by comparing the standards estimates of each model to its own corresponding base case estimates, a procedure which indicates a REEPS standards impact of about −3% in 1991 compared to an ORNL impact of less than −1%.

The total energy expenditures per household forecasts shown in Table VII.4 indicate substantial increases in real expenditures over the period shown for both models. Again, using the common initial value for 1977 of 513.3 (1975) $/hh (not shown), the 1991 base case projections indicate a 40–45% increase in real energy expenditures per household over 1977. Again, there are some differences between the projections of the two models for some of the intervening years but the overall trend is unmistakable. This

TABLE VII.4

Total Energy Expenditures per Household: REEPS versus ORNL Projections[a]

	Base case			Deregulation		Standards	
Year	REEPS	ORNL	% diff.	REEPS	ORNL	REEPS	ORNL
1979	575.1	558.1	−3.0	575.1	558.1	575.1	558.1
1981	623.5	598.5	−4.0	669.6	646.3	618.5	596.1
1983	668.3	647.7	−3.1	690.7	668.9	660.4	644.2
1985	727.3	705.3	−3.0	724.7	701.8	717.1	700.7
1987	732.0	706.8	−3.4	729.8	704.6	719.6	701.3
1989	734.9	711.5	−3.2	733.2	710.4	721.3	706.1
1991[b]	742.6	725.2	−2.4	741.9	723.8	728.4	718.9

[a] 1975 $/hh.   Source, REEPS, ORNL models.
[b] 1991 ORNL estimates based on linear interpolation between 1989 and 1995 projections.

trend also clearly indicates a significant slowing down in the rate of increase for the latter half of the 1980s, no doubt due to the reduced rate of price increases assumed for that period relative to the earlier years.

With respect to natural gas deregulation, both models indicate a substantial increase in real expenditures per household for 1981 and 1983, amounting to approximately 50 (1975) $/hh in 1981 or about 8% of the base case expenditures in that year.   This impact is reduced in 1983 and is considerably smaller in later years, indicating that the heaviest impact of immediate natural gas deregulation should occur in the early years since offsetting adjustments can be expected to set in increasingly after that.   In this respect, both models indicate a very rapid adjustment process.   Indeed, beginning with 1985, energy expenditures per household for both models are slightly lower than the corresponding base case projections, presumably due to 1981–1984 investments in more efficient appliances and housing induced by the higher natural gas prices.

The forecasts in the case of mandatory thermal efficiency standards indicate lower real expenditures per household, relative to the base case, as we would expect since the impact of the standards scenario is increased capital expenditures on the housing shell and a resulting reduction in energy consumption for space heating and air conditioning.   Both models indicate an estimated annual savings in real energy expenditures of from 5 to 15 (1975) $/hh/yr, with these annual savings generally increasing over time and with the REEPS model indicating annual savings which are approximately double those of the ORNL model.

C. Fuel-Specific Energy Consumption
   Projections

Projections of average annual household energy consumption for each of the three major residential fuels — electricity, natural gas, and fuel oil — are shown in Tables VII.5 and VII.6 for the base case scenario, and in Tables VII.7–VII.10 for the deregulation and standards scenarios. Note that the total energy consumption estimates correspond to those in Table VII.3. The percentage difference figures in Tables VII.5, VII.7, and VII.9 express the difference between the forecasts of the two models as a percentage of the corresponding REEPS estimates.

Looking first at the base case projection in Tables VII.5 and VII.6, both models predict that the consumption of electricity per household will decline slightly by 1985, by approximately $1 - 1\frac{1}{2}$ million Btu, or around 400 kWh/hh/yr, followed by a mild increase in demand. The two models differ somewhat in the magnitude of the increasing trend after 1985 since although both models project a level of electrical consumption per household by 1991 which is roughly equivalent to the original 1979 levels, REEPS indicates an increase of 1.7 million Btu/hh (or 6.2%) from 1985 to 1991 while ORNL only shows an increase of 0.8 million Btu/hh (or 3.0%) over the same period. Thus, in terms of the relative difference between the two sets of forecasts, there is an indication of an increasing divergence over time for estimated household electricity consumption after 1985, as shown by the numbers in the percentage difference column.

The story for natural gas is somewhat different. In this case, both models predict a sizable decline in the average consumption of natural gas per household, but ORNL predicts a considerably more severe downward trend than does REEPS. For example, by 1991 the ORNL model predicts that natural gas consumption per household will have fallen to 74% of its 1979 figure, while the REEPS projection for 1991 indicates average consumption per household at over 80% of its 1979 level. Thus, the ORNL projection implies an additional annual reduction of some 8.5 million Btu/hh (or 85 therms) by 1991 for the base case scenario.

With respect to average household fuel oil demand, there is also a significant disparity between the forecasts of the two models. While both models indicate a consistent decline in average fuel oil consumption over the period shown, the decline forecasted by the REEPS model is larger than that estimated by the ORNL model. By 1991, REEPS estimates that household fuel oil demand will be 63% of its 1979 level, while ORNL forecasts a 1991 household consumption of over 70% of its 1979 figure. This difference in the two projections amounts to 3.5 million Btu of fuel oil per household per year by 1991.

TABLE VII.5

Energy Consumption per Household by Fuel Type: REEPS versus ORNL—Base Case[a]

Year	Electricity			Natural gas			Fuel oil[c]			Total consumption		
	REEPS	ORNL	% diff.	REEPS	ORNL	% diff.	REEPS	ORNL	% diff.	REEPS	ORNL	% diff.
1979	29.3	27.7	−5.5	74.8	72.9	−2.5	23.9	25.4	+6.3	128.0	126.0	−1.6
1981	28.7	27.0	−5.9	71.4	67.6	−5.3	22.5	23.7	+5.3	122.6	118.2	−3.6
1983	27.9	26.7	−4.3	68.0	62.7	−7.8	20.2	21.7	+7.4	116.2	111.0	−4.5
1985	27.6	26.5	−4.0	65.5	58.7	−10.4	18.2	20.2	+11.0	111.3	105.4	−5.3
1987	28.3	26.7	−5.7	64.5	56.7	−12.1	17.0	19.6	+15.3	109.7	102.9	−6.2
1989	28.8	26.9	−6.6	63.5	55.1	−13.2	15.8	19.2	+21.5	108.1	101.1	−6.5
1991[b]	29.3	27.3	−6.8	62.2	53.7	−13.7	15.2	18.7	+23.0	106.8	99.6	−6.7

[a] 10^6 Btu/hh.   Source, REEPS, ORNL models.
[b] 1991 ORNL estimates based on linear interpolation between 1989 and 1995 projections.
[c] Fuel oil equals oil plus *other fuel* consumption.

238

VII. REEPS versus ORNL

TABLE VII.6

Energy Consumption per Household-Fuel Shares: REEPS versus
ORNL—Base Case[a]

	Electricity		Natural gas		Fuel oil[b]	
Year	REEPS	ORNL	REEPS	ORNL	REEPS	ORNL
1979	22.9	22.0	58.4	57.8	18.7	20.2
1981	23.4	22.8	58.2	57.2	18.4	20.0
1983	24.0	24.0	58.6	56.5	17.4	19.5
1985	24.8	25.1	58.8	55.7	16.4	19.2
1987	25.8	25.9	58.7	55.1	15.5	19.0
1989	26.6	26.6	58.8	54.4	14.6	19.0
1991[c]	27.4	27.4	58.4	53.8	14.2	18.8

[a] In percentage. Source, REEPS, ORNL models.

[b] Fuel oil equals oil plus *other fuel* consumption.

[c] 1991 ORNL estimates based on linear interpolation between 1989 and 1995 projections.

Overall, then, there are significant differences between the two sets of forecasts for the base case scenario at both the total household energy consumption level and by the three major residential fuels. With respect to total energy consumption per household, the ORNL model projects a substantially larger decline in energy consumption per household over the 1979–1991 period than does the REEPS model. For example, by 1991 the ORNL projection is almost 7% lower than the corresponding REEPS projection. Behind this difference in aggregate forecasts, however, there are even more striking differences with respect to the individual fuels, as can be seen from the fuel share estimates shown in Table VII.6. The projections for electricity consumption per household are in fairly close agreement, although the REEPS model does predict a slightly higher rate of increase after 1985. With respect to natural gas, however, the REEPS projections imply a fairly constant share of slightly less than 60% over the period shown, while the ORNL model estimates that the share of natural gas in total household energy consumption will fall steadily from about 58% in 1979 to a little under 54% by 1991. In the case of fuel oil, the third major residential source of energy, the projections are essentially reversed. The ORNL projections indicate a fairly constant share for fuel oil, in the 19–20% range, while the REEPS projections reveal a steady decline in the fuel oil share, from slightly less than 19% in 1979 to around 14% by 1991. Thus, the REEPS model predicts a fairly constant share of household energy consumption for natural gas and the gradual substitution away from fuel oil towards an increasing use of

TABLE VII.7

Energy Consumption per Household by Fuel Type: REEPS versus ORNL — Deregulation[a]

Year	Electricity			Natural gas			Fuel oil[c]			Total consumption		
	REEPS	ORNL	% diff.	REEPS	ORNL	% diff.	REEPS	ORNL	% diff.	REEPS	ORNL	% diff.
1979	29.3	27.7	−5.5	74.8	72.9	−2.5	23.9	25.4	+6.3	128.0	126.0	−1.6
1981	28.7	27.1	−5.6	66.8	63.6	−4.8	22.5	23.9	+6.2	118.0	114.6	−2.9
1983	28.1	26.8	−4.6	65.0	59.1	−9.1	20.2	22.1	+9.4	113.3	108.0	−4.7
1985	27.7	26.7	−3.6	64.5	56.9	−11.8	18.2	20.4	+12.1	110.4	104.0	−5.8
1987	28.3	26.8	−5.3	63.8	55.5	−13.0	17.0	19.8	+16.5	109.1	102.1	−6.4
1989	28.7	27.0	−5.9	63.0	54.2	−14.0	16.0	19.3	+20.6	107.7	100.5	−6.7
1991[b]	29.4	27.1	−7.8	61.6	53.2	−13.6	15.2	18.7	+23.1	106.2	99.0	−6.8

[a] 10^6 Btu/hh. Source, REEPS, ORNL models.
[b] 1991 ORNL estimates based on linear interpolation between 1989 and 1995 projections.
[c] Fuel oil equals oil plus "other fuel" consumption.

electricity. The ORNL model, on the other hand, projects a constant share for fuel oil and the gradual substitution of electricity for natural gas (instead of fuel oil) as a residential fuel.

An equivalent set of household energy consumption and fuel share forecasts for the natural gas deregulation scenario are shown in Tables VII.7 and VII.8. Both models indicate substantial reductions in the average annual consumption of natural gas per household for the two major impact years shown, 1981 and 1983. The REEPS model predicts a decrease in annual natural gas usage per household of 4.6 million Btu in 1981 and 3.0 million Btu in 1983, while the ORNL reductions amount to 4.0 and 3.6 million Btu, respectively. After 1983, both models indicate reduced levels of natural gas consumption per household but with the effects of natural gas deregulation steadily diminishing, so that by 1991 both forecasts are within 1% of the corresponding base case predictions. The projected impacts upon household consumption of the other two fuels, electricity and fuel oil, are minimal, although there is an interesting difference with respect to interfuel substitution possibilities. Both models indicate small increases in the consumption of electricity per household, but only the ORNL model also predicts a related increase in average fuel oil usage. Thus, the ORNL projections indicate substitution away from natural gas and towards increased consumption of both electricity and fuel oil, while the REEPS model indicates only substitution between natural gas and electricity, as a result of the deregulation-induced runup in natural gas prices. While these effects are not sizable in

TABLE VII.8

Energy Consumption per Household-Fuel Shares: REEPS versus
ORNL — Deregulation[a]

	Electricity		Natural gas		Fuel oil[b]	
Year	REEPS	ORNL	REEPS	ORNL	REEPS	ORNL
1979	22.9	22.0	58.4	57.8	18.7	20.2
1981	24.3	23.6	56.6	55.5	19.1	20.9
1983	24.8	24.8	57.4	54.7	17.8	20.5
1985	25.1	25.7	58.4	54.7	16.5	19.6
1987	25.9	26.2	58.5	54.4	15.6	19.4
1989	26.6	26.9	58.5	53.9	14.9	19.2
1991[c]	27.7	27.4	58.0	53.7	14.3	18.9

[a] Percentage. Source, REEPS, ORNL models.

[b] Fuel oil equals oil plus *other fuel* consumption.

[c] 1991 ORNL estimates based on linear interpolation between 1989 and 1995 projections.

TABLE VII.9

Energy Consumption per Household by Fuel Type: REEPS versus ORNL—Standards[a]

Year	Electricity			Natural gas			Fuel oil[b]			Total consumption		
	REEPS	ORNL	% diff.	REEPS	ORNL	% diff.	REEPS	ORNL	% diff.	REEPS	ORNL	% diff.
1979	29.3	27.7	−5.5	74.8	72.9	−2.5	23.9	25.4	+6.3	128.0	126.0	−1.6
1981	28.6	26.9	−5.9	70.2	67.3	−4.1	22.2	23.5	+5.9	121.0	117.7	−2.7
1983	27.8	26.5	−4.7	66.2	62.4	−5.7	20.2	21.5	+6.4	114.2	110.4	−3.3
1985	27.4	26.4	−3.6	63.5	58.4	−8.0	18.0	19.9	+10.6	108.9	104.7	−3.9
1987	28.0	26.5	−5.4	62.0	56.4	−9.0	16.8	19.2	+14.3	106.8	102.1	−4.4
1989	28.4	26.8	−5.6	60.9	54.7	−10.2	15.8	18.8	+19.0	105.1	100.3	−4.6
1991[c]	29.1	27.1	−6.9	59.5	53.3	−10.4	15.0	18.2	+21.3	103.6	98.6	−4.8

[a] 10^6 Btu/hh. Source, REEPS, ORNL models.
[b] Fuel oil equals oil plus "other fuel" consumption.
[c] 1991 ORNL estimates based on linear interpolation between 1989 and 1995 projections.

either case, due presumably to the fairly small shift in relative fuel prices that is assumed for the accelerated natural gas decontrol scenario, this difference does point out interesting contrasts in the underlying model structures.

Similar forecasts for both models for the case of mandatory thermal efficiency standards are shown in Tables VII.9 and VII.10. These estimates indicate reduced levels of household energy consumption in general, that is, for both models. However, the standards-induced reductions in energy consumption per household are larger in the case of the REEPS projections and indicate a major impact upon natural gas usage. The ORNL projections, on the other hand, indicate smaller reductions in general, reductions which are spread out fairly evenly over all three fuels. Since natural gas is the dominant space heating fuel in many parts of the country and given that the standards scenario as modeled in our study only impacts space heating and air conditioning consumption, the REEPS forecasts appear to be more reasonable. These differences between the two sets of projections also show up in the total consumption estimates which indicate a larger impact from the standards scenario in the case of the REEPS projections. Interestingly enough, this difference tends to reduce the disparity between the two sets of forecasts, relative to the corresponding set of base case estimates, since the base case projections indicate a slower rate of decline in total energy consumption per household for the REEPS model compared to the ORNL model.

In general, then, the two models tend to give rather different forecasts in terms of the impacts from the three alternative policy scenarios, both in

TABLE VII.10

Energy Consumption per Household-Fuel Shares: REEPS versus ORNL—Standards[a]

Year	Electricity		Natural gas		Fuel oil[b]	
	REEPS	ORNL	REEPS	ORNL	REEPS	ORNL
1979	22.9	22.0	58.4	57.8	18.7	20.2
1981	23.6	22.9	58.1	57.1	18.3	20.0
1983	24.3	24.0	58.0	56.5	17.7	19.5
1985	25.2	25.2	58.3	55.8	16.5	19.0
1987	26.2	26.0	58.1	55.2	15.7	18.8
1989	27.0	26.7	58.0	54.6	15.0	18.7
1991[c]	28.1	27.5	57.4	54.0	14.5	18.5

[a] Percentage. Source, REEPS, ORNL models.

[b] Fuel oil equals oil plus *other fuel* consumption.

[c] 1991 ORNL estimates based on linear interpolation between 1989 and 1995 projections.

terms of the general impact upon total household energy consumption and in terms of fuel substitution effects among the three major residential fuels. To determine whether these differences are primarily due to differential conservation effects caused by the rising real cost of household energy in general or to fuel-switching effects (primarily in new housing fuel choices) resulting from shifts in relative fuel prices, we turn to an analysis of projected patterns for the two models in energy usage by major residential end uses.

D. Energy Consumption by Major Residential End Use

Estimated total energy consumption and market shares — saturation rates in the case of existing housing and penetration rates for new housing — by fuel types for both space heating and water heating are shown in Tables VII.11 – VII.13. These two end uses are the primary residential end uses, accounting together for over 60% of total residential energy demand. All three residential fuels — electricity, natural gas, and fuel oil — are shown in the case of space heating, since fuel oil accounts generally for over 30% of total space heating energy consumption. In the case of water heating, however, only forecasts for natural gas and electricity are shown since together they account for over 85% of water heating energy consumption. The consumption and market share estimates for space heating are also broken down by type of housing — existing and new.

Looking at the fuel consumption estimates for space heating for the base case scenario in Table VII.11, we see that REEPS forecasts a rather small reduction in natural gas use between 1979 and 1991, the base case 1991 estimate being over 90% of the 1979 figure; a major increase in the use of electricity and a sizable decline in fuel oil consumption. In the case of fuel oil, the 1991 REEPS estimate is 25% lower than the 1979 figure. The overall result is a decline of about 12% in total space heating fuel consumption over the period 1979–1991 for the base case scenario. In contrast, ORNL projects a somewhat larger decline in natural gas consumption, with the base case estimate for 1991 being 87% of the 1979 figure. Again, as in the REEPS forecasts, this is offset partially by a substantial increase in electricity consumption. Finally, the ORNL model projects a relatively small decline in fuel oil consumption, about 12%, for space heating, in contrast with the 25% decline estimated by REEPS. Overall, ORNL ends up with a total space heating energy consumption forecast for 1991 which is only 5% larger than the corresponding REEPS projection for 1991, although ORNL estimates that the downward decline in energy consumption for space heating pur-

TABLE VII.11

Space Heat—Total Fuel Consumption by Fuel Type[a]

Year	Natural gas			Electricity			Fuel oil			Total		
	Base	Dereg	Std	Base	Dereg	Std	Base	Dereg	Std	Base	Dereg	Std
REEPS projections:												
1979	2.91	2.91	2.90	0.17	0.17	0.17	1.59	1.59	1.59	4.67	4.67	4.66
1981	2.85	2.64	2.74	0.17	0.17	0.16	1.54	1.55	1.53	4.56	4.36	4.43
1983	2.81	2.66	2.66	0.18	0.18	0.16	1.44	1.44	1.43	4.43	4.28	4.25
1985	2.71	2.65	2.54	0.19	0.19	0.17	1.33	1.34	1.32	4.23	4.18	4.03
1987	2.70	2.66	2.48	0.20	0.20	0.17	1.28	1.29	1.27	4.18	4.15	3.92
1989	2.71	2.67	2.47	0.21	0.21	0.18	1.23	1.24	1.22	4.15	4.12	3.87
1991	2.69	2.65	2.43	0.22	0.22	0.19	1.20	1.21	1.19	4.11	4.08	3.81
ORNL projections:												
1979	2.97	2.97	2.97	0.18	0.18	0.18	1.68	1.68	1.68	4.83	4.83	4.83
1981	2.79	2.59	2.77	0.18	0.18	0.17	1.61	1.63	1.60	4.58	4.40	4.55
1983	2.63	2.47	2.61	0.18	0.18	0.17	1.53	1.55	1.51	4.35	4.20	4.29
1985	2.54	2.47	2.51	0.18	0.18	0.18	1.47	1.49	1.44	4.20	4.14	4.14
1987	2.55	2.50	2.52	0.19	0.19	0.18	1.48	1.49	1.45	4.22	4.19	4.15
1989	2.58	2.54	2.55	0.21	0.21	0.20	1.49	1.51	1.46	4.28	4.26	4.20
1991	2.58	2.55	2.55	0.21	0.21	0.21	1.49	1.50	1.45	4.29	4.27	4.21
1995	2.59	2.56	2.55	0.23	0.23	0.22	1.48	1.49	1.44	4.31	4.29	4.22

[a] In quads. Source, REEPS, ORNL models.

poses will bottom out in 1985, followed by a small increase after that. REEPS, on the other hand, forecasts a constant decline over the entire period shown, averaging just over 1%/yr.

With respect to the impacts of the two alternative policy scenarios, natural gas deregulation and mandatory thermal efficiency standards, the estimated effects are generally rather small for both models, though still consistent with a priori expectations. Thus, accelerated natural gas deregulation results in reduced consumption of natural gas and increased demand for the two substitute fuels, while the standards scenario results in generally reduced consumption of all three fuels for residential space heating. There is one interesting difference between the two models, however. Looking at the forecasts for natural gas consumption for the standards scenario, REEPS predicts moderate declines reaching about 10% by 1991, relative to the base case projections, while ORNL forecasts a decline of only slightly more than 1%. Thus, in general, the REEPS projections seem to indicate a more sensitive residential demand for natural gas, at least for space heating, while ORNL, on the other hand, predicts a somewhat stronger role for fuel oil in residential energy consumption.

Table VII.12 contains saturation – penetration rate estimates for residential space heating for both natural gas and electricity, differentiated between existing and new housing, for each of the two models. These market share estimates represent saturation rates in the case of existing dwellings and penetration rates for new housing. The REEPS forecasts for natural gas indicate penetration rates for new housing which are only 10% (i.e., five percentage points) higher than those for existing housing, and which decline only slightly from 1979 to 1991. Furthermore, the two alternative policy scenarios—deregulation and standards—have little apparent impact on these market shares. In contrast, the ORNL natural gas penetration rates for new housing are 15–30% smaller than those shown for existing dwellings and are also considerably smaller than the REEPS penetration rates. Furthermore, the smaller natural gas penetration rates projected by ORNL decline by almost 15% between 1979 and 1991. The ORNL model also estimates mild declines in the natural gas saturation rates for existing housing as compared to the constant shares predicted by REEPS. Finally, with respect to the two alternative policy scenarios, both models indicate minimal impacts outside of the 1981 and 1983 reductions, primarily in new housing, as a result of natural gas deregulation.

There are also some interesting differences with respect to electricity demand, primarily in terms of the estimated penetration rates for new dwellings. On the one hand, the REEPS model indicates penetration rates of just under 30% for 1979 and a substantial increase by about one-third of this, to 40% or so, by 1991. ORNL, on the other hand, starts with slightly higher

TABLE VII.12

Space Heat—Saturation–Penetration Rates—Natural Gas and Electricity 1979–1995[a]

| Year | Natural gas | | | | | | Electric | | | | | |
| | Existing | | | New | | | Existing | | | New | | |
	Base	Dereg	Std	Base	Dereg	Std	Base	Dereg	Std	Base	Dereg	Std
REEPS projections:												
1979	52.4	52.4	52.4	57.2	57.2	57.2	15.6	15.6	15.6	29.9	29.9	29.9
1981	52.1	52.1	52.1	56.8	51.4	56.8	15.5	15.5	15.5	33.4	37.8	33.4
1983	51.6	52.3	52.6	57.0	54.4	57.0	16.4	16.6	16.4	34.6	36.6	34.6
1985	52.6	52.1	52.6	55.0	55.0	55.0	17.4	17.7	17.4	38.3	38.3	38.3
1987	52.5	52.2	52.5	57.5	57.5	57.5	18.3	18.6	18.3	38.0	38.0	38.0
1989	52.5	52.3	52.5	55.2	55.2	55.2	19.5	19.8	19.5	40.0	40.0	40.0
1991	52.1	51.9	52.1	55.5	55.5	55.5	20.6	20.8	20.6	41.0	41.0	41.0
ORNL projections:												
1979	53.5	53.5	53.5	45.8	45.8	45.8	16.3	16.3	16.3	34.0	34.0	34.0
1981	53.0	52.8	53.0	42.3	36.4	42.3	17.0	17.1	17.0	36.8	39.3	36.8
1983	52.5	51.9	52.6	39.3	34.4	43.0	17.7	17.9	17.6	39.7	41.8	38.8
1985	51.9	51.4	52.2	37.3	38.8	41.1	18.3	18.5	18.3	41.0	40.3	40.9
1987	51.5	51.1	51.8	37.9	40.0	39.9	18.9	19.0	18.9	39.6	38.7	41.2
1989	51.1	50.8	51.4	38.9	39.9	39.9	19.3	19.4	19.3	38.7	38.3	41.1
1991	50.8	50.6	51.1	39.0	39.9	39.8	19.7	19.8	19.9	38.6	38.3	41.2
1995	50.4	50.3	50.7	39.2	40.4	39.5	20.2	20.2	20.6	38.4	39.2	42.6

[a] Saturation rates refer to market shares for existing structures, while penetration rates refer to market shares for new structures. Source, REEPS, ORNL models.

penetration rates for 1979 and forecasts slightly slower rates of increase, so that by 1991 the ORNL estimates are actually smaller than the corresponding REEPS projections for 1991. Both models indicate about the same story in terms of saturation rates for existing dwellings, although the ORNL estimates increase by a somewhat smaller amount over the 1979 – 1991 period than do the REEPS estimates. Again, the REEPS forecasts indicate little differential impact from the two alternative policy scenarios, either for existing or for new dwellings, while the ORNL results register small impacts which are consistent with expectations.

Fuel saturation rate and energy consumption estimates for both models for water heating are shown in Table VII.13. REEPS indicates only minor changes in consumption for both natural gas and electricity, while ORNL projects a substantial decline in natural gas consumption, almost 20% by 1995, and a sizable increase in the residential use of electricity. These differences between the two models can be traced directly to differences in the estimated saturation rates of the two fuels. REEPS, on the one hand, projects fairly constant saturation rates for both residential fuels over the period 1979 – 1991, approximately 51% for natural gas and 34% for electricity. ORNL, on the other hand, forecasts saturation rates for natural gas which fall from about 53% in 1979 to just over 45% by 1995. In contrast, ORNL also estimates that the electricity saturation rate will rise by eight percentage points over the same period, from 33% in 1979 to 41% by 1995. Although a breakdown of these estimates between existing and new housing is not available, the fuel-switching behavior in favor of electric water heating predicted by ORNL is presumably due to new electric installations in both existing and new dwellings. Table VII.13 also indicates rather minimal impacts from the two alternative energy policies on water heating energy consumption on the part of both models.

Projections for total consumption and market saturation rates for cooking for both models are shown in Table VII.14. Although not as dominant a residential end use as either space heating or water heating, cooking still accounts for about 7% of total household energy consumption, making it the third major end-use category. The estimates in Table VII.14 indicate substantial differences between the forecasts of the two models. For example, the REEPS projections indicate a level of natural gas consumption for cooking purposes in 1979 which is almost double that shown for the ORNL model and which increases significantly over time, whereas the corresponding ORNL estimates indicate a reduction of about 10% in natural gas consumption by 1995, relative to 1979. In the case of electricity, the REEPS model projects a level of natural gas consumption in 1979 which is again almost double that shown for the ORNL model, although this time both models indicate a significant increase over the time period shown. With

TABLE VII.13

Water Heat—Fuel Saturation Rates and Energy Consumption: Natural Gas and Electricity 1979–1995[a]

Year	Natural gas						Electric					
	Consumption[b]			Saturation[c]			Consumption[b]			Saturation[c]		
	Base	Dereg	Std	Base	Dereg	Std	Base	Dereg	Std	Base	Dereg	Std
REEPS projections:												
1979	1.05	1.05	1.05	50.8	50.8	50.8	0.24	0.24	0.24	34.0	34.0	34.0
1981	1.04	0.99	1.04	50.8	50.8	50.8	0.24	0.24	0.24	34.3	34.3	34.3
1983	1.04	1.01	1.04	51.3	51.2	51.3	0.24	0.24	0.24	34.6	34.6	34.6
1985	1.03	1.01	1.03	51.8	51.5	51.8	0.24	0.24	0.24	34.2	34.7	34.2
1987	1.03	1.02	1.03	51.6	51.4	51.6	0.25	0.25	0.25	34.6	34.8	34.6
1989	1.04	1.03	1.04	51.7	51.4	51.7	0.25	0.25	0.25	34.8	35.1	34.8
1991	1.05	1.04	1.05	51.7	51.3	51.7	0.25	0.25	0.25	34.9	35.2	34.9
ORNL projections:												
1979	1.10	1.10	1.10	52.7	52.7	52.7	0.22	0.22	0.22	32.7	32.7	32.7
1981	1.07	1.00	1.07	51.9	51.5	51.9	0.23	0.23	0.23	33.6	33.9	33.6
1983	1.03	0.97	1.03	50.8	49.9	50.8	0.24	0.24	0.24	34.7	35.3	34.7
1985	0.98	0.95	0.98	49.7	48.8	49.7	0.24	0.24	0.24	35.9	36.6	35.9
1987	0.97	0.95	0.97	48.7	47.9	48.7	0.26	0.26	0.26	37.1	37.6	37.1
1989	0.96	0.95	0.96	47.8	47.1	47.8	0.26	0.27	0.26	38.1	38.6	38.1
1991	0.95	0.94	0.95	47.0	46.5	47.0	0.27	0.27	0.27	39.0	39.3	39.0
1995	0.92	0.92	0.92	45.8	45.4	45.8	0.29	0.29	0.29	40.6	40.8	40.6

[a] Source, REEPS, ORNL models.
[b] In quads.
[c] Percentage.

TABLE VII.14

Cooking Fuel — Energy Consumption and Saturation Rates: Natural Gas and Electricity
1979–1995[a]

| | Natural gas | | | | Electric | | | |
| | Consumption[b] | | Saturation[c] | | Consumption[b] | | Saturation[c] | |
Year	Base	Dereg	Base	Dereg	Base	Dereg	Base	Dereg
REEPS projections:								
1979	0.97	0.97	44.0	44.0	0.21	0.21	47.5	47.5
1981	1.04	1.01	44.3	44.3	0.24	0.24	47.5	47.5
1983	1.03	1.01	42.9	42.6	0.26	0.26	49.1	49.4
1985	1.14	1.12	42.7	42.3	0.28	0.28	49.8	50.0
1987	1.11	1.21	42.3	42.0	0.32	0.32	50.1	50.5
1989	1.26	1.27	41.1	40.9	0.35	0.35	51.3	51.6
1991	1.29	1.28	40.1	39.7	0.40	0.40	52.5	53.2
ORNL projections:								
1979	0.53	0.53	41.6	41.6	0.12	0.12	50.5	50.5
1981	0.52	0.50	40.8	40.6	0.13	0.13	51.4	51.5
1983	0.50	0.48	40.1	39.8	0.13	0.13	52.2	52.6
1985	0.50	0.48	39.5	39.1	0.15	0.15	53.0	53.4
1987	0.49	0.48	38.9	38.6	0.15	0.15	53.8	54.0
1989	0.49	0.47	38.5	38.2	0.16	0.16	54.4	54.6
1990	0.49	0.48	38.2	38.0	0.16	0.16	54.9	55.1
1995	0.48	0.47	37.8	37.6	0.17	0.17	55.7	55.8

[a] Source, REEPS, ORNL models.
[b] In quads.
[c] Percentage.

respect to the saturation rates shown, both models indicate a steadily declining market share for natural gas and a rising market share for electricity, although there are small differences indicated in the magnitudes of the projected shares. Both models also indicate rather small effects on natural gas consumption for cooking purposes from accelerated natural gas decontrol and essentially no effects on the residential use of electricity for this end use. This should not be surprising, given the relatively small share of cooking usage in total household energy demand.

These results on projected residential end-use energy consumption, at least for the two major residential end uses — space heating and water heating — provide some interesting contrasts between the two models. The REEPS results indicate a substantial shift away from fuel oil and towards electricity for residential space heating. Indeed, by 1991 REEPS predicts that less than 4% of new housing will use fuel oil for space heating. Natural gas appears to hold its own generally. The results for water heating are less clear although they do indicate a small movement away from the use of fuel oil. The ORNL results, on the other hand, indicate a significant shift towards electricity as a space heating fuel but, in this case, the shift is at the expense of natural gas rather than fuel oil. Indeed, the natural gas penetration rates projected by ORNL are significantly smaller than both the ORNL saturation rates and the REEPS penetration rates. Furthermore, ORNL continues to forecast a major role for fuel oil space heating since the combined penetration rates for natural gas and electricity sum to approximately 80%, leaving 20% for fuel oil. This general substitution in residential energy demand between natural gas and electricity also shows up in the ORNL forecasts for water heating. Thus, both models project an increasingly important role for electricity as a residential fuel but differ fundamentally as to the relative roles of the two remaining fuels, natural gas and fuel oil.

E. Differential Impacts across Income Groups

Tables VII.15–VII.17 show some of the residential energy forecasts for both models broken down by income group. The same six income groups were used defined in terms of 1975 dollars. Tables VII.15 and VII.16 contain estimates of energy consumption and expenditures per household for each of the three major residential fuels broken down by income group and by policy scenario for the two years 1983 and 1991, respectively. These two years were selected as being generally representative of the trends over the period of analysis, 1977–1991. Table VII.17 contains estimated household energy budget shares for the years 1979, 1983, and 1991 for each of the six income groups by policy scenario.

Table VII.15 includes estimated energy consumption and expenditure levels per household for each of the six income groups, as well as aggregate national projections, for the year 1983. In the following analysis, our focus will be on comparing the results of the two models, primarily with respect to the distributional impacts. Looking at the base case scenario results first, we see that the REEPS forecasts of total energy consumption per household, in million Btu/hh, are somewhat lower than the corresponding ORNL estimates for each of the lowest two income groups and considerably higher for the highest two income groups. For example, the REEPS 1983 estimated total energy consumption per household for income group 2 is 4% lower than the corresponding ORNL estimate, while the REEPS estimate for the highest income group, 6, is almost 40% higher than the corresponding ORNL estimate. Thus, the range in estimated household energy consumption by income group forecasted by REEPS is substantially larger than that estimated by ORNL, a critical difference in terms of analyzing the distributional impacts of alternative residential energy policies.

With respect to projected household energy consumption by fuel type, the differences between the two models are even more exaggerated. In the case of natural gas, the REEPS estimates are either larger than or equal to the corresponding ORNL estimates for all six income groups. On the other hand, the REEPS estimates for fuel oil are consistently smaller for all but the highest two income groups. Finally, the REEPS electricity forecasts mirror the differences in the total energy estimates, that is, they are smaller than the corresponding ORNL estimates for the lower two income groups and higher for the top two income groups. For example, in the case of income group 6, electricity consumption per household estimated by REEPS is almost 50% higher than the corresponding ORNL projections.

Perhaps the most important observation to be made from Table VII.15 with respect to the ability of the two models to estimate distributional impacts is to note that although the range of household energy consumption forecasts across income groups from REEPS is substantially larger than the range from the ORNL estimates, the average values for all households are fairly similar. Thus, it appears that although the models may give fairly close projections with respect to aggregate impacts, the estimates of the two models at more disaggregate levels — either by fuel type (as seen in the last section) or by income group — are considerably more varied.

The above observations relate to the base case projections for household energy consumption for 1983. Looking at the two alternative energy policy scenarios, there are also some interesting differences between the two models, although the two sets of results all have correct signs from an a priori point of view. In the case of natural gas deregulation, the relative declines in household energy consumption (relative to base case estimates) estimated by REEPS are slightly smaller than those estimated by ORNL for all income groups, although the absolute differences are similar. On the other hand, the REEPS estimates of the differential effects arising from the impact of mandatory thermal efficiency standards are larger than those estimated by ORNL for all income groups. Again, this difference between the two models is also reflected at the national or aggregate energy consumption level, shown at the bottom of the table.

Table VII.15 also includes estimated household energy expenditures by fuel type and by income group for each of the three policy scenarios. However, since the corresponding price sets for each of the three policy scenarios were used for each of the two models, these expenditure estimates

TABLE VII.15

Energy Consumption and Expenditures per Household by Fuel by Income Class 1983[a]

Income class	Case	Energy consumption per household[b]					Energy expenditures per household[c]				
		Gas	Oil	Elec.	Total	% dev.	Gas	Oil	Elec.	Total	% dev.
REEPS:											
1	B	45.07	17.90	11.26	74.23		144.39	88.96	135.12	368.47	
	D	43.20	17.86	11.24	72.36	−2.5	158.71	88.89	135.07	382.67	+3.9
	S	43.26	17.83	11.22	72.22	−2.7	138.66	88.72	133.82	361.21	−1.5
2	B	53.06	16.29	18.90	88.25		172.87	82.10	228.91	483.88	
	D	50.62	16.33	18.90	85.85	−2.7	179.66	82.40	228.43	490.49	+1.4
	S	51.62	16.25	18.69	86.56	−1.9	168.48	82.07	226.23	476.78	−1.5
3	B	60.78	20.12	24.75	105.56		200.40	99.46	297.76	597.62	
	D	57.63	20.17	24.80	102.60	−2.8	216.93	100.29	298.12	615.34	+3.0
	S	59.04	20.01	24.55	103.60	−1.9	195.04	99.43	295.55	590.02	−1.3
4	B	72.42	22.06	32.95	127.43		238.25	109.32	405.58	753.15	
	D	69.00	22.14	33.11	124.42	−2.4	259.24	109.97	407.57	777.28	+3.2
	S	70.72	21.96	32.78	125.16	−1.8	232.72	109.43	403.86	746.01	−1.0
5	B	107.36	24.08	49.34	180.78		357.35	120.03	618.14	1095.52	
	D	103.29	24.29	49.32	176.90	−2.1	343.50	131.43	618.15	1133.14	+3.4
	S	105.08	23.86	49.18	178.12	−1.5	350.45	119.15	616.96	1085.89	−0.9
6	B	129.62	26.55	68.27	224.44		433.96	131.18	873.49	1438.63	
	D	126.69	26.59	68.74	222.02	−1.1	487.41	131.67	880.31	1499.39	+4.1
	S	127.44	26.43	68.11	221.98	−1.1	427.25	130.84	871.76	1429.65	−0.6
National	B	68.01	20.17	28.04	116.19		223.63	100.31	344.57	668.51	
	D	65.09	20.23	28.05	113.37	−2.4	244.94	100.82	345.24	691.00	+3.4
	S	66.23	20.06	27.81	114.10	−1.8	218.10	100.00	342.58	660.68	−1.2

252

ORNL:

1	B	40.5	20.2	14.3	75.0		139.7	100.6	173.2	413.4	
	D	38.2	20.4	14.3	73.0	−2.7	150.8	101.8	173.8	425.8	+3.0
	S	40.4	20.1	14.2	74.8	−0.3	139.0	99.9	173.2	411.5	−0.5
2	B	51.0	20.6	20.4	92.0		175.5	102.0	247.8	525.4	
	D	48.3	20.8	20.5	89.6	−2.6	190.7	103.2	248.4	542.3	+3.2
	S	50.9	20.5	20.3	91.7	−0.3	174.9	101.5	246.6	523.6	−0.3
3	B	60.1	21.1	24.3	105.6		207.0	104.4	295.3	607.4	
	D	56.9	21.4	24.5	102.7	−2.7	224.3	106.2	297.1	627.1	+3.2
	S	59.8	20.9	24.2	105.0	−0.6	205.8	103.8	294.2	604.4	−0.5
4	B	70.7	24.3	31.4	126.5		243.2	120.8	382.2	746.2	
	D	66.9	24.7	31.6	123.2	−2.6	263.9	122.9	383.7	770.5	+3.3
	S	70.4	24.0	31.3	125.6	−0.7	242.2	118.8	380.2	741.7	−0.6
5	B	87.7	22.8	41.6	152.2		301.7	113.0	504.3	920.0	
	D	83.0	23.2	41.7	148.1	−2.7	327.8	115.7	507.0	949.6	+3.2
	S	87.1	22.4	41.3	151.0	−0.8	300.0	111.3	501.7	913.0	−0.8
6	B	93.3	22.9	46.1	162.3		321.7	113.0	559.4	994.2	
	D	88.4	23.2	46.4	158.0	−2.6	347.8	115.9	562.3	1026.0	+3.2
	S	92.8	22.3	45.8	160.9	−0.9	318.8	110.1	556.5	988.4	−0.6
National	B	62.7	21.7	26.7	111.0		215.9	107.8	323.9	647.7	
	D	59.3	22.0	26.8	108.1	−2.6	234.0	109.4	325.3	668.9	+3.3
	S	62.4	21.5	26.6	110.4	−0.5	214.8	106.8	322.4	644.2	−0.5

[a] Source, REEPS, ORNL models.
[b] 10^6 Btu/hh.
[c] 1975 $/hh.

TABLE VII.16

Energy Consumption and Expenditures per Household by Fuel by Income Class 1990–1991[a]

Income class	Case	Energy consumption per household[b]					Energy expenditures per household[c]				
		Gas	Oil	Elec.	Total	% dev.	Gas	Oil	Elec.	Total	% dev.
REEPS (1991):											
1	B	38.20	13.38	9.93	61.64		152.61	92.73	128.02	373.36	
	D	37.86	13.36	9.93	61.29	−0.6	151.16	92.78	127.95	371.89	−0.4
	S	35.61	13.26	9.71	58.71	−4.8	142.50	91.98	124.42	359.90	−3.0
2	B	43.35	13.26	17.78	74.33		172.64	93.02	229.30	494.96	
	D	42.89	13.31	17.78	73.98	−0.5	170.74	93.39	229.30	493.23	−0.1
	S	40.95	13.18	17.47	71.52	−3.8	163.43	92.68	225.74	481.85	−2.7
3	B	54.49	14.53	22.98	92.15		215.58	100.83	296.42	612.83	
	D	54.16	14.20	23.22	91.59	−0.6	214.31	98.73	299.45	612.49	−0.1
	S	51.84	14.52	22.60	88.97	−3.5	205.62	100.98	292.43	599.03	−2.3
4	B	62.48	16.30	31.87	110.46		249.44	112.29	420.20	781.93	
	D	61.79	16.39	31.86	109.86	−0.5	246.82	113.04	420.16	780.02	−0.2
	S	59.62	16.19	31.56	107.18	−3.0	238.45	111.74	416.79	766.98	−1.9
5	B	94.01	18.14	49.07	160.98		380.75	126.35	657.45	1164.55	
	D	92.90	18.63	49.19	160.53	−0.3	375.85	129.70	658.88	1164.43	0
	S	90.86	18.00	48.70	157.33	−2.3	368.63	125.56	653.49	1147.78	−1.4
6	B	116.67	16.42	70.46	202.27		458.63	114.85	941.09	1514.57	
	D	116.45	16.51	70.60	202.27	0	458.39	116.15	942.40	1516.94	+0.2
	S	114.29	16.40	70.21	199.67	−1.3	449.43	115.24	938.52	1503.19	−0.8
National	B	62.18	15.20	29.43	106.77		248.52	105.64	388.55	742.71	
	D	61.64	15.25	29.50	106.44	−0.4	246.32	106.09	389.58	741.99	−0.1
	S	59.48	15.04	29.11	103.73	−2.9	238.19	105.25	385.10	728.54	−1.9

254

ORNL (1990):

1 B	36.2	17.9	15.6	69.7		154.8	120.1	204.0	478.9	
D	35.7	18.1	15.6	69.4	−0.4	152.8	120.7	204.6	478.2	−0.1
S	36.1	17.7	15.5	69.3	−0.6	154.2	118.7	203.3	476.1	−0.6
2 B	44.2	18.2	20.6	83.0		188.8	122.1	270.4	581.3	
D	43.6	18.4	20.7	82.7	−0.4	186.7	122.7	270.9	580.3	−0.2
S	44.0	18.0	20.5	82.6	−0.5	188.3	120.5	268.8	577.6	−0.6
3 B	52.3	18.1	25.0	95.4		223.6	121.1	327.1	671.8	
D	51.5	18.3	25.0	94.8	−0.6	220.4	122.1	328.2	670.2	−0.2
S	51.9	17.8	24.8	94.5	−0.9	222.0	119.0	325.0	666.0	−0.9
4 B	60.3	21.6	32.2	114.1		258.3	144.3	422.5	824.6	
D	59.4	21.7	32.3	113.5	−0.5	254.1	145.2	423.5	822.7	−0.2
S	59.9	21.0	32.0	113.0	−1.0	256.4	140.5	419.3	816.2	−1.0
5 B	73.2	19.0	41.1	133.4		313.6	127.5	538.7	980.5	
D	72.1	19.2	41.3	132.5	−0.7	308.7	128.2	540.1	977.0	−0.4
S	72.5	18.5	40.8	131.8	−1.2	310.8	123.3	533.8	967.9	−1.3
6 B	71.3	19.2	39.9	130.4		304.5	128.3	524.0	956.7	
D	70.2	19.3	40.0	129.5	−0.7	299.8	129.8	524.0	953.6	−0.3
S	70.5	18.7	39.6	128.7	−1.3	301.4	125.2	517.8	944.4	−1.3
National										
B	54.5	18.8	27.4	100.7		233.4	125.8	358.8	717.9	
D	53.7	19.0	27.4	100.1	−0.6	230.0	126.7	359.6	716.2	−0.2
S	54.1	18.4	27.2	99.8	−0.9	231.8	123.1	356.3	711.0	−1.0

[a] Source, REEPS, ORNL models.
[b] 10^6 Btu/hh.
[c] 1975 $/hh.

should reflect the corresponding differences in consumption estimates. In general, this appears to be the case. For example, the range of income group forecasts from REEPS is again considerably larger than that for the ORNL estimates even though the aggregate forecasts at the bottom of the table are quite similar.

Similar sets of forecasts for 1990–1991 for the two models are shown in Table VII.16. The REEPS results are for 1991, while the ORNL estimates are for 1990 since 1991 forecasts were not run.

In general, as we have already seen, both models predict lower levels of household energy consumption in 1990–1991 relative to 1983, and this trend carries over to each of the individual income groups as well. As with the 1983 projections, REEPS still predicts lower levels of 1991 total energy consumption per household for the lower income groups and higher levels for the two highest groups, compared to the ORNL estimates. Thus, again the range of REEPS projection across income groups is considerably larger than the range of ORNL income group estimates. There also continues to be considerable disparity between the two sets of projections with respect to individual fuel consumption. For example, REEPS predicts higher levels of average household natural gas consumption for all six income groups, especially the highest two, and lower levels of both fuel oil and electricity consumption per household for the lower income groups. In the case of fuel oil, this difference between REEPS and ORNL estimates is true for all income groups, while in the case of electricity, REEPS projects considerably higher levels of average household electricity consumption for the highest income group. With respect to the two alternative policy scenarios, the two sets of accelerated natural gas deregulation forecasts are generally similar. On the other hand, the 1991 REEPS projections indicate higher impacts from mandatory thermal efficiency standards, relative to the corresponding ORNL projections, for all but the highest income group.

Another way of analyzing these differential impacts across income groups from various proposed energy policies is to estimate the share of household income which must be devoted to energy expenditures. Such estimates are shown in Table VII.17 for each of the two models for the years 1979, 1983, and 1990–1991. These budget shares are based on estimated mean incomes for the six income groups, derived from the 1977 U.S. population census. The budget shares shown for 1979 are constant across policy scenarios since the impacts of the two alternative policies were not assumed to begin until 1981.

The results shown in Table VII.17 indicate interesting differences between the estimates of the two models for both low and high income groups. For example, looking at the estimates for 1979, REEPS implies smaller budget shares for the two lowest income groups and larger budget shares for the two

TABLE VII.17
Estimated Household Energy Budget Shares^a

Income class	Policy scenario	1979		1983		1990–1991	
		REEPS	ORNL	REEPS	ORNL	REEPS	ORNL
1	B			10.6	11.8	10.7	13.6
	D	9.1	9.8	10.9	12.2	10.6	13.6
	S			10.3	11.8	10.3	13.6
2	B			6.1	6.5	6.2	7.3
	D	5.4	5.7	6.1	6.7	6.2	7.3
	S			6.0	6.5	6.0	7.2
3	B			4.6	4.7	4.7	5.2
	D	4.1	4.0	4.7	4.8	4.7	5.2
	S			4.5	4.6	4.6	5.1
4	B			4.0	3.9	4.1	4.3
	D	3.5	3.4	4.1	4.1	4.1	4.3
	S			3.9	3.9	4.0	4.3
5	B			3.0	2.6	3.2	2.7
	D	2.7	2.3	3.1	2.6	3.2	2.7
	S			3.0	2.5	3.2	2.7
6	B			2.8	1.9	3.0	1.9
	D	2.5	2.0	2.9	2.0	3.0	1.9
	S			2.8	1.9	2.9	1.8

^a Energy expenditure as a percentage of before-tax family income, assuming mean income levels of 3500, 8000, 13,000, 19,000, 36,000, 51,000 dollars, respectively, for the six income groups. Source, REEPS, ORNL models.

highest income groups. For the middle groups, the two sets of estimated energy budget shares are virtually identical. Put another way, the ORNL model predicts that the energy budget share of the average household will decline somewhat faster as family income rises. For the two post-1979 years shown in Table VII.17, the story is somewhat more complicated. In each of these two cases, the REEPS estimates for the lower four income groups are smaller than the corresponding ORNL projections for the base case. Only for income groups 5 and 6 are the REEPS forecasts larger than the ORNL forecast. The result is a much larger variation in estimated household energy budget shares across income groups for the ORNL model, from almost 14% for the lowest income group to slightly less than 2% for the highest income group for the base case scenario in 1990–1991. By contrast, the corresponding REEPS numbers are approximately 11% and 3%, respectively. Thus, ORNL appears to predict a substantially larger variation in the proportion of household income spent on energy across income groups than does REEPS, at least under the base case policy scenario.

With respect to the two alternative policy scenarios, natural gas deregulation and mandatory thermal efficiency standards, the two models generally forecast policy impacts with respect to household energy budget shares which are consistent with theory and rather small in magnitude.

F. The Mandatory Thermal Efficiency Standards

In contrast with the two price-related policy scenarios — base case and accelerated natural gas deregulation — mandatory thermal efficiency standards on new housing do not affect prices directly but do result in energy-saving investments in additional insulation and hence reductions in energy consumption. The resulting trade-off between additional thermal integrity investments and the related savings in reduced future energy expenditures is modeled by both the REEPS and ORNL models. Tables VII.18 – VII.20 contain a summary of these results, on both an aggregate and a household basis.

Table VII.18 shows aggregate annual estimates for additional capital investment and reduced energy expenditures for the odd years between 1981 and 1991 as a result of the imposition of a mandatory thermal efficiency standard. Note that in both cases, REEPS and ORNL, the additional capital investment required per year decreases over time while the annual savings in energy expenditures increases over time. The first trend is due to the general rise in the real cost of energy over this period, which brings about increased investment in thermal insulation *without* the standards. Since the estimated additional capital investment shown in Table VII.18 is simply the difference in new housing thermal integrity investment with and without mandatory standards, less additional capital investment will therefore be required to meet the standards in later years compared to earlier years. The increase in annual energy savings over time, the second trend, reflects the rising proportion of total existing homes which meet the mandatory standards as each annual new housing increment is designed to meet the standards, and is added to the total stock. A related issue of interest in analyzing these forecasts is that the energy savings estimates should not be truncated or cut off at the same point in time as the additional capital investment estimates. This procedure simply reflects the fact that energy savings from past thermal investments continue long after such investment in new housing ceases. For example, in the calculations shown in Table VII.20, we assume 10 yr of additional thermal integrity investment in new housing but 20 yr of energy expenditure savings from this accumulated investment.

TABLE VII.18

Mandatory Thermal Efficiency Standards — Aggregate Annual
Additional Capital Investment, Decreased Energy Expenditures

	REEPS annual estimates		ORNL annual estimates	
Year	additional capital investment	decreased energy expenditures	additional capital investment	decreased energy expenditures
1981	1.63	0.46	0.93	0.17
1983	1.45	0.67	0.64	0.30
1985	1.31	0.95	0.56	0.42
1987	1.32	1.26	0.50	0.51
1989	1.33	1.44	0.46	0.59
1991[a]	1.22	1.37	0.44	0.66

[a] 1991 ORNL estimates are based on linear interpolation between 1989 and 1995 projections. Source, REEPS, ORNL models.

Table VII.18 indicates that the REEPS model forecasts larger estimates for both annual additional capital investment and the related annual energy savings resulting from the use of mandatory thermal efficiency standards. For example, in 1981, REEPS predicts a level of required capital investment which is 1.75 times larger than the corresponding ORNL estimate. By 1991, this ratio of the two estimates has risen to almost 3. In addition, the 1981 REEPS estimate of annual savings in energy expenditures is slightly less than 3 times larger than the corresponding ORNL projection, while in 1991 the ratio is closer to 2.

REEPS and ORNL estimates of the additional annual capital expenditures and the associated annual savings in energy expenditures on a per-household basis, both for all households and by income group, are shown in Table VII.19 for the odd years between 1981 and 1991.

Looking first at the results for all households, we see that the REEPS model forecasts both higher investment expenditures and higher energy savings per household than does the ORNL model. However, the ORNL estimates for both additional capital investment and energy expenditures savings per year per household show greater variation across time. For example, according to the ORNL projections, the additional annual capital investment per household required by 1991 to meet mandatory thermal efficiency standards declines to only 40% of the corresponding 1981 figure, whereas for REEPS the 1991 estimate is over 60% of the 1981 estimate. In the case of the estimated annual household savings in energy expenditures, the ORNL model projects a 1991 estimate which is 3.3 times higher than the

TABLE VII.19

Mandatory Thermal Efficiency Standards — Additional Annual Capital Investment, Annual Savings in Energy Expenditures per Household by Income Group[a] (1975 $ per Household)

	Income group						All households
	1	2	3	4	5	6	
REEPS:							
1981							
% Capital (+)	7.88	10.73	18.75	26.02	36.32	34.96	19.87
% Expend. (−)	3.19	4.91	4.35	4.93	6.90	7.27	5.63
1983							
% Capital (+)	6.70	8.80	16.10	22.67	31.50	31.07	17.06
% Expend. (−)	7.26	7.10	7.60	7.14	9.63	8.98	7.83
1985							
% Capital (+)	5.70	9.82	13.33	19.05	28.54	24.08	14.86
% Expend. (−)	9.12	9.55	10.25	10.84	10.86	12.70	10.88
1987							
% Capital (+)	4.96	7.15	13.06	17.97	27.28	25.07	14.54
% Expend. (−)	11.36	11.96	12.72	13.11	12.69	11.79	12.37
1989							
% Capital (+)	5.46	7.27	12.27	18.28	25.54	22.83	14.24
% Expend. (−)	13.11	13.49	13.18	14.22	15.11	13.33	13.39
1991							
% Capital (+)	4.30	6.30	11.64	15.52	22.47	20.02	12.65
% Expend. (−)	13.46	13.11	13.80	14.95	16.77	11.38	14.25
ORNL:							
1981							
% Capital (+)	4.80	5.52	10.32	15.73	21.49	18.15	11.36
% Expend. (−)	0.63	1.21	1.87	3.13	4.55	3.18	2.08
1983							
% Capital (+)	3.23	3.91	6.86	10.01	13.83	12.46	7.54
% Expend. (−)	1.86	1.75	2.98	4.55	6.96	5.80	3.54
1985							
% Capital (+)	2.77	3.39	5.76	8.27	11.34	10.07	6.39
% Expend. (−)	1.89	2.26	4.61	6.40	8.91	9.59	4.79
1987							
% Capital (+)	2.29	2.86	4.89	6.93	9.59	8.46	5.50
% Expend. (−)	2.62	2.75	4.45	7.70	10.57	9.84	5.63
1989							
% Capital (+)	2.22	2.53	4.26	6.07	8.30	7.02	4.92
% Expend. (−)	2.69	3.23	5.93	8.00	11.36	11.71	6.32
1991[b]							
% Capital (+)	2.03	2.38	4.01	5.64	7.78	6.49	4.62
% Expend. (−)	2.90	3.67	6.29	8.58	11.98	11.97	6.92

[a] Source, REEPS, ORNL models.

[b] 1991 ORNL estimates are based on linear interpolation between 1989 and 1995 projections.

corresponding 1981 estimate, while for the REEPS model the ratio between 1991 and 1981 estimates is only 2.5.

Similar differences between the two sets of estimates are also apparent with respect to the forecasts shown for each of the six income group estimates. Here we also note that both additional annual capital expenditures and the savings in energy expenditures per year per household increase with income, an effect caused primarily by the increase in average house size with income. Thus, both models produce estimates which are qualitatively reasonable, i.e., in terms of their variation across both time and across income group.

Table VII.20 contains estimates of the net present discounted value per household, both for all households and by income group, based on the estimates in Table VII.19. These calculations assume a 5% real discount rate, 10 yr of increased capital expenditures, and 20 yr of related savings in energy expenditures. Thus, these estimates can be interpreted in terms of a specific policy of mandatory new housing thermal efficiency standards which are in place for the 10-yr period, 1981–1991.

Across all households, both models indicate positive levels of net discounted benefits from mandatory thermal efficiency standards, with an average net benefit per household of approximately $13/yr, in terms of 1975 dollars. Looking next at the forecasts for each of the six income groups, the contrast between the two sets of results is considerably more striking. On the one hand, the REEPS model estimates total net benefits per household

TABLE VII.20

Mandatory Thermal Efficiency Standards—Net Present Discounted Value per Household by Income Group[a]

Income group	REEPS	ORNL
1	$ 87.17	$ 5.75
2	65.85	7.32
3	14.22	12.23
4	−32.13	15.82
5	−97.35	25.11
6	−108.73	34.78
All households	12.71	13.60

[a] Calculations assume a real discount rate of 5%, 10 yr of increased capital expenditures and 20 yr of savings in energy expenditures. Source, REEPS, ORNL models.

which are large and positive for the lowest income group and which decline dramatically with income, from \$87/hh for the lowest income group to −\$109/hh for the highest income group. Indeed, the REEPS estimates for the highest three income groups are all negative. The ORNL model, on the other hand, estimates total net benefits per household which are small and positive for the lowest income group and which *increase* with income, from \$6 for the lowest income group to around \$35 for the highest. The policy implications of these two sets of estimates are, therefore, strikingly different. According to REEPS, thermal standards on new housing result in a small average gain per household, and a sizable redistribution of net benefits in favor of the lower income groups. In contrast, although ORNL predicts about the same level of average net benefits per household, i.e., averaged across all income groups, the ORNL results also suggest a redistribution of net benefits favoring higher income households. Thus, the two models yield similar results with respect to the average impact across all households but offer dramatically different results with respect to the distributional impacts across income groups.

VII.3. OTHER DIMENSIONS OF MODEL COMPARISON

In addition to empirical comparisons of model performance, there are other dimensions for comparing or evaluating microsimulation models in general, and the ORNL and REEPS models of residential energy demand in particular. These additional dimensions include model architecture or structure, calibration and validation problems, and the potential for and sources of model error. Unfortunately, in many cases it is difficult to be very precise when comparing models along these other dimensions, so that unlike the comparative discussion in the earlier sections in this chapter, our comments here will tend to be more impressionistic in tone. This should not be taken to imply that these additional dimensions of model comparison are any less important, however; they are simply more difficult to evaluate in general.

A. Model Architecture

The structure or architecture of microsimulation models can be compared along a variety of design dimensions, including model complexity; model

flexibility in terms of the range of alternative policy environments or conditions which can be handled satisfactorily by the model; the adaptability of
the model, particularly the extent to which and ease with which the model
can be modified and extended to fit new needs; and ultimately, the cost of
operating and maintaining the model and its associated databases.

Model complexity has two basic dimensions: complexity in structure and
data input complexity. Structural complexity refers to the complexity of the
equations and variables used, typically reflecting the behavioral variety and
technological detail assumed in the model. For example, an energy demand
model which disaggregates energy demand by fuel type – end use – region
may also include individual behavioral equations to capture differences in
energy demand by race, by age and/or size of household, by renters versus
owners, and by urban versus rural location. An alternative, and simplified,
approach would be to use more aggregate behavioral equations which average across these underlying differences to reduce model detail and complexity. Models can also differ in terms of the variety and detail of both inputs
and outputs, requiring more extensive input data to calibrate the model and
additional data handling to summarize and analyze the outputs. Unfortunately, while the structural detail found in more complex models may result
in increased forecast performance, there may also be offsetting analytical
and computational problems in handling the increased detail. Both of the
models analyzed in this study can be considered to be fairly complex, at least
by current standards, in terms of model detail and the variety of variables
included, although REEPS is somewhat more detailed in terms of the complexity and structure of the behavioral relationships included.

Model flexibility is an obvious characteristic of microsimulation models
designed primarily for use in policy analysis since the usefulness of the model
will generally depend in part on the variety and range of alternative policy
environments which can be accommodated. Model flexibility is also an
important part of the *to stock* or *to order* issue, since models which are more
specialized are less likely to be robust under a variety of simulation conditions. Thus, models which are not very flexible will either require that a
portfolio of complementary specialized models be on hand for use by the
policy analyst, or else a situation in which only a narrow range of policy
options need be considered. Both REEPS and ORNL are reasonably flexible at aggregate levels of analysis in terms of the variety of both price and
nonprice energy scenarios which can be handled, as we have already seen in
terms of the three representative policy scenarios included in our analysis.
However, as we have also seen, REEPS has the inherent capability of handling a larger variety of disaggregate dimensions, a capability which is crucial
if the distributive impacts of energy policy are important to the analyst.

Simulation models can also be more or less adaptable in terms of the extent to which structural modifications and variable changes can be permitted without requiring that the entire model be redesigned from the bottom up. While it is generally easier, and less costly in terms of the model builder's time, to design the basic model architecture to match the original policy problem or problems at hand, the ability to accommodate a variety of both structural and variable dimensions, including being able to link the model with other models, is an important attribute for model users. Model adaptability, however, must be designed into the original structure so that care and thought must be given at the very beginning of the design process. Once the initial foundation is set, it becomes difficult and costly to change model adaptability. In terms of the two models evaluated in this study, the modular structure of REEPS makes it easier to modify this model to suit other needs. In principle, the REEPS model can be expanded in a variety of variable dimensions simply by expanding the size of the contingency tables involved, although the related problems of behavioral structure and input calibration would also have to be handled.

Once designed, a simulation mode has at least three cost dimensions associated with its use: the cost of initializing the model, including the cost of acquiring and treating the necessary input data; the cost of operating the model; and the cost of analyzing the results. Since the last two components can be mechanized to a large extent, for example, using a data handler such as SPSS to process the large amount of REEPS output, implementation and calibration costs are probably subject to the most variation across different models. This is certainly true in the case of the REEPS model which clearly has more extensive input requirements in terms of both the behavioral and technological parameter values required and the baseline and forecast variable inputs required. Another cost factor for the REEPS model is the requirement of extensive multi-way contingency tables, typically derived from detailed household survey data such as the national Annual Housing Survey.

B. Calibration and Validation

All microsimulation models require calibration before they can be run, and should undergo validation analysis before being made operational. Indeed, model validation should be considered an integral and ongoing part of the model development and maintenance process.

With respect to calibration, both ORNL and REEPS contain a large number of behavioral and technological parameters whose values must be specified before the models can be run. In the case of the ORNL model, the parameter values used have come from three different sources: engineering studies, personal judgment, and previous econometric studies, with an emphasis on the first two. The result is likely to be considerable specification error, particularly when the model is used to carry out disaggregate analysis, e.g., regional or income distributions. Even though ORNL contains a module which attempts to reconcile disparate elasticity values, there is still room for considerable error given the general reliance on personal judgment and engineering studies. The REEPS model, on the other hand, contains a number of explicit behavioral equations which were estimated using detailed household survey data from the 1975 Washington Center for Metropolitan Studies (WCMS) Energy Survey. The result is a more objective set of parameter values, at least for the behavioral equations. Technological parameter values were obtained from a variety of sources, including both engineering and econometric studies.

In general, both models should be judged deficient in terms of the number and scope of validation studies carried out to date, both for the original versions and for more recent versions of the models. More careful and comprehensive validation studies are necessary to test model performance, highlight problem areas, and pinpoint areas where improvements can be made in later versions.

C. Model Error

Although, in general, there are a variety of sources of model error, two sources are of particular importance in evaluating the comparative performances of the ORNL and REEPS models, aggregation error and sampling error. Aggregation error refers to error from using equations at one level of aggregation (or disaggregation) to predict or forecast responses at another level of aggregation, while sampling error refers to using the behavioral responses of a subset (or sample) of the population to infer the overall responses of the population. Due to differences in model architecture, aggregation error is a potential problem for the ORNL model while sampling error is unique to the REEPS model.

Even though the ORNL model contains a relatively large amount of detail (e.g., residential energy demand by type of housing–fuel type–end use) there is still considerable aggregation involved. For example, all non-new dwellings are aggregated into a single class with representative characteristics in terms of efficiency and fuel usage, and all income classes are aggregated into a similar representative group. The advantages of such aggregation are, of course, reductions in the scope of data handling and computations involved, but at the same time a significant potential for aggregation error is also introduced. This error arises from the fact that many of the behavioral relationships are likely to be nonlinear. Since a nonlinear function of averages is not equal to the average of the corresponding nonlinear function, the result is aggregation bias. Furthermore, if the nonlinearity is predominantly concave or convex, this bias will be systematic. As noted earlier in this study, REEPS specifies its behavioral relationships at the household level for a representative sample and then magnifies or projects the resulting estimates to the desired level of aggregation, thus removing the source of aggregation error.

Although in principle it would not be difficult to assess the magnitude of the aggregation error inherent in the ORNL model—we simply run the model for each of a number of given subaggregates, and then compare the total of the subaggregate level forecasts to the forecast from running the model again at the aggregate level—this has apparently never been done in a systematic fashion. One possible explanation of this failure is the scope of the task; it would involve separate aggregation checks on all dimensions of the model. It is possible, however, to get some idea of the potential magnitude of the problem using some recent results from the REEPS model. These results were obtained by using the REEPS behavioral equations to forecast average residential electricity consumption at both the individual household and the aggregate levels; in the first case, individual household characteristics were used, while in the second, the average values across all households were used. The results for the four major electric appliances modeled by REEPS are shown in Table VII.21, and imply aggregation biases

TABLE VII.21

Aggregation Bias—Major End-Use Electricity Consumption[a]

	Household estimate E_i	Aggregate estimate E	Percent bias
Space heating	4910	5550	13.1
Water heating	2960	2880	2.6
Central air condition- ing	3130	2310	26.2
Cooking	1070	929	13.3

[a] Source, Goett et al., "Residential End-Use Energy Planning System (REEPS)," EPRI Report EA-2512, July, 1982, pp. 6–20, Electric Power Research Institute.

ranging from 2.6% in the case of electric water heating, to over 26% in the case of central air conditioning. The average error across the four major end uses appears to be in the 10–15% range, a magnitude which is clearly not insignificant.

As contrasted with the ORNL model, the REEPS model uses a simulated population of individual households rather than regional aggregates. As a result, REEPS avoids the aggregation problems which are inherent in the approach taken by the ORNL model. However, there is an offsetting problem in the form of sampling error. Statistical sampling error arises from the fact that a representative sample of households is used to infer or construct energy demand for the national population and various subsets. Since this sampling error can only be reduced to an acceptable range by using a relatively large simulation sample, the basic factor becomes the cost in terms of sample size and the associated model detail in reducing sample error to any given level. Estimates of this cost versus sampling error trade-off are not available so that precise quantification of this problem is not possible. It is perhaps sufficient to note that this problem is real and may occasionally result in reduced forecast accuracy, especially for small subsets, to avoid the increased computational costs associated with larger simulation samples.

VII.4. CONCLUSIONS

In general, at aggregate levels of analysis, both models yield results which are consistent with economic theory. For example, both models forecast reductions in total energy consumption per household over time under the base case scenario, a result which is consistent with the assumed rising real cost of residential energy. Furthermore, both models predict reduced consumption levels per household as a result of either accelerated natural gas deregulation or the imposition of mandatory thermal efficiency standards for new housing. In the deregulation case, this effect is due to the relative increase in the real price of natural gas, relative to the base case for the 1981–1984 period, while in the standards case the reduction in consumption is the result of increased insulation in new housing.

At more disaggregate levels of analysis, especially in terms of individual fuel effects, problems with consistent model performance begin to arise. For example, the projections in Table VII.5 indicate the increasing substitution from fuel oil towards electricity for the REEPS model, but substitution from natural gas toward electricity for the ORNL model. Thus, the two models yield rather different conclusions with respect to fuel switching behavior under the base case scenario. Moreover, as discussed in Chapter IV, the base case assumes real fuel oil, natural gas, and electricity prices in 1991 which are 151, 126, and 37% higher, respectively, than the corresponding 1977 fuel prices. Thus, the base case scenario assumes a fall in the price of electricity relative to both natural gas and fuel oil, and a rise in the price of fuel oil relative to natural gas. Assuming that the three major residential fuels are substitutes for each other, we might expect increases in the relative use of electricity between 1977 and 1991 but, on the other hand, we would not expect to find a relative shift away from natural gas and a fairly constant share of fuel oil consumption as forecasted by ORNL. Even income effects are not likely to bring about this result since we could reasonably expect both electricity and natural gas to be more income elastic than fuel oil. Thus, the ORNL projection of residential fuel switching between natural gas and electricity and a constant share for fuel oil over the period 1977–1991 does not seem plausible. A possible partial explanation for this ORNL projection could be future constraints on natural gas availability, but none of the three alternative policy scenarios were designed to capture this phenomenon. Thus, such effects should not show up in the analysis carried out in this study.

This perverse fuel switching behavior in the ORNL results also shows up in the analysis of residential space heating. Again, REEPS predicts the substitution of electricity for fuel oil and a small decline in natural gas consumption, while ORNL projects fairly constant fuel oil consumption and the substitution of electricity for natural gas. In both cases, however, total space heating energy usage is predicted to decline slowly, presumably the result of induced conservation effects from the general rise in real fuel prices. The water heating results, the only other end-use category examined in this report, do not allow us to differentiate between the two models in this respect since fuel oil is a very minor part of water heating usage. It is interesting to note, however, that in this case ORNL does indicate substitution towards electricity and away from natural gas. Indeed, the ORNL results indicate a substantially larger fuel switching effect for water heating than does REEPS.

We have already commented on the fact that both models in many cases give fairly similar projections at aggregate levels of analysis, i.e., total energy consumption and expenditures, but show substantial disparity at more disaggregate levels of analysis, e.g., by fuel type or income group. Actually, this is not very surprising given that the ORNL model was specifically designed to operate at the national level, while REEPS explicitly models individual household decisions with respect to energy choice and utilization. Accordingly, REEPS aggregates or adds up the individual household estimates to obtain its aggregate estimates, while ORNL must disaggregate by adjusting the exogenous variable and parameter values used in the model. The result

of using generally imprecise exogenous estimates and an inappropriate decision-making framework for disaggregate levels of analysis is quite likely to be
some degree of inaccuracy in the ORNL estimates of disaggregate behavior.

   This fundamental difference between the two models is of critical importance when it comes to analyzing the distributional impacts of various policies.   The ability of REEPS to model distributional effects directly by simply
adding up the individual household effects in whatever way is required gives
it an inherent and overwhelming advantage.   Moreover, it is not at all clear
that ORNL can be adjusted to give reasonably accurate projections at, for
example, state, income group, age group, or housing tenure categories.
There is of course an associated cost, namely, the cost of running a large
enough REEPS sample to give reasonably accurate *cell* estimates.   But this
trade-off between higher REEPS running costs and the unknown disaggregation errors associated with ORNL should be far from comforting to the
policy analyst using the ORNL model.   At the aggregate level, however,
ORNL may enjoy an advantage in computation cost with no associated
major disadvantage in terms of forecast error.

CHAPTER **VIII**

Implications

Based on the preceding analysis of the REEPS and ORNL models of residential energy demand and their forecasted energy policy impacts, a number of implications with respect to policy analysis and the use of microsimulation models to forecast policy effects can be drawn. For the most part, these implications go beyond the specific approaches and limitations inherent in the two models examined in this study, focusing rather on some of the more general issues involved in the use of microsimulation models to analyze economic policy in general and energy policy in particular. This discussion is organized into two parts: first, implications with respect to energy policy analysis, and second, implications with respect to microsimulation modeling.

VIII.1. LESSONS FOR ENERGY POLICY ANALYSIS

Several types of implications with respect to both current and future efforts in the area of energy policy analysis suggest themselves as a result of our study. These include:

(i) additional policy questions, including issues not covered within our specific analyses as well as issues not addressed in existing energy policy models;

(ii) the importance of addressing distributional effects, particularly in the case of energy policy analysis; and

(iii) limitations in using econometric models of energy markets for long-term forecasting.

No doubt there are other lessons which could be drawn as well, but we think that these three areas are especially important given the current state of energy demand modeling and energy policy analysis.

A. Additional Policy Questions

Although existing microsimulation models handle some policy issues well, there are a number of aspects of energy policy analysis, including specific types of programs, which are generally not handled satisfactorily or which in some cases cannot be handled at all. These issues are not limited to specific types of programs, but cover all types — energy conservation programs, price control programs, and programs involving direct and indirect transfer payments.

A basic criticism with respect to energy conservation programs, which is common to both the REEPS and ORNL models, is that the output or forecast variables are generally not expressed in the dimensions or units used by policy makers. For example, in terms of housing conservation programs, either voluntary or mandatory, program goals or guidelines are usually stated in terms of such dimensions as total (or additional) inches of insulation, amounts of caulking required, etc., whereas the REEPS and ORNL models dimension their output variables in terms of energy consumption, i.e., Btu or physical quantities of various kinds of residential fuels. Of course, such dimensions could be translated, for example, into the associated amounts of insulation and caulking required to attain such reductions in energy consumption, but the two models as currently structured do not contain this feature. The result is that the models do not converse in the working language of policy makers, at least in terms of specific guidelines, a limitation which may make such models less useful in translating their policy analyses into actual program designs.

Another aspect of energy conservation programs, at least voluntary programs, that is not captured by microsimulation models at present, is the role of information and incentives in the eventual success of such programs. For example, in the case of programs which focus upon such energy-saving areas such as increased attic or water heater insulation and cutting back thermostat settings at night, the *marketing* of such programs is of primary importance. If individuals do not have a good idea of the relevant costs and benefits to them of undertaking such actions, they are not likely to participate. Thus, essential information needs to be provided to prospective participants and the associated incentives for their participation need to be communicated in one form or another. In the case of programs where this informational or marketing role is crucial, current models of residential energy consumption are not capable of taking such features into account and therefore are likely to give inaccurate forecasts.

With respect to conservation programs which operate through mandatory efficiency standards, there is a potentially important feedback relationship between participation and costs which is not included within either of these models. If there are scale effects in meeting the new standards, due, for example, to the presence of scale effects in the manufacturing and/or installation of new appliances or efficiency-related housing characteristics, such economies of scale will induce more people to move to the standards who might otherwise have opted for *even more* efficient appliances and/or housing design features. This is because such scale effects will lower the cost of achieving the new standards relative to the costs of achieving above-standard levels of energy efficiency. The overall result is likely to be a relatively larger distribution of the population centered at the new standard and relatively fewer individuals at higher levels of efficiency, assuming that everyone is effectively constrained from choosing substandard efficiencies. Since both the REEPS and ORNL models treat such standards as an exogenous variable without considering the indirect effects of the standard in terms of revised relative costs, these models may overestimate the average energy efficiency attainable from such programs.

Another type of interdependency which is not included within existing models of residential energy demand is the potential interrelationship between two different policies, especially if they are both energy related. For example, an increased tax on automobile gasoline consumption or even a tax on automobiles which is inversely proportional to mileage will presumably reduce the use of automobiles but is also likely in the long run to affect residential location as consumers move closer to work and shopping locations to reduce transportation costs. If such relocation involves moving from suburban to urban areas, even perhaps into the central city, the result is likely to be a reduction in overall household energy consumption due to the presence of smaller and more efficient urban housing. Such indirect effects from other kinds of policies, both energy and nonenergy, are not included within either of the two models examined in this study. Redesigning models of residential energy demand to take into account such policy interactions is, of course, not a simple task, but the cost of not doing so may well be inaccurate assessments of energy policy impacts.

There is a more general lesson to be drawn from the last few comments concerning interrelationships in one form or another. That lesson is that energy policy should not be viewed in isolation, either from a conceptual point of view or in terms of policy analysis. Energy is a pervasive and significant component of any industrialized economy, with impacts which reach into all aspects of economic activity. Energy policy, therefore, is likely to become a transmitter of indirect and even unintended repercussions from one sector to others. And, as we have seen, there may also be significant linkages operating in the reverse direction. This does not necessarily mean that energy policy can only be analyzed within the framework of large-scale general equilibrium models which include all, or perhaps all major, sectors of the economy, but some further appreciation of at least the more important general equilibrium linkages among sectors and variables would certainly be desirable. These feedback and indirect effects are especially likely to be important, both qualitatively and quantitatively, for accurate energy policy analysis.

A more fundamental problem with both REEPS and ORNL, and similar energy demand models, is the level or type of policy decisions they focus on. For example, in both cases, these models forecast energy consumption under a given set of prices or nonprice constraints and conditional upon such residential characteristics as type of housing and geographical location. The result is that these residential characteristics cannot be endogenized in the form of policy-related decision variables. In the case of energy policy analysis, this may well lead to myopic policies since such alternative energy-conserving strategies as inducing people to move out of, say, mobile homes or reducing the size of new houses or moving to different locations, say, the south or west, are precluded from consideration. Of course, all variables cannot be made endogenous given data and modeling limitations, but it is clear that there are several tiers of energy-related variables which should be given consideration when designing energy policy. Depending on the exact nature of the problem at hand, we may wish to focus on either one, or both, of these sets of policy variables. Current models of residential energy demand do not give policy makers this option. The result is that first-best policy alternatives may be overlooked, resulting in the consideration of only second-best policy options.

One of the key and rather innovative aspects of both the REEPS and ORNL models is the consideration of the efficiency – cost trade-off involved in the selection of optimal appliance stocks. In both cases, an explicit functional representation of this trade-off is included, based primarily on the results of a small number of engineering appliance cost studies. Clearly, there is a need for more extensive research on the structure of this trade-off in a static sense, but perhaps more importantly, there is also considerable room for improving the way in which these models take new technologies into account. Conceptually, this would not seem to be a particularly difficult problem; new technologies can simply be represented by efficiency–cost points which lie within or underneath the existing trade-off frontier. The problem is that this frontier is not parameterized in a way which makes it convenient to accommodate new technologies. In the existing models, the trade-off curve has to be refit to include the new points, involving adjustments in several of the parameters. The basic point here is that additional thought needs to be given to the form or specification of this trade-off frontier so that new appliance technologies can be included in an easier and more convenient fashion. Along these lines, additional thought might also be given to the dynamic nature of this frontier, including the roles of learning-by-doing and induced technological change. The current specifications used in both models are entirely static, making it impossible to accommodate more dynamic types of effects.

Turning from energy conservation issues, there are also a number of issues related to energy pricing. One of the more fundamental problems here is the total lack of feedback relationships linking demand and supply. Since energy prices in general affect both demand and supply decisions, policy analysts must be careful that the final price effects they assume take proper account of pricing impacts on both sides of the market. The failure to do this means that the assumed set of post-policy prices used in the analysis are not likely to be consistent with market equilibrium, so that the resulting policy analysis will be biased. In the case of REEPS and ORNL, both models limit themselves to a partial equilibrium analysis of demand-side effects only, thereby failing to take proper account of downstream price effects operating via the supply side. A dramatic example of this general failure involves the role of electricity, electricity being both a final residential fuel which is a substitute for both natural gas and fuel oil but also an energy source on the supply side which is produced from natural gas and fuel oil, as well as coal. This means that there is a linkage between fossil fuel prices and the price of electricity via generation costs, and that failure to take proper account of this linkage will result in an inconsistent set of residential fuel prices. Furthermore, this linkage will affect residential fuel prices differentially across regions, since the energy mix in the electrical generating sector will vary across regions in response to variation in local relative fossil-fuel prices. In the case of both REEPS and ORNL, proper account can be taken of these linkages by using exogenous fuel price forecasts in the analysis which are consistent with supply–demand and other general equilibrium interrelationships thought to be important. However, a conceptually more satisfying approach in the case of the electricity supply problem would be to include an electric generation module within the model which forecasts fuel mix and hence electricity costs and prices from a set of given fossil fuel prices. This endogeneity of electricity prices would guarantee a set of consistent residential fuel prices which could then be used to drive the household decision module.

Another price dimension of the energy sector which existing models of energy demand do not handle well, and in some cases not at all, is the general area of price or rate structure. One of the unique features of the energy sector is that customers typically face a structure of prices, rather than a single price, with marginal prices by type of customer which depend on both the quantity consumed and, increasingly, the time of day. Under such circumstances, a rational customer will use marginal price, rather than average price, in energy decisions so that energy demand models need to include marginal prices as the appropriate exogenous price variables. In some cases, information on the entire rate structure, or at least key aspects of the structure, needs to be included. This would be the case, for example, when analyzing the impact of lifeline rates and other rate structures involving substantially different initial prices. In the case of the ORNL model, only average prices are used which severely limits the types of energy policies that can be analyzed and which also probably means some degree of forecast error if average prices differ substantially from marginal prices. The REEPS model, on the other hand, does make limited use of marginal price data, but household behavior relative to this information is not modeled adequately. In general, there is considerable room for improving both the price structure inputs and the related household behavioral specifications in both of these models.

A third aspect of energy pricing which is not handled satisfactorily by either of these two models is the role of price expectations. Both models essentially assume naive expectations in which current prices in any given period are assumed to last forever, even though the given forecasted prices change in the next period. Not only is this an inconsistent treatment of price expectations within the framework of each model, but it also is likely to be a very inaccurate specification. Again, given the pervasive nature of energy and the long-run impact of energy policies operating through appliance and housing choice decisions, the correct modeling of expectations in this sector is especially likely to be important. Furthermore, one of the primary focuses of energy policies may be directly upon the structure of price expectations — for example, Jimmy Carter's attempt to depict the energy crisis in 1977 as the *moral equivalent of war*. Thus, for several reasons, the modeling of energy price expectations needs to be given further consideration.

With respect to energy policies which incorporate direct or indirect transfer payments programs, there are also several issues that should be pointed out. In the past, such programs have been important components of energy and economic policy at both national and state levels. They have included such programs as low-income energy assistance, housing subsidies to low-income families, and tax write-offs for residential investments in energy efficiency improvements. Since these programs have significant impacts on residential energy consumption, both in the short run and in the long run, the related decision-making process on the part of households must be modeled appropriately if accurate forecasts of policy effects are to result. At present, neither of the two models is capable of accommodating such policy impacts in other than rather ad hoc fashion. Given the importance of such programs as integral parts of energy policy in general and given the significant impact of such programs on residential energy consumption in both aggregate and distributional terms, there is a clear need to expand or modify existing models of energy demand to accommodate these types of programs.

B. Importance of Distributional Effects

The two primary dimensions of economic analysis in general are efficiency and equity. In terms of policy analysis, efficiency is concerned with total or aggregate costs and benefits, and the associated issue of optimal levels for policy variables. Given the size of the target population, it is also possible to consider average effects but these average effects are essentially aggregate effects averaged across the entire population. In contrast, equity is concerned with the incidence or distribution of both costs and benefits where the associated disaggregation or partitioning of the population can occur in a variety of alternative ways depending on the specific issues at hand. Thus, the equity or distributional effects of economic policies are a legitimate concern of policy makers in general, and are fully as fundamental as the more typical aggregate efficiency effects. Furthermore, in microeconomic policy analysis, distributional effects take on additional significance since the behavioral relationships involved may vary fundamentally across subsections of the population. In the case of energy policy analysis, for example, type of housing, owners versus renters and urban versus rural are basic household characteristics which are likely to affect household energy consumption in substantially different ways.

One of the primary focuses of our study has been upon the importance of accurate distributional analyses of economic policy in general and particularly, energy policy. One reason for this emphasis is that policies with similar aggregate effects can have quite different distributional implications. For example, a policy with socially desirable average impacts can have very undesirable distributional consequences, which may not necessarily cause us to discard the policy but most certainly would make it desirable to add a transfer scheme to compensate those sectors of the population unfairly impacted by the policy. Clearly, this can only be done if the original distributional consequences can be measured with reasonable accuracy.

The two models of residential energy demand examined in this study, ORNL and REEPS, both have some capacity for analyzing distributional dimensions. Of the two, the ORNL model can only handle such dimensions as regional location and type of housing, but even in these cases the general lack of differentiated behavioral relationships renders the associated distributional forecasts imprecise at best. REEPS includes additional dimensions — age and size of household, family income, and housing tenure — as well as employing a more disaggregated specification of the behavioral equations and forecasting aggregate results from the *bottom up* to avoid aggregation error, but even so there is considerable room for improvement. Such obvious dimensions of distributional analysis as race, education, and urban versus rural location are not included within the REEPS model in its present version. Furthermore, there is no differentiation in terms of the underlying behavioral relationships for some of the dimensions which are included; age of head of household is an example here. Thus, there is considerable scope for improvement if these models are to become effective tools for analyzing distributional, as well as aggregate, policy impacts.

An interesting aspect of the distributional analysis of energy policy is the issue of who ultimately bears the burden of mandatory energy efficiency standards, such as the new housing standards scenario modeled in our analysis. This is not to suggest that distributional aspects of price-related policies are not important; they clearly are, but the distributional analysis of mandatory standards is a considerably more complex question. This is partly because the distribution of existing energy appliance efficiencies, and hence the burden of constraining current efficiencies, is not well known, and partly because mandatory standards programs may well have indirect and unintended consequences upon less fortunate groups in the economy. An example is the case of thermal efficiency standards for new housing which result in higher prices for used housing in the future due to the increased initial investment in additional insulation in new housing. If the new housing market is dominated primarily by higher income groups who then resell to lower income groups in the future, the final burden of the mandatory efficiency standards will be borne by both current and future generations of homeowners, the latter in the form of higher used-housing prices. Models which concentrate only on the initial burden in the form of higher new-housing prices will overestimate the relative burden on higher income groups and correspondingly underestimate the burden for lower income groups. Since residential energy demand is closely related to the choice of energy-using appliance stocks, including houses, there is considerable room for this kind of analytical error.

In general, the analysis of mandatory efficiency standards on new appliances is both complicated and difficult. In particular, the distributional effects from such policies depend critically upon the discount rate assumed and upon whether or not we assume different discount rates for different segments of the population. For example, recent research — McFadden and Dubin (1982) and Hausman (1979) — suggests that lower income groups may have significantly higher discount rates than higher income groups because of either borrowing constraints or systematic differences in time preference. Thus, we would not want to assume a constant discount rate across income groups. This problem of discount rate specification is doubly important since the distributional analysis of mandatory standards is especially sensitive to the particular set of discount rates assumed.

A final aspect of this general criticism which merits brief mention is the importance of distributional analysis in terms of assessing the political feasibility of any given policy proposal. This is certainly true of such household characteristics as geographic location, race, and income, but is also true of other distributional dimensions as well. Since to be effective, a policy must first be implemented in a legislative sense, it should be clear that distributional analysis can be useful in this regard as well.

C. Limitations of Long-Term Forecasting

We commented earlier that in general microsimulation models will perform better under simulation conditions which are closer to the time periods used to design and calibrate the model in the first place and are not likely to do as well under assumed conditions which vary widely from historical experience. Since it is critical to the success and usefulness of these tools in policy analysis and to the avoidance of unnecessary failures caused by the inappropriate use of such models, this admonition bears repeating; namely, that for a variety of reasons, microsimulation models should not be expected to do particularly well under conditions which differ dramatically from recent historical experience. Such influences as major economic shocks, basic technological innovations and fundamental shifts in consumer tastes represent structural changes whose timing and impact are difficult at best to capture within the framework of economic models. Of course, it is not clear what alternative analytical tools would perform any better, so that resorting to substantial judgment and large forecast variances may be in order.

One procedure for reducing the error inherent in long-term forecasting, both model error and the potential for misrepresenting or misinterpreting the associated analysis, is the use of *conditional* forecasts: conditional upon given (and stated) values of some of the strategic exogenous variables. An obvious example in the case of recent history would be world oil prices. A related procedure would be to prepare several conditional forecasts, one for each of a reasonable set of possible exogenous variable values. Of course, the total number of such cases can quickly become overwhelming so that decisions must be made early in the analysis as to which variables and which set of values to concentrate on. Other exogenous variables which can be used as conditioning factors in the case of energy policy analysis include consumer behavior and tastes, and technological innovation.

VIII.2. LESSONS FOR MODEL CONSTRUCTION

With respect to the implications of our results for microsimulation model development and use, there are probably a number of questions which could be discussed. We will concentrate on four which seem to us to be particularly important given the current state of the art. These include both the advantages and limitations of microsimulation in general, the issue of whether to use general-purpose or specialty models, the adequacy of documentation standards, and suggestions for a future agenda of ideas for model designers.

A. Power and Limitation of Microsimulation Models

The fundamental power or advantage of microsimulation models is two-fold: first, they force the model builder to work through the various relationships involved in a consistent and orderly fashion at the design stage; and second, at the operational stage, they correctly account for energy consumption by, say, either end use or type of housing. That is, the aggregates across these dimensions are consistent with the disaggregate values used. However, both the ORNL and REEPS models are extremely complex models of residential energy demand and, accordingly, cannot reasonably be expected to do everything either correctly or even adequately. A case in point are the behavioral specifications and the related parameter values used, which tend to be based on inadequate econometric research, personal judgment, and accepted consensus values. Clearly, a substantial amount of additional research and modeling effort needs to be carried out in this area.

Other sources of model limitations include the cost of designing, initializing, and running these models and interpreting the results; the presence of unacceptable levels of statistical noise in the form of sampling error; the burden of collecting and preparing the input data; and the fact that such models often demand data, both parameter values and exogenous variable values, which are not readily available. The result in this latter case is that a resort must be made to judgmental values, further increasing the potential for forecast error.

B. Modeling "To Stock" or "To Order"

For the model user faced with the decision as to the optimal portfolio of models to keep on hand for ready use, two polar strategies suggest themselves: one is to have a single general purpose and highly flexible model which can be adapted to particular circumstances as they arise, and the second is to maintain a repertoire of specialized models and to simply select the most appropriate model for use in any given occasion. A variation on this theme is the *to stock* option, i.e., to either keep on hand several fairly standard models, one of which can be selected each time and modified appropriately, or the *to order* option in which a new model is designed for each new situation. Obviously, there are some basic trade-offs involved here. The *to stock* alternative minimizes model development costs but probably does so at the expense of model performance since *retrofitted* models are not likely to do as well as specialty models designed for a given situation. On the other hand, the *to order* option involves model development and testing costs which are likely to be both substantial and time-consuming. The optimal course of action will ultimately depend on the relative importance of timely results versus more accurate forecasts.

Given this basic trade-off between model flexibility on the one hand and model specialization on the other, however, there are some additional considerations related to initial model design. One relevant aspect is that model adaptability, that is, the ability of a model to be modified easily to fit new circumstances, is a design characteristic which can often be designed into the original structure with little or no additional cost. The only prerequisite is thoughtful design and an appreciation of the possible environments within which the model may have to operate in the future. A second consideration is that too much flexibility is not likely to be optimal since, after some point, additional model flexibility may be had only at the expense of model performance. An interesting analogy here is the difference between ordinary passenger cars and specialty vehicles such as 4-wheel-drive jeeps and dune buggies. The latter are admirably suited to a rather narrow range of conditions, but their performance characteristics generally fall off rather quickly under different conditions. On the other hand, ordinary passenger cars can cope with a wider variety of driving conditions, but are not likely to perform as well in either rough or sandy terrain.

Another aspect of good program design which is important to users of a model is structuring the model to be user friendly. Such a model will be easier for the analyst to use in its current version, as well as making it easier to both adapt the model to different uses and accommodate the model to analyzing different policies. Again, making the model user friendly does not necessarily entail additional costs if good design practices are followed initially and if a complete picture of model requirements is on hand at the beginning. On the other hand, if the model builder does not have an adequate notion of the range of future possible uses, the result is likely to be a less adaptable model for which significant retrofit costs will be necessary to accommodate future needs.

C. Documentation Standards

One of the absolute prerequisites of microsimulation models, especially given the complexity of model structure and the variables involved, is good documentation. Unfortunately, in the past, such documentation typically has not been available, due either to pressures to get the model *on line* quickly or because new versions have been started before adequate documentation for the older versions could be prepared. This complaint in general applies to all program development, but is even more important in the area of simulation models and policy analysis where timeliness on the part of the user is often of paramount importance. A potential source of model misperformance due to improper initialization is inadequate documentation, a problem which generally can be rather easily avoided.

Good documentation has at least four separate dimensions:

(i) clear and complete user instructions,
(ii) updated documentation concerning model modifications and new versions of the original model,
(iii) program documentation so that the user can self-modify the model when necessary, and
(iv) documentation concerning model calibration and validation.

In a general sense, inadequate model documentation is like selling a new automobile without providing either the owner or the mechanic with operating and design specifications concerning the basic design, modifications inherent in new designs and design failures which have been discovered after the fact.

D. Future Agenda

Perhaps the most valuable service that an analysis such as this can perform is providing a list of suggestions with respect to model modifications and new developments which are needed. There are several areas here which suggest themselves to us by way of a future agenda for model designers.

The most important area is the need for better specification of the behavioral relationships and parameter values used in predicting end-use residential energy consumption. In general, current specifications of these relationships do not do an adequate job of reflecting either economic theory or casual empirical observation. A strategy for improving model performance in this regard would consist of a thorough review of both the behavioral and technological relationships involved for each end use, followed by careful validation and consistency checking in each case. A case in point is the efficiency–cost specification which has generally been based on rather casual engineering information. There is a clear need here for more careful consideration of the nature of this trade-off and for more thorough validation studies of the final specifications used.

Attention should also be paid to improving the timeliness with which models can be updated to reflect new trends in consumer tastes, new technologies and relevant new information in general. Essentially this involves designing model structure so that the necessary updating data can be entered conveniently without reinitializing the entire model. We have already commented on the awkwardness with which existing models accommodate new technologies in terms of the efficiency–cost frontier, but there are also similar problems with respect to updating behavioral relationships as well as new consumer tastes and other information.

A final area for needed improvement is related to the market equilibrium problem. Both the REEPS and ORNL models are concerned only with the demand side of residential energy, so that supply side effects are totally ignored. What is needed here is a matched and compatible supply side so that both models can be run as a complete and integrated simulation. For example, a supply model for REEPS would forecast energy quantities by state by type of fuel so that a regional set of equilibrium fuel prices could be derived. There is also a similar need to include nonresidential demand as well to capture important interdependencies among residential, commercial, and industrial demands. These nonresidential demand models should be compatible with respect to the residential demand model in terms of the fuel types and regional level of disaggregation used. The overall result would be a model for residential energy demand in which a complete set of feedback relationship vis-à-vis both supply and nonresidential demand could be captured and incorporated within the final set of forecasts.

CHAPTER **IX**

Concluding Remarks

Given the variety of prescriptive advice which has been offered in Chapters VII and VIII, remarks pertaining to both the comparative evaluation of the two models in Chapter VII and various implications with respect to energy policy analysis and microsimulation outlined in Chapter VIII, it seems appropriate to conclude this study by way of a brief summary of our results. In general, while these results follow rather directly from our evaluation of the two specific residential energy demand models examined in this study, these concluding remarks also have a more general importance. This generality stems, we think, in part from the fact that the two models represent state-of-the-art models on the cutting edge of microsimulation model development and the fact that we have tried throughout this volume to place our evaluation within a broader context to give some perspective to our results. Thus, our results should be of interest in many areas, including econometric modeling in general and energy demand simulation in particular.

With respect to the specific performances of each of the two models, REEPS and ORNL, Table IX.1 summarizes the more important model dimensions or attributes on a comparative basis. As we saw earlier in this

284

TABLE IX.1

Comparative Model Evaluation — Summary

Performance dimensions	REEPS model	ORNL model
Aggregate forecasts — energy consumption and expenditures	comparable	comparable
Disaggregate forecasts — type of housing, type of fuel, end use	generally comparable, although REEPS appears to produce more reasonable results with respect to fuel choice by end use	
Disaggregate forecasts — income group, state location, family size	can be handled consistently within the existing framework	not likely to yield very accurate forecasts in these dimensions
Disaggregate forecasts — race, education, urban location, owners – renters	not handled at all in existing versions of either model, although REEPS is capable of being expanded to cover these additional dimensions in a consistent way	
Structural complexity	both models are reasonably complex, although REEPS has a somewhat more complex behavioral structure	
Flexibility — with respect to range of conditions which can be handled	REEPS can handle a variety of both aggregate and distributional analyses	comparable flexibility with respect to aggregate analyses only
Adaptability — with respect to ease with which modifications can be made	modular structure and use of individual household behavioral specifications makes REEPS relatively easier to modify	
Cost-operating – maintenance	the increased data requirements and simulation architecture used by REEPS make it more costly to run, especially if a relatively large simulation sample is used	
Cost-modification	REEPS is likely to be somewhat more expensive to modify, although it can in principle be modified to meet a larger range of alternative environments	
Data requirements	REEPS requires slightly more data inputs, particularly with respect to behavioral equation parameters and the conditional probability matrix	
Primary sources of error	(i) sampling error, related to size of simulation sample (ii) specification error in behavioral equations	(i) aggregation error, due to nonlinear behavioral equations (ii) specification error in behavioral equations

study, both models give forecasts at the aggregate level of analysis which are quite comparable. At disaggregate levels of analysis, especially with respect to income group, the two sets of forecasts tend to diverge substantially in at least several cases. Thus, it appears that the REEPS model would give more accurate predictions with respect to the distributional analysis of energy policy, in a variety of possible dimensions, while either model is generally acceptable for more aggregate analysis.

With respect to other dimensions of model performance, there are some interesting trade-offs; trade-offs which are relevant to the choice of a micro-simulation model for any particular situation. In general, REEPS is a more complex model in terms of both behavioral specification and data requirements. However, this increased structural complexity also gives it distinct advantages with respect to flexibility and adaptability, due primarily to the structure of the behavioral equations based on individual household decision making and the modular design of the model architecture. At the same time, this additional structural detail also carries an associated cost in terms of the costs of operating, maintaining, and modifying the model. Thus, one basic trade-off between the two models involves the more expensive but more accurate disaggregate forecasts produced by REEPS versus the less costly but also probably less accurate distributional analyses obtained from the ORNL model.

Another important dimension of model performance is forecast error. Here the two models differ rather fundamentally due to differences in model design. On the one hand, the REEPS model uses a simulation sample of representative households as the central pivot in its forecasting system, with the sample forecasts being appropriately scaled to produce population forecasts. Although this approach has a number of distinct advantages, as we have already seen, it also has the unfortunate consequence of introducing sampling error. Perhaps the one good thing that can be said about sampling error is that it can be controlled, i.e., reduced, albeit at the cost of increasing the simulation sample and the associated cost of running REEPS. Unfortunately, after some point, the marginal operating costs of further increasing sample size, for example, in response to an increase in model disaggregation, may become prohibitive.

The ORNL model, on the other hand, while it does not suffer from the same kind of sample error, does have an important source of intrinsic error of its own. This aggregation error results basically from aggregation across nonlinear behavioral equations and reflects the fact that in such cases the mean of the estimates is not equal to the estimate based on the means. This aggregation error has two unfortunate consequences: its magnitude is difficult to measure, at least in more than a few dimensions; and it is essentially impossible to control or reduce, given fundamental behavioral nonlinearities.

Finally, both models probably suffer from some degree of misspecification in many of the behavioral equations, a result which implies the need for better and more current validation studies of both models. Furthermore, there is a sense in which this problem of specification error is likely to be more important for the REEPS model given the increased detail and the resulting larger number of individual behavioral equations involved.

As we have also seen, there are a number of dimensions, primarily design in nature, which represent limitations or shortcomings for both models, and for many other microsimulation models in general. The associated areas for improvement include model rigidities which prevent several important types of energy policies from being analyzed, a generally myopic framework which does not adequately account for possible linkages between different energy programs, the general inability to carry out long-term forecasting accurately or to include some of the more important dynamic dimensions within the analysis, and finally, the lack of general equilibrium types of feedback relationships between either energy demand and supply or between energy and nonenergy sectors of the economy.

Although we have been critical at a number of junctures within this volume, perhaps overly so occasionally, it is certainly appropriate to be optimistic in retrospect. Microsimulation modeling, and especially residential energy demand modeling, has come a long way in the last decade or so. From the relatively small number of primarily single-equation microeconomic energy models which existed prior to, say, 1970, a variety of complex econometric models for analyzing energy policy have been developed of which the two included within this study represent the most sophisticated in terms of structure and the most ambitious in terms of detail. However, there still remain critical areas where further model development and improvement are both desirable and feasible. We have already commented on a few by way of suggesting a future agenda of needed research in Chapter VIII. We would only further note here that the current, and probably temporary, state of relative calm in most energy markets, both national and worldwide, should not be interpreted as a demand for slackened or complacent efforts. Energy has always been, and will continue to be, of central importance to industrialized and nonindustrialized economies alike, and further research into energy markets in general and energy policy analysis in particular must still rate high on the nation's agenda of unfinished business.

References

Acton, J. P., B. M. Mitchell, and R. S. Mowill. (1976). "Residential Demand for Electricity in Los Angeles: An Econometric Study of Disaggregated Data," Rand Report R-1899-NSF. Rand Corporation, Santa Monica, California.

Amemiya, T. (1981). Qualitative response models: a survey. *Journal of Economic Literature,* **19,** 1483–1536.

American Society of Heating, Refrigeration and Air Conditioning Engineers. (1977). "Handbook and Product Directory—Fundamentals" ASHRAE, New York.

American Society of Heating, Refrigeration and Air Conditioning Engineers. (1978). "Handbook and Product Directory—Appliances" ASHRAE, New York.

American Society of Heating, Refrigeration and Air Conditioning Engineers. (1979). "Handbook and Product Directory—Equipment" ASHRAE, New York.

Anderson, K. P. (1972). "Residential Demand for Electricity: Econometric Estimates for California and the U.S.," Rand Report R-905-NSF. Rand Corporation, Santa Monica, California.

Anderson, K. P. (1973). "Residential Energy Use: An Econometric Analysis," Rand Report R-1296-NSF. Rand Corporation, Santa Monica, California.

Balestra, P. (1967). "The Demand for Natural Gas in the United States," North-Holland, Amsterdam.

Baughman, M. L., and P. L. Joskow. (1975). The effects of fuel prices on residential appliance choice in the United States, *Land Economics,* **51,** 41–49.

Berkovec, J., T. Cowing, D. McFadden, and J. Rust. (1982a). "An Analysis of the Distributional Impacts of Energy Policies Affecting Residential Energy Demand: The ORNL Model," discussion paper No. 22, Studies in Energy and the American Economy, MIT Energy Laboratory, Massachusetts Institute of Technology.

Berkovec, J., T. Cowing, D. McFadden, and J. Rust. (1982b). "An Analysis of the Distributional Impacts of Energy Policies Affecting Residential Energy Demand: The REEPS Model," discussion paper No. 26, Studies in Energy and the American Economy, MIT Energy Laboratory, Massachusetts Institute of Technology.

Berkovec, J., T. Cowing, D. McFadden, and J. Rust. (1982c). "A Comparative Evaluation of the ORNL and REEPS Models of Residential Energy Demand for Forecasting Residential Energy Policy Impacts," discussion paper No. 29, Studies in Energy and the American Economy, MIT Energy Laboratory, Massachusetts Institute of Technology.

Berndt, E. R., and G. C. Watkins. (1977). Demand for natural gas: Residential and commercial markets in Ontario and British Columbia, *Canadian Journal of Economics,* **10,** 97–111.

Bishop, Y. M. M., S. E. Fienberg, and P. W. Holland. (1975). "Discrete Multivariate Analysis: Theory and Practice." MIT Press, Cambridge, Massachusetts.

Bohi, D. R. (1981). "Analyzing Demand Behavior: A Study of Energy Elasticities. published for Resources for the Future by Johns Hopkins University Press, Baltimore.

Brownstone, D. (1980). "An Econometric Model of Consumer Durable Choice and Utilization Rates," unpublished PhD dissertation. Department of Economics, University of California, Berkeley.

Chern, W. S. (1976). "Energy Demand and Interfuel Substitution in the Combined Residential and Commercial Sector," ORNL Report RM-5557. Oak Ridge National Laboratory, Oak Ridge, Tennessee

Chow, G. (1975). "Analysis and Control of Dynamic Economic Systems." Wiley, New York.

Cohn, S., E. Hirst, and J. Jackson. (1977). "Econometric Analyses of Household Fuel Demands," ORNL Report CON-7. Oak Ridge National Laboratory, Oak Ridge, Tennessee.

288

Data Resources, Inc. (1977). "The Residential Demand for Energy," final report, vol. 1, EPRI Report EA-235. Electric Power Research Institute, Palo Alto, California.

Dubin, J. A. (1984). "Consumer Durable Choice and the Demand for Electricity." North-Holland, Amsterdam.

Dubin, J. A. and D. L. McFadden. (1984), An econometric analysis of residential electric appliance holdings and consumption." *Econometrica,* **52,** 345–362.

Energy Information Administration. (1980). "Residential Energy Consumption Survey: Conservation," DOE/EIA-0207/3. U.S. Department of Energy, Washington, D.C.

Erickson, E., R. Spann, and R. Ciliano (1973). Substitution and usage in energy demand: an econometric estimation of long-run and short-run effects. *In* "Energy Modeling." (M. Searl, ed.) Resources for the Future, Washington, D.C.

Federal Energy Administration. (1974). "Project Independence Report." U.S. Government Printing Office, Washington, D.C.

Fisher, F. M., and C. Kaysen. (1962). "A Study in Econometrics: The Demand for Electricity in the United States." North-Holland, Amsterdam.

Freedman, D., T. Rothenberg, and R. Sutch. (1980a). "Progress Report on a Review of the Hirst–Carney Model of Residential Energy Use." Report prepared for the National Bureau of Standards, Washington, D.C.

Freedman, D., T. Rothenberg, and R. Sutch. (1980b). "Second Progress Report on a Review of the Hirst–Carney Model of Residential Energy Use." Report prepared for the National Bureau of Standards, Washington, D.C.

Freedman, D., T. Rothenberg, and R. Sutch (1981). "Analysis Quality Report on Midterm Energy Demand: The Hirst–Carney ORNL Model for the Residential Sector." Report prepared for the National Bureau of Standards, Washington, D.C.

George, S. (1979). "Short-Run Residential Electricity Demand: A Policy Oriented Look," unpublished Ph.D. dissertation. University of California, Davis.

Goett, A. A. (1978). "Appliance Fuel Choice: An Application of Discrete Multivariate Analysis," unpublished Ph.D. dissertation. Department of Economics, University of California, Davis.

Goett, A. A. (1984). "Household Appliance Choice: Revision of REEPS Behavioral Models," Final report, EPRI Report EA-3409 (February). Electric Power Research Institute, Palo Alto, California.

Goett, A., and D. McFadden. (1984). The residential end-use energy planning system: simulation model structure and empirical analysis," *In* "Advances in the Economics of Energy and Resources," (J. R. Moroney, ed.). JAI Press, Greenwich, Connecticut.

Goett, A., and D. McFadden. (1982). "Residential End-Use Energy Planning System (REEPS)," final report, EPRI Report EA-2512. Electric Power Research Institute, Palo Alto, California.

Griffin, J. M. (1974). The effects of higher prices on electricity consumption. *Bell Journal of Economics and Management Science,* **5,** 515–539.

Halvorsen, R. (1975). Residential demand for electric energy. *Review of Economics and Statistics,* **57,** 12–18.

Halvorsen, R. (1978). "Econometric Models of U.S. Energy Demand." D. C. Heath, Lexington, Massachusetts.

Hamblin, D. M. (1981). "Conversions from ORNL/CON-3 Estimation Coefficients to Residential Model Simulation Coefficients," working paper (September). Oak Ridge National Laboratory, Oak Ridge, Tennessee.

Hansen, L. P., and T. Sargent. (1981). "Formulating and Estimating Continuous Time Rational Expectations Models," working paper. Department of Economics, University of Minnesota, Minneapolis, Minnesota.

Hartman, R. S. (1979). Frontiers in energy demand modeling. *Annual Review of Energy*, **4**, 433–466.

Hausman, J. A. (1979). Individual discount rates and the purchase and utilization of energy-using durables. *Bell Journal of Economics*, **10**, 33–54.

Herbert, J. H. (1980). "Selected Comments on the ORNL Residential Energy Use Model," DOE/EIA/TR-0244 (June). U.S. Department of Energy, Energy Information Administration, Washington, D.C.

Hirst, E., and J. Carney. (1977a). "Analysis of Federal Residential Energy Conservation Programs." Oak Ridge National Laboratory, Oak Ridge, Tennessee.

Hirst, E., and J. Carney. (1977b). "Residential Energy Use to the Year 2000: Conservation and Economics," ORNL Report CON-13. Oak Ridge National Laboratory, Oak Ridge, Tennessee.

Hirst, E., and J. Carney. (1978). "The ORNL Engineering-Economic Model of Residential Energy Use," ORNL Report CON-24. Oak Ridge National Laboratory, Oak Ridge, Tennessee.

Hirst, E., R. Goeltz, and J. Carney. (1981). "Residential Energy Use and Conservation Actions: Analysis of Disaggregate Household Data," ORNL Report CON-68 (March). Oak Ridge National Laboratory, Oak Ridge, Tennessee.

Hittman Associates, Inc. (1976). "Development of a Method to Determine Energy Utilization of Existing Utility Systems," vol. II—Manual, prepared for U.S. Army Construction Engineering Research Laboratory.

Houthakker, H.S. (1951). Some calculations on electricity consumption in Great Britain. *Journal of the Royal Statistical Society*, Series A, **114**, Part III, 351–371.

Houthakker, H. S., and L. D. Taylor (1970). "Consumer Demand in the United States: 1929–1970," 2nd ed. Harvard University Press, Cambridge, Massachusetts.

Houthakker, H. S., P. K. Verleger, and D. P. Sheehan. (1974). Dynamic demand analyses for gasoline and residential electricity. *American Journal of Agricultural Economics*, **56**, 412–418.

Howard, R. (1960). "Dynamic Programming and Markov Processes." Wiley, New York.

Hudson, E. A., and D. W. Jorgenson (1974). U.S. energy policy and economic growth, 1975–2000, *Bell Journal of Economics and Management Science*, **5** (Autumn, 1974), 461–514.

Lin, W., E. Hirst, and S. Cohn. (1976). "Fuel Choice in the Household Sector," ORNL Report CON-3. Oak Ridge National Laboratory, Oak Ridge, Tennessee.

McFadden, D. (1974). Conditional logit analysis of qualitative choice behavior. *In* "Frontiers in Econometrics" (P. Zarembka, ed.) Academic Press, New York.

McFadden, D. (1982). "An Evaluation of the ORNL Residential Energy Use Model," EPRI Report EA-2442, Interim Report. Electric Power Research Institute, Palo Alto, California.

McFadden, D., and J. Dubin. (1982). "A Thermal Model for Single-Family Owner-Occupied Detached Dwellings in the National Interim Energy Consumption Survey," Discussion Paper 25, Studies in Energy and the American Economy, MIT Energy Laboratory, Massachusetts Institute of Technology. [Also in Dubin, J. A. (1984). Consumer Durable Choice and the Demand for Electricity. North-Holland, Amsterdam.]

McFadden, D., K. Train, and W. Tye (1977). An application of diagnostic tests for the IIA property of the MNL. *Transportation Research Record*.

McFadden, D., C. Puig, and D. Kirshner. (1978). Determinants of the long-run demand for electricity. *In* American Statistical Association, "1977 Proceedings of the Business and Economic Statistics Section" (Part 2), 109–117.

Merton, R. (1978). On the microeconomic theory of investment under uncertainty, *In*

"Handbook of Mathematical Economics," Vol. II. (K. Arrow and M. Intrilligator eds.) North-Holland, Amsterdam.

Moselle, G. (1978). "National Construction Estimator," 6th Ed. Craftsman Book Company, Solana Beach, California.

Mount, T. D., L. D. Chapman, and T. J. Tyrrell. (1973). "Electricity Demand in the United States: An Econometric Analysis," ORNL Report NSF-EP-49. Oak Ridge National Laboratory, Oak Ridge, Tennessee

"National Construction Estimator." 6th ed. (1978). (G. Moselle, ed.) Craftsman Book Co., Solana Beach, California.

Newman, D. K., and D. Day. (1975). "The American Energy Consumer." Ballinger, Cambridge, Massachusetts.

Oak Ridge National Laboratory. (1981). "RESENU: A Model of Residential Energy Use," CET-002/RESENU. Engineering Physics Information Centers, Oak Ridge, Tennessee.

Parti, M., and C. Parti. (1980). The total and appliance-specific conditional demand for electricity in the household sector. *Bell Journal of Economics,* **11**, 309–321.

Pindyck, R. S. (1979). "The Structure of World Energy Demand" MIT Press, Cambridge, Massachusetts.

R. S. Means Company. (1981). "Mechanical and Electrical Cost Data—1981," 4th annual ed. R. S. Means Company, Kingston, Massachusetts.

Response Analysis Corporation. (1976). "Report on Methodology: 1975 National Survey—Lifestyles and Household Energy Use." Response Analysis Corporation, Princeton, New Jersey.

Rust, J. (1983). "Stationary Equilibrium in a Market for Durable Assets," unpublished Ph.D. dissertation. Department of Economics, Massachusetts Institute of Technology, Cambridge, Massachusetts.

Taylor, L. D. (1975). The demand for electricity: a survey. *Bell Journal of Economics,* **6**, 74–110.

Taylor, L. D., G. R. Blattenberger, and P. K. Verleger. (1977). "The Residential Demand for Energy," EPRI Report EA-235. Electric Power Research Institute, Palo Alto, California.

U.S. Bureau of the Census, "Curent Population Report," Money income in 1977 of families and persons in the United States. U.S. Government Printing Office, Washington, D.C.

U.S. Department of Energy, Energy Information Administration. (1981), "1980 Annual Report to Congress," DOE/EIA-0173(80). U.S. Government Printing Office, Washington, D.C.

U.S. Department of Energy, Energy Information Administration. (1982). "1981 Annual Report to Congress," DOE/EIA-0173(81). U.S. Government Printing Office, Washington, D.C.

Weatherwax, R. (1981). Task 2.3: Comparison of the capabilities of the ORNL and CEC residential energy consumption forecasting models, *Information Validation of Energy Consumption in California: Final Report,* (July). Report ERG-81-1, California Energy Commission, Sacramento.

Wilson, J. W. (1971). Residential demand for electricity. *Quarterly Review of Economics and Business,* **11**, 7–19.

Index

ECONOMIC THEORY, ECONOMETRICS, AND MATHEMATICAL ECONOMICS

Consulting Editor: Karl Shell

UNIVERSITY OF PENNSYLVANIA
PHILADELPHIA, PENNSYLVANIA

Marc Nerlove, David M. Grether, and José L. Carvalho. Analysis of Economic Time Series: *A Synthesis*

Thomas J. Sargent. Macroeconomic Theory

Jerry Green and José Alexander Scheinkman (Eds.). General Equilibrium, Growth and Trade: *Essays in Honor of Lionel McKenzie*

Michael J. Boskin (Ed.). Economics and Human Welfare: *Essays in Honor of Tibor Scitovsky*

Carlos Daganzo. Multinomial Probit: *The Theory and Its Application to Demand Forecasting*

L. R. Klein, M. Nerlove, and S. C. Tsiang (Eds.), Quantitative Economics and Development: *Essays in Memory of Ta-Chung Liu*

Giorgio P. Szegö. Portfolio Theory: *With Application to Bank Asset Management*

M June Flanders and Assaf Razin (Eds.). Development in an Inflationary World

Thomas G. Cowing and Rodney E. Stevenson (Eds.). Productivity Measurement in Regulated Industries

Robert J. Barro (Ed.). Money, Expectations, and Business Cycles: *Essays in Macroeconomics*

Ryuzo Sato. Theory of Technical Change and Economic Invariance: *Application of Lie Groups*

Iosif A. Krass and Shawkat M. Hammoudeh. The Theory of Positional Games: *With Applications in Economics*

Giorgio Szegö (Ed.). New Quantitative Techniques for Economic Analysis

John M. Letiche (Ed.). International Economic Policies and Their Theoretical Foundations: A Source Book

Murray C. Kemp (Ed.). Production Sets

Andreu Mas-Colell (Ed.). Noncooperative Approaches to the Theory of Perfect Competition

Jean-Pascal Benassy. The Economics of Market Disequilibrium

Tatsuro Ichiishi. Game Theory for Economic Analysis

David P. Baron. The Export-Import Bank: *An Economic Analysis*

Réal P. Lavergne. The Political Economy of U. S. Tariffs: An Empirical Analysis

Halbert White. Asymptotic Theory for Econometricians

Thomas G. Cowing and Daniel L. McFadden. Microeconomic Modeling and Policy Analysis: *Studies in Residential Energy Demand*

In preparation

V. I. Arkin and I. V. Evstigneev. Translated and edited by E. A. Medova-Dempster and M. A. H. Dempster. Stochastic Models of Control and Economic Dynamics